THE WAC CASEBOOK

Scenes for Faculty Reflection and Program Development

Edited by

Chris M. Anson

North Carolina State University

Foreword by
Barbara Walvoord

New York   Oxford
OXFORD UNIVERSITY PRESS
2002

Oxford University Press

Oxford   New York
Athens   Auckland   Bangkok   Bogotá   Buenos Aires   Cape Town
Chennai   Dar es Salaam   Delhi   Florence   Hong Kong   Istanbul   Karachi
Kolkata   Kuala Lumpur   Madrid   Melbourne   Mexico City   Mumbai   Nairobi
Paris   São Paulo   Shanghai   Singapore   Taipei   Tokyo   Toronto   Warsaw

and associated companies in
Berlin   Ibadan

Copyright © 2002 Oxford University Press, Inc.

Published by Oxford University Press, Inc.
198 Madison Avenue, New York, New York 10016
http//www.oup-usa.org

Library of Congress Cataloging-in-Publication Data

The WAC casebook: scenes for faculty reflection and program development/editor,
Chris M. Anson.
    p. cm.
    ISBN 0-19-512775-7 (paper)
    1. English language—Rhetoric—Study and teaching.   2. Interdisciplinary approach in
education.   3. Academic writing—Study and teaching.   I. Anson, Christopher, M., 1954–

PE1404.W727 2001
808'.042'0711—dc21
                                                                        2001032153

Printing number: 9 8 7 6 5 4 3 2 1

Printed in the United States of America
on acid-free paper

CONTENTS

PART EIGHT. Tending the Garden: Scenes of Program Development

Barbara Walvoord

This collection of cases, intended for discussion by teachers and graduate teaching assistants, is a treasure-chest that I predict will be plundered by all kinds of people, inside and outside of WAC programs. I will plunder it myself, in all my roles as director of a center for "teaching and learning." That's what these cases are really about.

I have often been disappointed by "cases" that are too cute, too flimsy, too vague, that talk down to the reader, or that create sexist stereotypes or typecast characters. These cases do none of those things. They have a ring of authenticity that makes them highly usable with faculty. They are detailed enough to provide meat for discussion; some even include actual student papers or conversations. They present real people in real situations. Written by people whose names are highly visible in WAC nationally, but also by writers who bring a wide range of valuable perspectives, including student and TA perspectives, the collection addresses the tough and complex issues that teachers, administrators, and institutions face.

I might use these cases in workshops with many different titles. For example, the technology cases (Part 5) would fit a workshop on using technology wisely for classroom learning. The cases that highlight ideology and interaction (Part 4) would be useful in any workshop that discussed "reflective" teaching—that is, coming to understand the unspoken assumptions, cultural concepts, and expectations that one enacts in the classroom. Any faculty group that talks about responding to student work or creating assignments will benefit from the cases on those topics.

I could see using these cases, too, with summer reading groups, which, at the University of Notre Dame, involve four to ten faculty who meet several times over the summer for discussion of a book or a collection of articles. They have no formal leader, only a facilitator who calls the group together. Groups have read, for example, Parker Palmer's *The Courage to Teach*, Mark Schwen's *Exile from Eden*, and more practical advice-giving texts such as my own and Virginia Anderson's *Effective Grading* or John Bean's *Engaging Ideas*. A book of cases would provide a somewhat different experience for such a group—forcing them to focus on their own assumptions and experiences rather than on an author's thesis. I'm eager to have a group try using these cases on their own. I think they might choose one or two cases per meeting, or focus on one section of cases. Or they might read an article or book on a particular topic and then use a case or two to test the book's thesis and their own reactions.

And of course, I would use the book with groups of faculty who are engaged in writing-intensive courses. The cases address many of the tough questions that arise in actual settings where faculty of great dedication and thoughtfulness are trying to make WAC function as it was meant to—as a way to enhance student engagement, to deepen students' learning, and to allow faculty members to get inside the learning process in new ways.

The cases will be valuable with groups of graduate students, whether in a teaching course, workshop, or discussion group in any discipline. Because the cases reflect real faculty lives, I can imagine that for graduate students, they will have the additional benefit of illuminating some of the cultures and complexities of faculty life at various types of institutions. I will recommend this book to all the faculty in various departments at my institution who teach courses about teaching to graduate students. Some of the cases address administrative and organizational issues; I would use these with gatherings of WAC committees, administrators, or taskforces planning learning communities or general-education reform.

Though Anson's initial chapter discusses the problems of faculty who neglect their teaching in favor of research, and faculty who are content to transmit information with little student involvement, no such faculty are pictured in these cases. The sociologists, biologists, engineers, composition teachers, and others reflected in these cases are struggling, as all of us struggle, to balance time demands while giving full measure to our students, to understand the culture of the human beings who people our classrooms, and to find new ways of engaging our students and our subjects. The cases show teachers doing good things, right things, that have good outcomes, but that also raise problems. The questions at the end of each case are challenging and provocative.

If you take the book in your hands and wonder which one, or which few, of the many cases will be best for your purposes, the section titles will be helpful. However, the cases are so rich that most of them raise more than one issue. One way to skim them quickly is to read only the questions at the end of each case; that will give you an idea of the issues each case might raise. The cases are of such uniform quality that you can hardly go wrong. Just pick one, get a group of faculty or teaching assistants together in a friendly place with some cookies, and let them go at it.

Reflection, Faculty Development, and Writing Across the Curriculum
The Power of Scene

Chris M. Anson

T he movement now almost universally known as "writing across the curriculum" (WAC) had its beginnings in a conviction: writing belongs in all courses in every discipline. In part, the movement was a reaction against decades of compartmentalization and increasing specialization in our college and university curriculums. Over time, the responsibility for teaching writing had fallen to English departments, where the emerging subdiscipline of composition studies was providing a substantial research base that complemented and reinforced the belief that writing instruction has a specific domain. Knowing that students were taking required composition courses that presumably prepared them for advanced literacy in college and beyond, many teachers in other disciplines were not particularly worried if students wrote little in their own courses. With the increasing pressures on faculty to engage in research and scholarship, what appeared to be a student-intensive and time-consuming activity was easily and readily replaced with prepared lectures and objective tests. Yet when students did write, teachers often expressed concerns about the jumbled, inarticulate prose they collected. A new challenge best solved by the entire campus community turned into a refrain heard, often defensively, by many composition program administrators: What's the matter with the required first-year course in composition? Why isn't it fixing the problem?

The WAC movement has sought to reverse this trend toward compartmentalization for reasons broader than simple writing proficiency or preparation for the work place. There is little doubt, of course, that students best learn the specialized conventions, standards, and processes of writing in their chosen fields when they do so in the context of their own majors, in their discipline-based courses. It can hardly be otherwise: teachers of composition aren't thoroughly familiar with the dozens of fields in which students must learn to write competently, and even if they were, the prospect of organizing a curriculum of such specialized writing courses boggles the mind of any composition program administrator. Teachers of all subject matters are those best prepared to help students write in their own fields; after all, they read the field's literature and they themselves usually contribute to its base of knowledge. They are the field's readers and writers, its gatherers and distributors of intellect.

But other advantages to such a model soon appear. As the movement has spread, many faculty who have newly incorporated writing into their courses find that students become more active learners, more thoughtful readers, and more engaged participants in class as a result of putting their knowledge, uncertainties, speculations, and intellectual connections into words on a page. No other mode of language yields such recursiveness of thinking. As writers formulate thoughts into written propositions, their emerging texts loop back into their own thinking. Words written become words reconsidered, ideas put to new tests. Gaps in information appear, revealing the need for further learning. Accumulated knowledge takes on the voice of authority, creating in the writer a new sense of expertise.

What has started privately in the interaction between a writer's silent thoughts and a blank page or computer screen can magically transform a dull, lifeless, information-driven classroom into a lively meeting where minds work collectively and productively. Students can share their ideas or work together to improve their papers. Even collecting students' quickly penned "freewrites" about the course material can give teachers a window into the learning processes of their students and reveal confusions and misunderstandings as well as unconsidered connections and insights. Teachers soon find themselves not only learning about their own teaching, but learning new ideas, sometimes quite sophisticated, from their own students. Without some record of students' thinking, we have little sense, beyond test results or the spontaneously uttered thoughts of our most confident students in class, of what is really happening in their minds.

But incorporating writing into college courses is not accomplished only from conviction and quick action, as thousands of instructors have discovered. The process offers challenges and conundrums that show quite clearly why teaching is not something anyone can do with a few facts, a textbook, and a syllabus. Nor is WAC an area of instructional knowledge learned all at once and put into place mechanically: renowned experts in the movement are the first to admit that using writing successfully in the classroom is, like learning to become a good teacher, a continuing and lifelong pursuit. If complacency atrophies teaching, it does far more damage to WAC by encouraging methodological failure, which leads to abandonment of principle and the eventual exile of writing from the classroom.

In combating instructional complacency, this book is not designed to offer faculty across the curriculum lots of procedural knowledge, tips for assignment design, or quick fixes to complicated questions about teaching. Excellent resources already exist to help faculty learn new approaches to WAC and to provide models of successful strategies (see, for example, Bean, as well as the extensive online resources provided in the appendix to the present volume). Instead, this book is designed to engage teachers in sustained reflection on and discussions of the many problems and complexities associated with incorporating writing into their courses.

The WAC Casebook consists of forty-five "scenes"—real or realistic descriptions of writing across the curriculum put into action on campuses, in courses, by faculty, and among students. The scenes describe problems faced by instructors in all sorts of institutions as they try to create writing-intensive courses, as they work with students who bring their own share of frustrations to the learning process, as they collect and grade the products of their assignments, and as they interact with other faculty who do not always share their beliefs about the role and nature of writing across the curriculum.

In using narrative accounts of teaching situations, the book adopts a recent innovation in faculty development: discussion cases. Case methodology has precedents in several disciplines, such as business, medicine, and law, that use descriptions of real events or situations to encourage reflection and learning. Not all cases, of course, look the same. Cases for faculty development typically involve problems or conflicts that require solutions—but the solutions are not provided with the case (Anson, Joliffe, and Shapiro; Anson et al.). Readers must analyze such cases using their own knowledge, experience, and intuitions. Deliberately complex and multifaceted, the scenes in this book do not suggest easy answers; they are designed to encourage a variety of interpretations, courses of action, and implications for readers' own contexts. Because they are open-ended, they lead to different interpretations and different uses of facts and evidence. Responses, therefore, are varied.

The scenes here are learner centered, and foster collaboration and discussion. Drawing on many sources of teachers' knowledge (social, political, textual, interpersonal), they encourage readers to move beyond the abstract "idea" of an issue by considering it in a particular context. These contexts naturally call up similar or related experiences. After discussing a narrative scene, teachers often have mixed feelings—that they haven't been given an answer (which can be unsettling) but that they've puzzled their way through a situation and developed a strategic way of dealing with a similar circumstance (which can build confidence and a sense of expertise).

The scenes also respect the many differences in learning styles among faculty who represent diverse disciplines and ways of creating knowledge. Those of us predisposed toward philosophizing can engage in the conceptual puzzles offered by a scene, to extend its implications into related areas of teaching and learning. For the more pragmatic among us, the scenes provide situations and possible solutions that add to our repertoire of strategies for dealing with our own experiences. For those who enjoy working with other people, the scenes are ideally suited to the sort of dialogue and collaboration that can be found in many faculty-development efforts.

As aficionados of narrative cases have pointed out (e.g., Hutchings; Silverman, Welty, and Lyon) the goal of a good case discussion is to engage in reflection. Reflection, or "reflective practice" (Schön, *Reflective Practitioner; Educating the Reflective Practitioner*), is a process of thoughtfully interrogating what we do in a particular activity. Successful experts in various fields are constantly experiencing their work, standing back from it and assessing its effectiveness, thinking and hypothesizing about how to improve it, then applying these ideas and insights to their ongoing work. Because as faculty we are often preoccupied with our own scholarship, we do not always find opportunities to reflect on the teaching process, even though it makes up an important part of our professional lives. Historically, this lack of reflection in teaching has been especially true on campuses where teaching isn't seen as true "scholarly" work or even as the most important work of a professor, whose own research may overshadow classroom instruction.

The term "reflection" may suggest a kind of turning inward, a privately introspective activity—and it is, at least sometimes. As Brookfield puts it, the process of critical reflection means "recognizing and generating [one's] own contextually sensitive theories of practice" through "continuous investigation and monitoring" of our teaching (Brookfield 215). But such investigations work most successfully when they become public—when we talk about our teaching, share ideas, and solve problems with our colleagues. By immersing us in a shared context, the scenes in this collection allow us to be reflective together, to propose hypotheses, to discuss issues, to relate our own experiences, and to examine alternative solutions to the same problem.

Part 1, "Writing to Learn: Scenes of Intellectual Growth," considers the uses of writing as a medium for students' thinking, learning, and intellectual development. How can writing help students to learn effectively? What potential problems arise when we use informal writing, or writing in unexpected genres, in our classrooms? Part 2, "Effective Assignments: Scenes of the Craft," contains seven narratives about the nature and design of writing assignments, raising important questions about what constitutes a "good" occasion for students' writing, how much constraint or freedom students should be granted in responding to our assignments, and how students and teachers conceive of their respective roles in the process of writing. The chapters in Part 3, "Reading Student Work: Scenes of Response and Evaluation," describe scenes in which teachers face the difficult and complicated task of explaining to their students what counts as successful and unsuccessful writing and, in most cases, giving them a grade.

Part 4, "Coaching Writing: Scenes of Ideology and Interaction," extends response into other ways in which we coach or interact with students around their writing, and raises various interpersonal issues—clashes between teachers and students involving miscommunications or differences of values and ideology. Part 5, "Cybertext: Scenes of Writing and New Technologies," offers several cases in which faculty are struggling to accommodate writing to the new electronic capacities offered by the Web and multimedia technologies. Part 6, "Fences and Neighbors: Scenes of Cross-Disciplinary Work and Faculty Collaboration," tells the stories of teachers and administrators trying hard, not always successfully, to implement writing-across-the-curriculum programs and writing-intensive courses that require faculty interaction and consensus. Part 7, "Seeds of Change: Scenes of Apprenticeship and the Role of Graduate Students," takes up important questions about how WAC is taught to, or learned by, new and prospective teachers. Should graduate teaching assistants be permitted to design and teaching writing-intensive courses? What sort of guidance should TAs receive about WAC from faculty mentors who themselves may still be learning new methods for incorporating writing into their courses? The final section of the book, "Tending the Garden: Scenes of Program Development," contains six scenes that focus on how WAC programs are best created and maintained. Should they be a permanent part of a campus? Who should run them? How do they relate to other aspects of education at different levels? What happens when faculty resist the idea of WAC for various reasons?

Each scene in the book ends with a list of questions for discussion and a brief list of readings or Web sites for further consultation. The additional readings can be consulted beforehand, to enrich the discussion of the scene, or they can provide further information and perspectives after the scene is discussed. The cases also represent a wide range of disciplines: history, psychology, anthropology, women's studies, math, philosophy, political science, agronomy, mechanical engineering, music, sociology, food science, geography, civil engineering, forestry, economics, and others. Although it may seem appealing to jump to the scenes that are situated in, or closest to, one's own disciplinary area, it is probably more useful not to become preoccupied with finding a "match."

By gathering together scenes from many different institutions, crafted by several dozen experts and frequent consultants in the writing-across-the-curriculum movement, it is my hope that this collection provides new opportunities for teachers in all disciplines to engage in productive discussions about a critically important part of our curriculums.

WORKS CITED

Anson, Chris M., David A. Jolliffe, and Nancy Shapiro. "Stories to Teach By: Using Narrative Cases in TA and Faculty Development." *WPA: Writing Program Administration* 19 (1995): 25–38.

Anson, Chris M., et. al., eds. *Dilemmas in Teaching: Cases for Collaborative Faculty Reflection.* Madison: Mendota, 1998.

Bean, John C. *Engaging Ideas:* The Professor's Guide to Integrating Writing, Critical Thinking, and Active Learning in the Classroom. San Francisco: Jossey-Bass, 1996.

Brookfield, Stephen. *Becoming a Critical Reflective Teacher.* San Francisco: Jossey-Bass, 1995.

Hutchings, Patricia. *Using Cases to Improve College Teaching: A Guide to More Reflective Practice.* Washington, DC: AAHE, 1991.

Schön, Donald. *The Reflective Practitioner: How Professionals Think in Action.* New York: Basic, 1983.

Schön, Donald A. *Educating the Reflective Practitioner.* San Francisco: Jossey-Bass, 1987.

Silverman, Rita, William Welty, and Sally Lyon, eds. *Case Studies for Teacher Problem Solving.* New York: McGraw-Hill, 1996.

Part 1

Writing to Learn
Scenes of Intellectual Growth

The Misbegotten Journal of Dennis Wong

Toby Fulwiler

Assistant professor John Wilson, Columbia Ph.D., teaches a first-year seminar in American intellectual history, a writing-intensive course focusing on nineteenth-century thinkers who shaped twentieth-century thought. John believes passionately in the power of journals to generate, shape, and record thinking. He keeps one himself, writing in it, if not daily, at least weekly, sometimes early in the morning, in the student union with a cup of coffee and a chocolate donut, other times relaxed at home in an easy chair, writing about ideas for his classes as well as working out the kinks in his current research project.

Hoping to train his students in the intellectual habits of serious writers and scholars, Wilson requires them to keep journals too. He believes strongly in the principle of "writing to learn" and hopes to teach his students that the more they write about the readings, the better they will understand and remember them, and the better equipped they will be to participate in seminar discussions. His syllabus requires the students to "Write responses to each of the assigned daily readings, and bring the journals to class to facilitate class discussion." He collects the journals four times during each term—at weeks three, six, nine, and twelve. Each time he assigns a grade based on "a combination of quantity (the number and length of entries) and quality (the amount of personal intellectual engagement displayed in the entries)." Each succeeding grade counts more than the last, as Wilson wants to reward those who learn to write good journals.

Dennis Wong, one of the quietest students in Wilson's seminar, received the highest grade in class on the mid-term take-home exam and the second highest grade on his five-page biography paper on Mark Twain. Dennis's journal is also first rate, containing as it does dated entries for every assigned reading and, often, several entries dated the same day about a single reading. Unlike the journals of many of his classmates, Dennis' journal meticulously records author's names, book titles, dates of publication, and quotations with page numbers. But what especially sets Dennis' entries apart from his classmates is (1) his engagement with specific passages in assigned texts, which he copies verbatim and comments upon with intelligence, and (2) the amount of cross-referencing, as each new entry refers to passages in previous readings Dennis has written about before.

Wilson is immensely pleased with Dennis Wong's journal, one of the most powerful demonstrations of writing-to-learn that he has ever witnessed. It illustrates concretely the wonderfully integrative thinking that regular writing promotes over time. In fact, once the course is over, he plans to ask Dennis' permission to photocopy the whole journal to use for an article on "The Role of Journals in Teaching History."

The fourth and final time Wilson is scheduled to collect the journals, he arrives in class early and has occasion to overhear Dennis confiding in a classmate that he's exhausted from spending all weekend fabricating journal entries about four weeks worth of assigned readings on Friedrich Nietszche, William James, and Herbert Spencer. Dennis does, in fact, look exhausted. Wilson, however, looks dismayed.

After class, Wilson pulls Dennis aside for a frank conversation. "Yeah, I always get so busy," Dennis confesses, "and I'm taking theatre, and I'm not a very fast reader, and I get behind on the daily readings, so I don't write about them until I have to—until the journals are due or there's an exam or something—then I catch up all at once. I know that's not what you want us to do, but that's the way I do it, and it works—I get good grades."

"Dennis, faking all those dates is not good. Journal writing is an important part of the course, a habit of mind that I'm trying to instill in you and your classmates—my goal is written right on the syllabus. You defeat the whole reason for keeping a journal, which is to help you keep up with the readings and learn as you go along and make connections between the readings. When you write in it weekly, you learn the course material better. When you bring your entries to class, our discussions are better."

"Well, I do bring the journal to class; it's just that there's nothing in it. And I do like to write—I always find my best ideas when I write, but I just don't have time to keep a daily journal. Besides, I'd much rather think about all the material all at once. I learn better that way. I still learn just as much, which my grade on the mid-term proves."

"Your grade on the mid-term only proves you're good at cramming and deadline writing. When you study that way, you don't retain what you learn. You really disappoint me, Dennis. You're sharp enough to get away with cutting corners like this—you really had me fooled. You get by with good enough grades, but you'll never know how good you really could be. You realize, don't you, that I'll have to lower your grade for not doing this assignment correctly?

"But, Professor Wilson, it really helps when I just read and think and write about issues such as Social Darwinism at the same time. I really do learn just as much writing the journal this way—you should have seen me this weekend. Reading all those guys at once—and they are all guys, you know. Anyway, reading Spencer, then reading James, seeing the connections and being able to use a yellow highlighter to mark the relevant quotes. I really got into the material and saw the connections, saw clearly how the Europeans influenced the Americans and then how it sort of reversed."

"Ah, Dennis. What am I going to do with you?"

QUESTIONS FOR REFLECTION AND DISCUSSION

1. What is Wilson going to do about grading Dennis? Lower his grade? Forgive and forget?
2. Does Wilson's pedagogy represent high standards or unreal expectations?
3. List three things Wilson could do to avoid this situation next time he teaches the seminar.
4. Should Wilson continue his plan to write an article called "The Role of Journals in Teaching History"?
5. What should Dennis do next time he is faced with a similar requirement?

READINGS FOR FURTHER CONSIDERATION

Fulwiler, Toby. "Journals Across the Disciplines." *English Journal* 69.9 (1980): 14–19.
———, ed. *The Journal Book.* Portsmouth: Boynton/Cook, 1987.
———. "Responding to Student Journals." *Writing and Response: Theory, Practice, and Research.* Ed. Chris M. Anson. Urbana: National Council of Teachers of English, 1989. 149–73.
Gardner, Susan, and Toby Fulwiler, eds. *The Journal Book for At-Risk Writers.* Portsmouth: Boynton/Cook, 1999.
———, eds. *The Journal Book for Teachers of Technical and Professional Programs.* Portsmouth, NH: Boynton/Cook, 1999.

2

Writing for Empathy

Patricia Connor-Greene, Hayley Shilling, and Art Young

"Informed empathy." That's how Diane Arnold summed up her goals for the interdisciplinary honors seminar she was teaching, The Social Construction of Madness. She wanted her undergraduate students to develop a solid grasp of the history and controversies surrounding theories and treatment of psychiatric disorders (the "informed" part), but she also hoped the course would foster a sense of empathy for people with mental illnesses. In an attempt to encourage students to feel rather than just think about the material, she assigned readings from Anne Sexton, Clifford Geertz, Sylvia Plath, Janet Frame, and others who had been hospitalized for psychiatric difficulties.

"Have you considered asking them to write a poem?" When her friend, Paul McNulty, her campus's writing-across-the-curriculum (WAC) coordinator, raised this question, Diane had to admit that she'd never thought of assigning poetry. She considered herself a WAC workshop "groupie" and emphasized student writing in all of her psychology courses. She was convinced of the value of writing as a way of thinking. But poetry . . . the idea had never occurred to her.

"Some of our colleagues around campus, in accounting, biology, and entomology, have tried poetry assignments," Paul continued, "and they were surprised and pleased with the results. They've told me that it is a good way for students to develop new perspectives on the course material, to express thoughts and feelings that don't usually get expressed orally or on tests and research essays, and to engage the subject matter in creative ways. These teachers also like the way the poems, when read aloud in class, increased student-teacher communication and students' interaction with each other in collegial ways."

Diane wondered how her students would react to this assignment. What would she, a psychology professor, *do* with the assignment? But then again, this Madness class is an interdisciplinary seminar, so why not give it a try? "Why not ask the students directly how they felt about the assignment," said Paul. "Ask them to do a brief freewrite at the end of class, and you'll get some sense of how the assignment worked for them."

"For next Tuesday's class, I'd like you to write a poem. It can be from any perspective, rhymed or unrhymed, any type of poem; the only requirement is that it relate to mental illness in some way. The poem won't be graded, but it will count as your daily participation." Around the seminar table, student faces registered the entire spectrum from delight to dread, and a shout of "yes!" coincided with a low moan.

Over lunch, Diane told a friend in another department about the assignment, who listened, paused, and then hesitantly responded, "I would have hated to have to do that when I was a student—and I'll bet you would have too." But then he hastily added, "But it would have been good for us." Later that day, in her office, she told a colleague in her department what she was asking her students to write. "You've got guts," her colleague replied, "I'd be afraid the students would laugh at me. If they asked me what this assignment had to do with studying mental illness, I wouldn't know how to answer them."

In Tuesday's class, students met in small groups of four and distributed copies of poems within their group. After readings in small groups, Diane asked for volunteers to read their work to the entire class. "Thank you," Diane responded awkwardly after each volunteer read a poem, wanting to comment on her students' ideas but feeling constrained by her lack of expertise with poetry. Although she enjoyed listening to the poems, Diane felt as if she had entered a foreign country in which she didn't know enough of the language to make an intelligent comment.

After there were no more volunteers, all of the students in one of the groups encouraged Hayley to read her poem to the class.

Dread and Butter

I'm a stick-to-the-roof-of-your-mouth kind of Pilgrim
Do my sailing on Maywheatflower days.
Sticky salty vanity, congealing crunch-style mind
    arcades
It's my inner child that's calling
Down into that sippy cup soul.
Send soldiers to free up this barracks!
I need a parachute roll.
George Washington Carver didn't raise no fool
Not spread or beaten or bound or cut
Legumes like me have the best legs.
But Almonds are the dumbest Nut!!
Pry me out of this sandwich, tan-brown and wrapped
    too tight
A straight jacket's fine for a loony,
But nuts like me need Rye or White!

After spontaneous applause from the rest of the students, Hayley fielded questions from the visibly appreciative class. "How did you do that?" "How long did it take you?" "Have you written a lot of poetry before?" They complimented her success at capturing the spirit of psychosis, and they wanted to know how she did it. Hayley was touched by their enthusiastic response to her poem, and the students were surprised and impressed to hear that she had written the poem relatively quickly. The class seemed energized by the assignment and when Diane asked the class if they would like their poems compiled into a booklet so that all the class members could have a copy of each other's work, their response was overwhelmingly positive.

During the last few minutes of class, Diane asked students to write brief reflections on their experience of writing the poems. John, an electrical engineering major, found the poetry assignment difficult and discouraging:

> First, I don't consider myself a poet. Second, I like to read poetry; I am aware of its power. Therefore I feel powerless when I write a poem (much more than when I write prose). I have a feeling that I want to put on paper, but it would take an epic to get that feeling across.

Susan, a psychology major, also found the assignment difficult, but her response to this challenge was quite different from John's:

> Writing these poems made me feel uncomfortable because I didn't feel confident about my own abilities. Through that process I probably learned much more about what it feels like to be mentally ill than to read books about mental illness. My perception of mental illness is being "out of your comfort zone" every minute of every day. I am lucky that I can return to other things to regain my confidence, but often mental illness infiltrates every area of the person's life.

For David, majoring in speech and communication, writing the poem accomplished exactly what Diane had hoped:

> In simply reading (and even in reflection and discussion) it is possible to maintain emotional distance. Writing, however, necessitates involvement—to step into the shoes of the schizophrenic and walk a while. When emotions are called to the surface, it becomes possible to identify—to connect in some way—with the experience of those about whom we have read so much.

James, an outstanding student in engineering who was usually one of the most vocal students in the class, was silent throughout the class, didn't write a reflection paper, and avoided eye contact with Diane. As he was leaving at the end of class, Diane asked him if he was feeling okay. James's response was short and direct: "Ridiculous assignment."

QUESTIONS FOR REFLECTION AND DISCUSSION

1. Diane felt justified in assigning a poem because this was an interdisciplinary class. Would it be legitimate to assign poetry in a psychology course (or history, or physics, . . .)?
2. Is it appropriate for Diane to assign writing that is ungraded? If she assigns writing but does not grade it, does it send the message that she doesn't value

it? Does an assignment include an implicit agreement that the teacher will respond in some way, even if the assignment itself is ungraded? If she doesn't comment on the poems, how will the students interpret her lack of response?

3. How can Diane support exceptional work (e.g., Hayley's poem) without demoralizing other students' efforts? What can or should a teacher with no training or experience in writing poetry say about her students' poems?

4. Is it fair to ask students to share their poetry with others in the class?

5. Almost all of the poems presented a sympathetic view of mental illness; none was from the viewpoint of anyone who was destructive or dangerous. Does a poetry writing assignment encourage an overly romantic view of a problem?

6. Should students be given some direction or guidance in how to write poetry? If so, what would that include? Should the class discuss how to assess poetry? If so, what criteria would be addressed?

READINGS FOR FURTHER CONSIDERATION

Young, Art. "Considering Values: The Poetic Function of Language." *Language Connections: Writing and Reading Across the Curriculum*. Ed. Toby Fulwiler and Art Young. Urbana: National Council of Teachers of English, 1982. 77–99.

———. *Teaching Writing Across the Curriculum*. 3rd ed. New York: Prentice-Hall, 1999.

———. "Mentoring, Modeling, Monitoring, Motivating: Response to Students' Ungraded Writing as Academic Conversation." *Writing to Learn: Strategies for Assessing and Responding to Writing Across the Disciplines*. Ed. Mary Deane Sorcinelli and Peter Elbow. San Francisco: Jossey-Bass, 1997. 27–39.

3

Writing Intensity

Chris M. Anson

I t had been almost five years since Steve Scott had joined the faculty as an assistant professor of anthropology at Pound Ridge University, a mid-sized, private institution with an enrollment of about ten thousand. Steve regularly taught a general-education course, Introduction to Culture and Society, which enrolled about forty students, most of them nonmajors. As part of a faculty development project in support of the university's "writing-intensive" curriculum, Steve had tried putting more writing in his course. In the first year of the project, Steve's faculty group focused on the design of effective writing assignments. Steve more than doubled the number of papers he assigned in his course, from three (two short analyses plus a term paper) to seven—four reaction papers, two summaries of readings, and the term paper, which he shortened to five to seven pages.

After teaching his new writing-rich course, Steve felt that his assignments were helping students to concentrate harder, read better, and learn the material more fully. At the urging of his department chair, he sent the syllabus along to the committee that oversees the writing-intensive curriculum, and it was approved with one or two minor suggestions.

But after a year of his revised course, Steve had come to feel the weight of the increased writing in his workload, especially in the time he spent reading, responding to, and grading the students' work. His department chair had also asked the faculty to take on an extra course because of an unexpected rise in enrollments, and, as he neared the end of his tenure-track period and faced the imminent review for promotion, Steve felt even more pressure to be active in research and publication. Now, at the start of a new term, he was becoming increasingly concerned about his writing-intensive course and his own role in students' writing experiences.

It was the first week of the term. To kick off his course, Steve gave his usual assignment to create, in a couple of pages, a utopian society. The first of four short papers, the assignment allowed Steve to focus the discussion on what principles govern the way we live and think about our social, political, and cultural systems—a good introduction to the idea of culture and socially inscribed institutional practices. It was Steve's practice to collect the papers, read and grade them, and then pass them back within one or two class sessions. His assignment sheet, which he handed out to the students, was designed to give some structure to the students' papers while still allowing some freedom and creativity:

> *Short assignment #1*: All of us imagine ways in which our lives could be different—better, perhaps—in alternative kinds of societies. These visions of different worlds come, at base, from our cultural and social beliefs. In this class, we want to think about culture and society not just as grand theories rendered in abstract language, but also as part of who we are and how we think about our lives. To that end, this assignment asks you to try creating, in a couple of pages, a utopian society. What kind of ideal world would you like to create and live in? What makes it unique or different from the present society and sets of beliefs and practices that govern your existence? Due: Sept. 10.

Two class meetings after collecting the batch of short utopian papers, Steve apologized to his students that he had not had time to read them, but promised to have them back by the Friday class. Now it was already Thursday, and the stack of papers was still sitting on his desk. As he returned to his office after lunch, three students were waiting for him, and he could hardly hide his impatience as he tried to deal with their questions quickly so he could return to his work. After the students had left, he checked his voicemail; there was a message from the editor of a journal for which he was a reviewer. Steve knew he was late with his review of a long, problematic essay the editor had sent him, and had come to work prepared to finish and fax the review that morning. Perhaps he was reading too much into it, Steve thought as he listened, but the editor's message sounded almost angry. After hanging up, Steve immediately turned on his computer and opened the file with his review. But just as soon as he had settled down to finish his comments, there was a knock at his door. It was Paul Kim, a senior colleague who had befriended Steve early on. Paul, coffee in hand, had come to talk about a major planning document the chair of the anthropology department had circulated in preparation for a long departmental meeting later that day. "Have you read this, Steve?" Paul asked, looking very serious.

"I was hoping to do that over lunch," Steve replied, trying to look distracted so that maybe Paul wouldn't stay. He really liked Paul, but didn't feel so at ease with him that he could simply ask him to leave.

"We've got to talk," Paul said, plopping himself down in the chair across from Steve's desk. "The department simply must oppose this proposal."

"Why?" Steve asked as he found his copy of the proposal in his briefcase.

"Well, take some time to read through it and then I'll tell you what I've been telling other faculty about how we should respond," Paul said, waiting.

After the department meeting ended at 5:30 that afternoon, Steve returned to his office and faxed a short note to the editor of the journal promising he would send his review first thing in the morning. He knew that his students would expect their essays at his nine o'clock class (and the class session depended on it), but if he could read through them quickly, say, by eight or nine that evening, he could try to finish his review of the journal essay before midnight. Caught in heavy highway traffic on his way home, Steve tried to read some more of the journal article whenever the cars came to a stop.

"Did you forget that I have a meeting with my book club tonight?" Linda asked when Steve came into the house. She already had her coat on and was bustling around. "There's lasagna to microwave, and the baby's already eaten. Just be sure to change her before she goes to bed. She took a long nap this afternoon, so she can stay up later."

"God, I'm sorry, Linda. I got caught up in traffic," Steve said, feeling dazed. "When will you be back?"

"Probably about ten or so," Linda said, holding her keys. "Maybe we can catch up then; I've got lots to tell you." And she was out the door.

After trying three times to rock the baby to sleep, Steve finally got her down at 9:15. Coffee in hand, he sat down in his study in front of the stack of forty papers from his class. Tired and anxious about his journal review, Steve felt his concentration ebbing. The papers looked terrible. "How can students like this be admitted to college?" he thought, gripping his pen tighter. It was deplorable; they just couldn't write at all. What were the high schools doing, anyway? "Look at this," he muttered, glancing through a paper titled "My Utopia," by Thomas Dooley.[1] "This guy can't even think!"

MY UTOPIA

From my point of view the perfect society would be a small community nestled in the mountains—away from the masses of people and cities. There would be small businesses, but mainly crafts would be the large portion of employment. It would be a closed society in the sence that any one who didn't live there could not come in and find employment. Therefore only enough people could live there that there was jobs available for and there were only enough jobs to support about 5,000.

The economic nature would be as follows: All jobs would have a fixed salary the only way to get increased wages would be to move up in position or status. There would be no inflation because all prices would be fixed. There wouldn't be room for competition because there would only be one firm or one shop for each craft. With no unemployment or inflation people would never have to worry about a decrease in their standard of living. Everyone can still be in whatever class they want, as far as lower, upper or middle classes, as long as they are productive members of society. You must want to earn a living in order to live here. There are no taxes: no welfare programs—the incomes received would allow them to purchase anything they want and they would be able to work as long as they want, age wise.

The goverment would be composed of a few people who would act more like a committee than a Pres, vice pres., partlimentary group. There purpose is to see that the fixed prices were followed and act kind of like a supreme court. The only rules would be the 10 commandments and if any of these are broken, this is cause enough to expell them from the society.

After spending almost fifteen minutes writing comments on Thomas' paper, Steve glanced at his watch: it was already after ten. As he raced through another three or four papers, he found himself writing the same things over and over: "Give *evidence* for your assertions," "This makes no sense," "You need to *think this through* more carefully," "*PROOFREAD!*" Exhausted and angered by the lack of skill and care in the essays, Steve also felt his comments becoming harsher. But without the time to read the essays carefully, how could he give much constructive commentary? Besides, it was *their* problem, wasn't it? Why should he be their editor?

Steve's concentration was broken by the sound of Linda returning from her meeting. He pictured her bright face and smile. It seemed as if he hadn't seen her in weeks. Pushing the papers aside, he went out of the study to greet her.

At midnight, Steve still had fifteen papers to read, and the journal article kept glaring at him from the other stack of work on his desk. He felt almost numb, alternately lulled into submission by the late hour and slapped awake by the nagging image of his nine o'clock class the next morning. But there had to be something . . . . "I just can't do all this," he muttered to himself, vowing to make a change.

Glancing over his syllabus for "Introduction to Culture and Society," he wondered how much resistance he would get from the class if he made a few adjustments. Three more short papers were due that term—120 pieces of lousy writing to read and grade. Not to mention eighty summaries and forty term papers at the end of the course, just before he had to present a paper at a convention. "No," he thought suddenly, "this is a writing-intensive course; what would the committee say if they knew I was altering what they approved? And what about the curriculum—this would work against its whole spirit." He wondered how other faculty coped. He couldn't think of more than one full professor in his department who was teaching a writing-intensive course.

"Damn," he muttered. Feeling suddenly exploited and overworked, he continued to stare at his syllabus. Who on earth would know or even care whether he made some alterations? Maybe he could justify them somehow on pedagogical grounds. What if he . . . he circled the four papers on his syllabus and made a note in the margin: "Reduce to one more short reaction paper. Cut one summary. Make remaining papers count more." "There," he said. "Probably get cheers from the class."

QUESTIONS FOR REFLECTION AND DISCUSSION

1. Should Steve reduce the amount of writing in his class?
2. What's the source of Steve's feeling that he is overworked? How much is the writing-intensive course contributing to his overall workload?
3. What strategies might Steve use to continue his writing-rich course without compromising his other work or driving himself crazy?
4. How might Steve rethink the role of writing in his course?

NOTE

1. Thanks to Art Young for the use of Thomas's paper.

READINGS FOR FURTHER CONSIDERATION

Bean, John C. *Engaging Ideas*. San Francisco: Jossey-Bass, 1996. (See especially parts 3 and 4.)

Sorcinelli, Mary Deane, and Peter Elbow, eds. *Writing to Learn: Strategies for Assigning and Responding to Writing Across the Disciplines*. San Francisco: Jossey-Bass, 1997. See especially chapter 1 (Peter Elbow, "High Stakes and Low Stakes in Assigning and Responding to Writing"), chapter 5 (Stephen M. Fishman, "Student Writing in Philosophy: A Sketch of Five Techniques") and chapter 8 (Ronald F. Lunsford, "When Less Is More: Principles for Responding to Writing in the Disciplines").

4

WAC Meets WMS
Not Love at First Sight

Hephzibah Roskelly

Tess read the evaluations once more. Thirty or so students in an introductory course in women's studies, and many with the same comments. "Good readings, but we didn't talk about them much," one complained. "I didn't really learn much that was new to me." "I hated the tests!" "I loved hearing the voices of the women we read," one said. That was practically the only admiring comment. No one had rated the course very highly, and no one had gotten excited enough about the material or the work to declare a women's studies major or minor, something that had always happened in the near past. Well, in the near past it had been taught by a dedicated part-time lecturer, underpaid and driving to four different campuses to craft a full-time job. She had left when she found better employment. Laurinda had been great, Tess thought. She had also taught the course with a W. Writing intensive. Looking back once more at the evaluations, Tess noticed none talked about writing. They hadn't written much, she guessed.

The problem with women's studies, Tess thought, is that it's an all-volunteer army. You get what you get and you make do. She herself was on loan for the year from the English department, charged with improving curriculum. When Mary Kay had volunteered to teach the introductory women's studies course a year or so ago, Tess had been thrilled. It meant that for the first time the Intro course, the one that loomed so large in maintaining and expanding the program as a whole, would be taught by a full-time faculty member. Mary Kay was tenured in her own Department of Sociology, and she seemed excited by the chance to explore gender and cultural issues with the students, who, Tess knew, were curious about women's studies, but not too sure what they thought about feminism or gender concerns. They needed both a knowledgeable source and a good facilitator; they needed someone who could make the atmosphere comfortable, since the topics often weren't. Laurinda had created that, easily it seemed. Unlike Mary Kay, who clearly was having trouble.

Students obviously hadn't been happy with the course. And this was the second semester in a row that the course taught by Mary Kay had received uncomplimentary reviews. Once, in the middle of last semester, a student had dropped by the women's studies office to pick up an article Mary Kay had left there. Tess had been standing at the desk, and she casually had asked the student about the course.

"Oh, it's fine," the student had said. "Dr. Abernathy is a stickler, that's for sure. But that's good." She had paused and looked down, her face almost hidden by the brown hair that fell over it. "I wish there was more time to deal with what we're reading."

Tess hadn't wanted to press it, but she couldn't help herself from asking. "What do you write?" she said.

"Oh, we'll do a final paper. We've already had one test. And it's essay." She laughed and made a face. "I'm a terrible writer anyway." The student stuffed the article into her backpack and left.

Tess sighed and then picked up the phone and dialed Mary Kay's number. "Let's talk about your course, OK? You know we're thinking about how to improve what we do in the early courses to make them more appealing."

Mary Kay had been willing. "Bring some of your stuff, maybe some things the students are doing, and we can look at it."

———————

Mary Kay walked into the office late that afternoon. The women's studies office was located on the second floor of the oldest building on campus. It was the building where once all the students—who were all women for the first seventy years of the university's existence—took their classes. The top floor, closed off for years, had once been the gymnasium, and Tess sometimes told the old ghost story that if you were in the building late at night you could hear the girls' feet bouncing as they did their calisthenics.

Mary Kay didn't seem in the mood for fantasy. She sat carefully, negotiating the stacks of folders grouped around the chair. It was portfolio time for Tess's students, and she had been reading most of the day.

"I know you've been hearing from some of these students," Mary Kay began. "I know they don't like the class much. But, and I hate to say this, it's really their own fault. One of them told me she didn't want to answer a question because she hated people looking at her."

"That's often a problem, especially with young women. And especially with material that pushes a lot of buttons. Haven't you found that to be true in your sociology classes?"

"They seem to know the drill better, I think. They know how to take notes, ask questions, be prepared. They seem ready to do the work. I just don't know about these women. And the three men—well, they're a little better. At least they talk more."

Mary Kay showed Tess her syllabus. Tess had seen it already. She knew that it was designed very much as the student who had come in last semester had described it. One long paper at the end of the semester. "And a real research paper," Mary Kay said. "I want them to know that women's studies is a subject worthy of research. That's one of their problems, in fact.

They don't think of something called women's studies as a serious, rigorous pursuit." She made a face and laughed. "At least I think that's one of their problems."

Tess nodded. This was going to be tough. She looked down at the syllabus. A midterm and a final exam. Two required texts and a group of articles on gender.

"Do you think I'm asking too much?" Mary Kay lifted her eyebrows and waited for Tess's response.

"No. I don't think you're too demanding. I think they need to write."

"They hand in a prospectus for the research paper. And I make extensive comments on it." Mary Kay shook her head slightly. "The problem isn't writing. It's that they don't get this material. They're in here to learn about sex roles and women's issues, but they *resist* learning about it. When I ask them what they think, they almost shrug at me."

"What would you say to making this class writing intensive next time?"

Mary Kay shrugged herself, and then laughed. "I'm like my students!" She paused. "What do you think that will do?"

"I think writing is a way for these students to find a way to talk about what they're learning, to figure out what they think. You know."

Mary Kay was frowning now. "You may think that because you're in English that writing about your grandmother and what you *feel* about Asian women's problems is the answer to every problem in a class. But in sociology we don't operate that way. And to me that 'W' just means work."

Tess tried another tack. "Well, how about the research? How about opening up what they do and how they do it? Women's studies and feminism in general is trying to break down some of those categories about what constitutes research and evidence, trying to make form more a matter of—"

"Research is research. Do you really think students should create their own citation form? Decide they don't need a bibliography?

"Well," Tess pushed her glasses back on her nose. "I do think students need the chance to hear their voices, to play with forms. The whole problem with voice, finding one, learning to hear it, that's a feminist concern."

Mary Kay was suddenly angry, and about more than writing; Tess could feel it.

"It doesn't have a place here. It's all well and good to make them feel good about themselves and what they've done. But this is no therapy session and too often that's what the kind of writing you're talking about is about."

Mary Kay straightened her books and sat up in her chair, as though she were ready to leave. "What I want to know is this: are you saying that if I don't teach a course writing intensive I am not teaching as a feminist?" Mary Kay's face reddened.

"It's a student issue. Look at what your students write. They don't get enough chance to reflect, to rethink, to examine assumptions together. How can a test help them see into their own set of cultural assumptions about gender? And none of them is choosing to go on into WMS."

"What about all the sociology classes I teach? Should they all be WAC courses if I'm to be a good feminist? It's not just my field we're calling into question, but my credentials as a feminist. I don't think that's fair, Tess."

Mary Kay stood up. Tess had the distinct and uncomfortable feeling she had said way too much. Was WAC a feminist issue? Was she calling into question Mary Kay's interest in her students? Was she so certain that students were really not learning about feminism and gender because they couldn't write about it?

She needed to make amends and quickly. "I'm not sure about any of this," she said. "I'm just trying to figure out how we can improve what we're trying to do."

"I know. And I know this is one of those thankless jobs. And I see you've got lots of your own work to do." She tapped a stack of portfolios with her shoe.

They walked to the door together. They would have this discussion again, Tess assured herself. It was late, dark outside. If she stayed any longer, she'd be hearing the girls doing exercises upstairs. She locked the evaluations in the filing cabinet and picked up a couple of portfolios from the floor before turning out the lights.

QUESTIONS FOR REFLECTION AND DISCUSSION

1. How should Tess talk to Mary Kay about her course?
2. Is writing-for-knowing a feminist concern as well as a learning one?
3. As a faculty member, how have you dealt with pedagogical issues in conversation with your colleagues?
4. What are the power issues involved in cross-disciplinary programs? How does a faculty member reconcile different priorities and different assumptions from one program to another?

READINGS FOR FURTHER CONSIDERATION

hooks, bell. *Teaching to Transgress.* New York: Routledge, 1995.
Lerner, Gerda. *Why History Matters.* New York: Oxford UP, 1977.
Martin, Jane Roland. *Coming of Age in Academe: New York: Rekindling Women's Hopes and Reforming the Academy.* New York Routledge, 2000.

5

What's Appropriate?

Monica Stitt-Bergh, Thomas Hilgers, and Joan Perkins

J eff Walcourt walked into the WAC program director's office and found a seat at the conference table. The director welcomed him and the other eight professors to the semester's first meeting of the WAC Program Faculty Board, which sets WAC policies and approves courses as "writing intensive." Jeff had joined the University's zoology department five years earlier—the same year the WAC program and writing-intensive (WI) requirement were established. He had volunteered to teach at least one WI class each year because he felt that writing should play an important role in all fields, and he found that it was often neglected in natural sciences. Jeff's dean and other colleagues noticed his interest in WAC and recommended that he be appointed to the WAC Program Faculty Board.

During the first meeting, Jeff found himself nodding in agreement when the director explained that the program and WI course requirement were established to satisfy the community and employers who complained about the quality of graduates' writing abilities. The director added that the faculty who developed the criteria for WI classes were also influenced by write-to-learn pedagogy. Jeff remembered those folks and a WAC workshop he had attended during his first year. It was that workshop which gave him an alternative to traditional lecture-based teaching. He took the WAC teaching strategies—reaction papers, journal writing, short in-class writing assignments—and applied them to his own classroom. After several challenging semesters of experimenting with different approaches, he believed he had worked out the kinks: his small-group activities, "lab process logs," and in-class writing assignments had increased students' participation and their engagement with the material. Because of his success, he was committed to using informal, reflective writing assignments.

At the end of the meeting, Jeff jotted down a few notes as the director explained the process the board would follow to review and approve courses as writing intensive for the upcoming semester: each board member would receive a folder with WI application forms and syllabi to review. At the next Monday meeting, each member would recommend that the board approve the class as WI or ask the professor to revise the syllabus to better meet the WI criteria. Jeff left the meeting with a stack of application forms and syllabi to review.

At the end of the week, Jeff still hadn't begun reviewing the WI applications because his own workload demanded too much of his time. So on Saturday afternoon, he rifled through his teaching files and pulled out the folder of handouts from the WAC workshop he had attended. After glancing through the folders' contents to refresh his memory about what should happen in a WI class, he decided to approach the WI applications like a group of student reports: skim all first before making any comments or decisions.

Halfway through the bunch, he came across an application and syllabus from a professor in plant pathology that seemed to exemplify all that's good about the WI program: a student-centered approach with an academic journal requirement. He set it aside. Close to the end of the stack, he came across another application that troubled him more than any other. A meteorology professor's syllabus contained enough writing, but the majority was writing on in-class exams and quizzes. Jeff sat for a moment looking at his desk. On his left lay the plant pathology application, on his right lay the meteorology application, and the remaining ones lay in the middle. "Very different," he murmured. If all of these are approved as WI, he thought, what does that say about our program? Can both the plant pathology and meteorology classes be WI? What should he tell the board on Monday? He wished that he hadn't waited until the weekend before the meeting to review the WI applications.

Jeff searched his memory for someone to help him, someone with WI experience who wouldn't mind a phone call on Saturday. Jim Rausch, a botany professor, came to mind. Jeff had worked with him about other issues related to teaching and he knew Jim had been on the WAC Faculty Board several years ago. Jeff tried his home phone number.

"Jim—it's Jeff Walcourt here," he said when Jim answered. "I'm reviewing applications for writing-intensive classes next semester and I'm stuck. I need to be clear on what 'writing intensive' means," he explained. "Each application is different—everyone doing different kinds of writing. I don't know what a WI class should be anymore. I thought that instructors should be using writing to make student thinking visible and to push students into new areas. You know, journals and learning logs."

Jim quickly agreed with him, "Yeah, I had a lot of success with my students last semester when I asked them to keep observation logs on the plants in their neighborhood. They really engaged with the material and started refining their views on what plants were appropriate for the climate and soil. It was a great addition to the ideas covered in the textbook."

Jeff picked up the meteorology course's syllabus and said, "Listen to this. Here's an application for a WI class and the professor writes, 'The course format is traditional lecture with a lab. Questions from students are strongly encouraged. This class is writing intensive so exams, quizzes, and lab reports will be marked down for mistakes in grammar and poor organization. All writing will receive comments on poorly constructed sentences. Occasionally I will read some examples of good and bad prose in class.' Geez, I don't know where this professor has been for the last five years."

Before Jim could comment, Jeff rushed on, "Oh, and listen to his assignments: 'Quizzes will be given in class each Friday and require a written interpretation of the results. If a question is poorly done on the quiz, the student will be required to write a second version of the answer. Students will write two laboratory reports. Groups of four or five will perform the experiment; each group member will write a separate report of approximately 4–5 pages plus calculations, charts, and diagrams.' That's it for the writing in his proposed WI class. Most of the writing is on in-class exams and quizzes—and he's grading them on grammar. It's hard to write in a timed situation and get it right the first time."

There was a moment of silence as Jim pondered Jeff's words. "Hmmm, it does appear that this professor has the wrong idea about writing intensive. It sounds like he sees WI as classes on grammar and correctness and not much else. But don't give up on him yet. Perhaps if he attended a workshop like you did, he'd learn how to use journals and reading logs."

Jeff sighed and as he picked up the plant pathology syllabus, said, "I'm not giving up. That application's the worst of them all. I have another one here that's a 300-level plant pathology course which sounds like an excellent WI course. The majority of writing is done in an academic journal and the syllabus includes a full-page description of what an academic journal is—reminds me of what I read in that Toby Fulwiler book. These students will be pushed to take charge of their own learning and reflect thoughtfully on the course readings and discussions. I don't know why all the WI courses can't be like this. This is great."

The phone conversation ended on that positive note. Jeff decided to recommend that the meteorology course not be approved as a WI course unless the professor agreed to include write-to-learn activities. And he planned to bring several other courses to the board's attention because their focus was on students producing a perfect final paper.

On Monday morning he met the other faculty board members in the WAC program office. The first three board members who reported on their applications seemed pleased with the course descriptions and syllabi. One would contact a professor for clarification, but overall, the applications were fine. Jeff adjusted himself in his chair thinking, "Why did I get all the lousy ones?"

The director turned to him next and asked what he observed about the applications and which ones needed more attention. Jeff decided to start with the positive and talked for several minutes about the plant pathology course. Then he moved on to why he believed the meteorology professor should be contacted.

To his surprise, another board member questioned the heavy reliance on journals in the 300-level plant pathology course. He came on a bit forcefully for Jeff's tastes when he said, "Journals are important tools for learning, but a professor who teaches juniors and seniors has a responsibility to help students improve their writing skills—improve their ability to write for a job after they graduate. If students go through the WI program only writing journals, they'll never be prepared to do work place writing. They'll never learn to revise and edit. Correctness is important. I think the meteorology professor is on the right track. You should be calling the plant pathology professor to talk about writing skills."

QUESTIONS FOR REFLECTION AND DISCUSSION

1. Is it appropriate to assign only journal writing in a 300-level class? Should WI courses at the upper division help prepare students to do the types of professional writing that will be required in their future jobs?
2. Is the plant pathology professor avoiding his responsibility to help students with their writing because no formal writing and no revision are required?
3. Should a class be considered writing intensive if the professor assigns mostly in-class, timed writing (exams and quizzes)? How much out-of-class writing should be required?
4. When students are allowed to rewrite answers on a quiz or exam, should the professor give suggestions for content revision? Should he give editing suggestions?
5. Is it appropriate to grade grammar and language use on an in-class exam or quiz? Writing under pressure is common in the work place. Employees must meet deadlines and cannot make mistakes. Should the professor be commended for mirroring a work place setting and demonstrating that correctness is valued?
6. If the WAC Faculty Board decides that the meteorology professor should be contacted, what should the board member say? And if the plant pathology professor is contacted, what should be said to him?
7. Writing-intensive courses at this university are limited to twenty students. Is a lecture format appropriate?
8. Jeff found a variety of teaching approaches and writing assignments when he reviewed the applications. What should the common elements of a "writing-intensive" or WAC course be? Should they be the same for all courses, regardless of level or field?

READINGS FOR FURTHER CONSIDERATION

Bartholomae, David. "Inventing the University." *Journal of Basic Writing* 5 (1986): 4–23.

Bazerman, Charles. "Living with Powerful Words." *Writing, Teaching, and Learning in the Disciplines.* Ed. Anne Herrington and Charles Moran. New York: MLA, 1992. 61–68.

Fulwiler, Toby. *Teaching with Writing.* Upper Montclair: Boynton/Cook, 1987. See especially chapter 1, "Writing and Learning" (1–14), chapter 2, "Student Journals," (15–34), and chapter 3, "Composing" (35–47).

Gardner, Susan. "Introduction: To Use or Not to Use Journals in a Technical or Professional Program." *The Journal Book for Teachers in Technical and Professional Programs.* Ed. Susan Gardner and Toby Fulwiler. Portsmouth: Heinemann, 1999. 1–9.

Hilgers, Thomas, Edna Hussey, and Monica Stitt-Bergh. "'As You're Writing You Have These Epiphanies': What College Students Say About Writing and Learning in Their Majors." *Written Communication* 16 (1999): 317–53.

Part 2

Effective Assignments
Scenes of the Craft

6

Great Assignment, but Nobody's Happy

David A. Jolliffe

Derek Jellinek had been hired by his university, a large Catholic institution with a strong teaching mission, to accomplish a big job: to create a new, state-of-the-art, general-education mathematics course for students whose majors did not require calculus or more advanced math; and to head up a faculty-development initiative designed to get faculty members from many different disciplines to agree to teach the class. The course, which Derek developed with the help of a small steering committee composed of the associate dean of arts and sciences (herself a mathematician) and three other math professors, was called Quantitative Reasoning. Its main goals were three. The course was designed to teach students how to: (1) read and understand written arguments involving quantification that they might encounter, either in their courses throughout the curriculum or in their civic and professional lives beyond the university; (2) create their own expository and argumentative texts about topics that involve quantification and to present these texts either orally or in writing; and (3) access the tools of technology they would need to accomplish the aforementioned reading, writing, and speaking goals.

Since Quantitative Reasoning was required for so many students—about 1,250 per year would take it—Derek needed to identify and prepare enough faculty members to offer about fifty sections of the course a year. He had his hands full.

Within two years of undertaking the task, Derek had the course up and running and had recruited an impressive array of faculty members to teach in the program, people with training not only in mathematics and computer science, but also in the social sciences—professors from psychology, communication, and public policy regularly pitched in—and in the humanities: one philosopher and one historian were among the faculty. And these faculty members created a curriculum and pedagogy that, they hoped, addressed the three basic learning goals. Students read and heard lectures about principles from mathematics, statistics, and computer science, and they did problem sets as homework. They scoured the popular media for stories about quantitative reasoning at work in business, industrial, and governmental settings, and they delivered oral reports about what they discovered. They wrote examinations that included both problems and explanations of their problem-solving activities. They learned how to read and create spreadsheets and how to download, manipulate, and analyze data from the Internet. They were reading about quantification; writing and speaking expository texts about it; and using both their personal computers and their Internet browsers to gather, process, and produce information about their quantitative reasoning.

What seemed missing in the curriculum, though, was argumentative writing. In a previous job, Derek had worked at a mid-sized state university that had a very successful writing-across-the-curriculum program, and he believed strongly that students could really only fully understand the principles of quantitative reasoning if they used them as part of their own arguments, as the building blocks for formulating claims and as the starting points for generating evidence. Derek, therefore, decided to require a final paper in his section of Quantitative Reasoning, and he persuaded several of his faculty colleagues to assign the same project. Here is Derek's assignment:

> You are presidential advisor, and you have been asked to give a briefing on a specific aspect of the United States: population, vital statistics, health, crime, etc. The president needs to be informed of important trends in each area. Using the data from this year's *Statistical Abstract of the United States*, prepare a three-page paper analyzing some of the most recent data available in the area you have been assigned. You should focus on areas that have public policy implications for our nation. You will present your findings to the class in a five-minute PowerPoint presentation. Your analysis must use three related tables from the *Statistical Abstract*; it should include one mathematical model and a prediction based upon it; and it should, where appropriate, refer to ideas from the course such as percentage change, rates, and consumer price index. Your paper should have a well-written introduction and conclusion, and it should use proper bibliographic references, referring to tables by number.

Students were randomly assigned a topic for their briefing; in addition to the aforementioned population, vital statistics, health, and crime, other topics were education, voting patterns, child care, and salaries and wages. In most sections of Quantitative Reasoning, at least three students were assigned to each topic, but they were not expected to work together on their papers or presentations.

Derek seemed pleased with the assignment. He had piloted it in his own section of a course similar to Quantitative Reasoning at his previous university, and students there performed well. They wrote interesting, lively papers that made strong claims about trends in the data and supported those claims by clearly citing evidence from the *Statistical Abstract*. Derek had no problem figuring out which student papers were the best ones, why they were the best, and how others might be improved. So Derek had every reason to be optimistic that the assignment would work well at his new university.

Unfortunately, it didn't. As director of the Quantitative Reasoning program, Derek had to field complaints both from students and from faculty colleagues about the final project. "It's boring," students said. "We don't know what you want us to do in this paper. How are we supposed to know what to write to the president, for heaven's sake? What's more, we don't want to write about those topics. Why can't we choose our own topics? Why can't we work together, if there are three of us with the same topic?"

His colleagues were miffed about other issues. One of them asked, "How do we help students get started on this paper?" Another queried, "Do students really know enough by this point in the course to do this project?" Yet another posed this problem: "So what's going to count on this paper—the quality of the writing or the quality of the mathematics? How are we going to be able to tell students what a good paper is?"

Sheesh, Derek thought to himself. What a good assignment I've got here, and what uncooperative students and colleagues.

QUESTIONS FOR REFLECTION AND DISCUSSION

1. What do you think of Derek's assignment? Do you agree that it provides an appropriate opportunity for students to produce argumentative writing at the end of a Quantitative Reasoning course?

2. In what ways might you suggest that Derek and his colleagues restructure the assignment so that some of the students' concerns are addressed? How might you build in the provision for students to choose the topics they would investigate and analyze? How might you break the task into smaller parts and provide some sort of instructional sequence so the students would "know what you want us to do in this paper?" What pedagogical activities would help students not only get started on this project but also move through its phases to completion successfully?

READINGS FOR FURTHER CONSIDERATION

White, Edward M. *Teaching and Assessing Writing*. 2nd ed. Portland: Calendar Islands Press, 1998. See especially chapter 2, "Assessment and the Design of Writing Assignments."

Wolcott, Willa, and Sue M. Legg. *An Overview of Writing Assessment: Theory, Research, and Practice*. Urbana: National Council of Teachers of English, 1998. See especially chapter 10, "Writing Assessment in the Disciplines."

Yancey, Kathleen Blake, and Brian Huot, eds. *Assessing Writing Across the Curriculum: Diverse Approaches and Practices*. Greenwich: Ablex, 1997.

7

Trudy Does Comics

Chris M. Anson

"Great seminar!" Howard Pruett exclaimed to the group leaders as he and his colleagues filed out of the room. For the past two days, Howard had been participating in a faculty development workshop at his school (along with two dozen colleagues from various departments) focusing on teaching and assessing writing in the disciplines. Inspired by the many ways that the seminar leaders had helped the group to think about writing, Howard was determined to make some major changes in the way he taught philosophy. "I can't believe I've been so dull in my teaching," he observed to Amanda Shall, one of the seminar participants he had befriended. "Lecture, test, lecture, test . . . it's a wonder that my students have tolerated me for this long. And my writing assignments—sheer boredom!"

"Mea culpa," Amanda said, laughing. "I think this seminar has been a breath of fresh air. But are you ready to put all that work into redesigning your courses?"

"Actually, I'm looking forward to it," Howard replied as they left the building. "And the first thing I'm changing is the way I use writing in my Principles course."

For over a decade, Howard had assigned occasional short, formal papers in his Principles of Philosophy course. As a supporter of writing across the curriculum, he had become known in his department for his opinion that students should write at least one paper in every course they took. While he teasingly admitted to his English department colleagues that he was not versed in the "higher arts of teaching the lower verbal skills," he had—until the faculty seminar—felt quite confident assigning and grading his short academic papers. In these papers, he expected his students to explain philosophical concepts and provide examples for generalizations, or to argue a position on a philosophical controversy using a standard essay structure that included a thesis statement and carefully developed supporting paragraphs. His students rarely contested his grades and comments, which tended to be rigorous.

But now he was about to throw out what he had been doing for ten years: a course so "automatic" that he usually prepared for his new term the day before it began. Later that day, he dug out a copy of his syllabus from the previous term and began marking it up. Still inspired by the seminar, he found himself putting big slashes through the section describing his writing assignments, then jotting down lists of ideas on the back of the pages. He hadn't felt this excited about teaching since he collaborated with a close colleague on a team-taught course.

––––––––––

"How can you say that?" Trudy almost yelled, clutching her second paper and looking defiantly at Howard as the rest of the class filed out of the room. It was a few weeks into Howard's philosophy course, and not all was well.

"Look, Trudy, I wrote to you about this on your last paper," Howard replied, gathering his books and notes. "When I asked you to develop ways of understanding the material of the course, I had in mind all sorts of possibilities—traditional papers, invented dialogues with the philosophers we're reading, double-entry notebooks, the annotated page idea in which you critique major concepts point by point. I did *not* have in mind comic books. I'm afraid I just can't accept what you're doing."

In redesigning his course, Howard had decided to give the students an opportunity not only to write in different ways about the course material, but to define these ways themselves and assemble their work into a course portfolio. According to the leaders of his faculty-development seminar, providing such opportunities can help students to respond in ways that better match their learning styles and intellectual dispositions. In his syllabus, Howard had included the following passage reflecting his new expectations for students' writing:

> *Writing assignments:* These will be worth one-half of your final grade. There will be five assignments due on the dates specified and collected into a course portfolio. I will grade each piece as it is turned in. *You* will decide what kind of writing you would like to do; you may choose typical school writing such as essays and formal analyses of the readings, or you may be more inventive, perhaps writing an imaginary dialogue with one of the five philosophers we are reading, or a dialogue *between* two different philosophers, or perhaps a parody of an author's writings. Be inventive but insightful, and write enough to explore a subject well, please. The final assignment will appear first in your portfolio; it will be a 1–2 page reflection on what all the writing in the portfolio adds up to. Explain the portfolio to a reader so that the pieces make sense together. In other words, give us an introduction.

In drafting these new requirements for his course, Howard had worried a little that he would be unable to make clear judgments on the quality of the students' work. After all, they would be turning in different kinds of writing, some of which would not resemble papers he was used to reading in his course. Partly to reassure himself and partly to be more specific to his class about the assignments, he spent ten minutes during the first class meeting discussing what he meant by "free choice" in the assignments. "What will I be looking for in these, then?" he asked rhetorically. "First, that you have become engaged with the subject matter—not just that you have read the material but that you have actually reflected on it, swirled it around in your thinking like a sip of fine wine. These papers are first and foremost a tool for your own learning, and second, a tool for me to assess the extent to which you are actively and critically exploring the subject matter." He realized as he said this that he was echoing some concepts from the summer seminar—terms like "active learning" and "critical thinking." But he had found it all so compelling that certainly his class would, too. A glance around the room at the twenty young students confirmed it, he thought: many of them seemed eager to get to work.

But now, a few weeks into the term, here was Trudy, visibly upset, holding her paper and demanding an explanation.

"But it says right here," Trudy went on, searching through his syllabus. "Well, it says we decide about what kind of writing. Maybe it was what you said on the first day, but I remember reading or hearing something about just wanting to know if we were reading the stuff and thinking about it. And I'm doing that here. I mean, look at all the different things other people are writing. Why can't I use these little scenes as my way of showing that I've done the reading?"

Howard had to admit that he was intrigued the first time he saw Trudy's comics after the class had read Plato's allegory of the cave in the course text, *The Endless Questions*. Most of the students had taken a safe path on this first essay, discussing the idea of Forms or critiquing the relationship between ideals and what is tangible in the world. A few students had tried something different, most notably Kurt Nichols, who had imagined himself being on the other side of the cave wall and seeing not shadows but what he called the Real Thing. When he reached Trudy's comics a few papers after Kurt's, Howard was excited to think that at least a few students were using alternative methods of analyzing the material.

In that first paper, Trudy had drawn two imaginary characters (Hip and Zip) shackled on one side of the cave. The drawings themselves were quite good—and he expected it: on the first day, during the introductions, Trudy had pointed out that she was a studio arts major specializing in drawing, and wanted to enter the field of advertising as a commercial artist.

But as he read the comics, Howard began feeling unsure about how he should grade Trudy's work. The two characters spoke to each other in short sentences that appeared in the usual cartoon balloons above their heads. Their discussion seemed to Howard rather unsophisticated, rendered in a kind of teenage speech not characteristic of discussions in his course. It was hard to tell from the short exchanges just how much Trudy really understood of the Plato readings. When he had finished the page of comic frames, he was utterly at a loss to decide what to say to Trudy about her work. He had put the comics aside, finished the rest of the papers, and then returned to Trudy's work the next day. Finally, pressured by the upcoming class meeting, he jotted down some notes on the back of the comic page:

Trudy—this is fine work visually speaking, and I like the *idea* (if not entirely the substance) of the comics. I think that in some ways, however, the choice of comics has limited your opportunities to explore the readings very fully. It's not clear, for example, whether Zip really knows what Plato means by Forms, and most of the time Hip is just saying "yup" to Zip's pronouncements (were you trying to be Socratic here? If so, it's not entirely clear to me). So while the idea is innovative, it may not work, finally, as a method of writing in the course. C−

When he had handed back these first papers, he noticed that Trudy seemed upset, but she didn't approach him. Now, after the second paper (and another, longer batch of comics on a reading by Kant), she was confronting him directly about his assessment. On this batch, Howard had given Trudy another C−, mainly to recognize that she had, in fact, read the selection and tried to say something about it in her comics. But again Howard had been at a loss to grade her work. Hip was clearly more vocal this time, and there were a lot more frames in the comics as the two characters carried on their discussion about Kant's positions. But after all, Howard had thought, there was simply *less text* here than in the other students' papers. Trudy just wasn't writing as much, even in several pages of comics, and it was again difficult for him to know how deeply she understood Kant.

"Trudy, I know how much you enjoy art," Howard had said, trying not to be confrontational. "But this is a course that turns around the written language, around words that stand on their own. Your comics are fun and interesting, but they go only halfway toward what I see as the proper way to explore the field of philosophy. Why don't you put the comics aside for the third paper and try something a little different? Besides, you might find some other new ways of exploring the material and becoming engaged with it."

"Fine," Trudy said abruptly, thrusting the syllabus and her paper into her bag. "But I don't consider that freedom." And she swiftly left the room.

QUESTIONS FOR REFLECTION AND DISCUSSION

1. Is Howard wise in asking Trudy to stop using the comics in her responses to the required writing assignments? How do you assess his course of action?
2. Should Howard have been more explicit in his expectations to students for their experimental writing? If so, could that squelch the "freedom" he wants to give them? What could he have said about his expectations?
3. Is there a way for Howard to recognize Trudy's strongly visual learning style (and creative talents) in his expectations for students' papers?
4. Could Trudy have done anything in her responses to meet Howard's expectations, as expressed in his syllabus and in what he said to the class?
5. What is the relationship between the course portfolio and the individual assignments? What further potential do you see in this relationship?

6. What issues does this case raise about diverse forms of writing, teachers' expectations, criteria for assessing learning, power versus freedom in discourse, and the relationship between learning to write and writing to learn?

READINGS FOR FURTHER CONSIDERATION

Anson, Chris M. "Reflective Reading: Developing Thoughtful Ways to Respond to Students' Writing." *Evaluating Writing: The Role of Teachers' Knowledge About Text, Learning, and Culture*. Ed. Charles R. Cooper and Lee Odell. Urbana: National Council of Teachers of English, 1999. 302–24.

Anson, Chris M., and Richard Beach. *Journals in the Classroom: Writing to Learn*. Norwood: Christopher-Gordon, 1996.

Straub, Richard. *The Practice of Response: Strategies for Commenting on Student Writing*. Cresskill: Hampton, 2000.

8

Who Has the Power?

Christine Farris

Jack Hastings has been teaching the introductory political science course at his college for several years. Like many introductory poli sci courses, the course is concerned with comparative political systems and the nature of ideology. Before completing his doctorate, Jack served in the Peace Corps and worked as a political speech writer in Washington. Students generally appreciate his lectures, which are informative and sprinkled with witty real-life anecdotes. However, the first year that Jack taught the course as "writing intensive," neither he nor his students were happy with the changes writing made in the course. Several students came to office hours to discuss his evaluation of their papers. One student complained that Jack wrote so little on the paper that she had no clue why she got the grade she did. Another student pointed out to him that all he had marked were the surface errors. Still another wanted to know why he hardly ever mentioned anything about writing in lecture. "Do you think of the writing assignments as exams—so you don't want to give anything away?" she asked him. While Jack did not think he was guilty of merely using writing to test rather than to learn, he had hoped his students would bring to their papers more of the critical analysis he believed he encouraged in lecture and discussion.

Jack belongs to a brown-bag group of faculty who, under the auspices of the WAC program, have recently incorporated writing into their general education courses. They meet regularly for lunch to discuss how things are going and take turns presenting an assignment or concern about writing. When it is his turn, Jack brings his most recent writing assignment and three student papers to the group. "I'm wondering if my students even understand my assignments," he confesses to the group. "And if what I'm grading for on papers has anything to do with what distinguishes my strongest students from my weakest students in this course. These were three of the best papers, but even the student who got an A on the third paper came to see me, saying he couldn't tell from the comments what he had done right, and he wanted to know so he could do it again next time."

Miranda Ruiz, the WAC consultant who leads the group, suggests that the group use their discussion of Jack's students' papers to reexamine Jack's assignment and criteria for evaluation. "First," Miranda says, "let's imagine what each of these three students thought the assignment called for. Then let's talk about which of the papers we think made the most of the assignment. Then we can look at how Jack's assignment did or didn't enable what he and the rest of us think students were able to do."

Jack distributed copies of his assignment and the three student papers, and the group set to work.

ASSIGNMENT

Political scientists approach the role of the people in determining governmental policy differently. Considering the countries we have examined in this course, how do you deal with the question of who has the power? Discuss the various approaches and then argue one of the positions. You will be graded according to the following criteria on a 10-point scale: Thesis (2 points), Supporting Evidence (3 points), and Mechanics (5 points).

STUDENT PAPER #1 : WHO HAS THE POWER?

All governments have similar goals, but the ways in which they meet these goals differ a great deal. When we compare governing institutions, three theories represent how power structures operate in society: elitism, neo-Marxism, and pluralism. These theories help explain the relationship between society and politics and why systems work or fail. In order to answer who makes the political decisions, we can use these theories to see whether a society gives the greatest power to the elite, the capitalist ruling class, or to other interest groups.

The elitist theory divides a society into three categories: the governing elite, the non-governing elite, and the non-elite. This structure gives control to a small minority. The status of the ruling class is based on wealth, birth, military prowess, or knowledge. If there is a revolution, however, the non-elite may become powerful and new blood comes into the decision-making process.

The neo-Marxist theory also divides society into three categories: capitalist ruling class, middle class and working class. With this theory, a government is a reflection of underlying economic forces, primarily the pattern of ownership and the means of production. The ruling class controls the basic conditions of the working class. The distribution of wealth is concentrated in the upper class and much of the working class lives in poverty. Power, in this theory, lies with the upper class, which makes decisions that support the interests of their class and exploit the middle and lower classes.

In the theory of pluralism, the class structure changes constantly. Interest groups seek to influence public policy. Some issues cause interest groups to join together and form coalitions. This is good for small groups, because they can be influential by being allied with each other. No one group can win all the time or get a monopoly on political resources. This division of power provides a good representation of the people.

The United States is a good example of pluralism. Political parties must bargain and compromise to get bills passed. While doing so, they must keep in mind the interests of both the party and the public. If a party has a majority, it wants to keep it, but public elections can change that. So it is important to satisfy the public, as well as the party's interests if they want to stay in power. The pluralistic society is one that maintains the active support of the people. Various interest groups may fight for different objectives, but no single party will always win. Because pluralism is full of compromises, wins and losses, it serves the best interests of the people to the greatest extent.

STUDENT PAPER #2: ELITIXISM RULES

Since there have been thinking men and women, the question of who has the power has been on their minds. It's natural to wonder who's the boss. In attempting to answer this question, people struggle with answers, none of which are foolproof. The three answers with the greatest following are elitism, neo-Marxism and pluralism.

Imagine the world in the shape of a pyramid. At the very top are the biggest houses, the greenest grass, the cleanest water, the fastest cars, and the smartest people. Further down lie the average homes, okay grass, muddy water, slow cars, and average people. According to the elitist theory, the very top is the home of the elites. The power structure. At the bottom of the pyramid lives the non-elites, the masses. The very top control the government, the economy, the country.

Birth, wealth and intelligence are usually needed for elite status. But determined non-elites can push their way in. Pluralism really grew out of the counter-elites and is a way to bust up the power structure. The shape of pluralism changes continually. Power is distributed among many. There are no winners or losers. Everyone has a fair chance. Life is a group effort in pluralism. All issues get discussed among the interest groups whose constituents are the masses.

The neo-Marxists reject this kind of fluidity. They agree with the elites that there is a ruling class, but this ruling class is not just made up of the born rich or super intelligent. It is instead made up of those in power positions in industry—those who control the food, clothing, water and energy supply to the masses. Without these things, the masses cannot survive. This explains why the company executives hold all the cards and call all the shots.

In studying these ideologies, I find fault with all three. I have, therefore, developed my own theory, borrowing some of my assumptions from elitism and neo-Marxism. I call my theory neo-elitixism. The neo-elitix world is shaped much like the elitist world. At the top of the pyramid is the power structure. Those who live at the top own all the major industry or are the family of these tycoons. They have all the money to get the best education, therefore they are the most intelligent. Their relatives will eventually take their place when the power players grow too old to run the power structure. The counter-neo-elitixs will only spend their parents money to party and buy things and will amount to nothing. A few of these neo-elitixs will enter into politics. But most will wield their influence and their money to get things done the way they want them to be.

All those in the power structure were once part of the masses. At some time, their ancestors were living in average homes, driving average cars and making average salaries. By either dumb luck or smarts (or murder as with the Mafia) each family member pushed its way to the top of the pyramid. And by the same virtues they have been able to remain there.

But some will fall due to losing their money and be replaced. Why? Because all humankind strives to be part of that power structure and keeps pushing until they succeed. After all, is that not the American Dream? So the world is ruled by both the very rich and those who own industry. They are usually one and the same. Elitism and neo-Marxism both believe in a ruling class which resides in the upper crust of society, with the only difference being capitalism's power.

By combining these two theories they become a very strong argument: neo-Elixitism.

STUDENT PAPER #3: POLITICAL LENSES, NOT ANSWERS

Despite the existence of many different methods of political evaluation, none of them can stand alone as a definitive answer to the question of who has the power, because every system of government is unique and, therefore, defies the over-simplistic restrictions of political theory, Political theories, however, can be helpful lenses for viewing and understanding political perspectives, and that's where their true value lies.

Three of the most popular political theories are elitism, pluralism, and neo-Marxism. Elitism is the political theory which contends that power rests in the hands of a ruling elite who hold their positions because they are the most capable. Pluralist theorists contend that the main political units are interest groups, and political power exists in a constantly changing combination of these groups. Neo-Marxism, like elitism, stresses the existence of power in the hands of a small minority, but neo-Marxists believe that this minority possesses political power because it is a capitalist class which owns the means of production and the banks.

Because economic considerations are always a key factor in any political decision making, the neo-Marxist view, which stresses economic influence, is the most definitive of these three theories. Karl Marx actually believed that a superior economic method existed that would eventually do away with capitalism. Today this possibility appears to have been no more than a pipe dream or an ideal that lies in the future. Both the Soviet Union and China, the two largest states which claim Marxist goals, have moved in the direction of capitalism. During the past 80 years of Russian history, attempts at developing a successful Marxist economy have not proven as successful as the capitalist alternative. Because capitalism remains the most influential economic alternative, neo-Marxist theory, which directly addresses the effects of capitalism on political power, is the most accurate.

Neo-Marxism, like all political theories, however, is not without its weaknesses. The neo-Marxist contention that power rests in the hands of those who own the majority of influential economic institutions is not true in every case. Two of the most politically effective forces in the 80 year history of the Soviet Union were the army and the KGB. Neither were economic institutions or owned a significant portion of the means of production, yet they possessed much political power. While the actual ruling elite were selected from the most elite positions within the CPSU, no rulers since Stalin have been able to rule without pressure from these two institutions. Indeed, without the support of the army and the secret police, a member of the party would not have had a chance of becoming politically powerful.

Within the same nation, however, evidence exists which lends support to the neo-Marxist political theory. Even though the Soviet Union always shunned capitalism, the political regime always monopolized control over the powerful state institutions. The CPSU, because of its autonomous economic influence, is very similar to what neo-Marxists term the capitalist ruling class. And as Russia continued to face many of the same economic problems, especially regarding agriculture, it has been facing since 1917, it has moved toward capitalism as the only feasible alternative. Even outside the realm of "capitalism" the neo-Marxist political theory makes a good argument in response to the question of who holds political power.

Obviously the neo-Marxist political theory is not independent or flawless. The most important thing to remember when using political theory to address questions of power is that no theory used exclusively can provide an accurate understanding of political power. Political theories, in fact, are much better at pointing out the weakness of opposing theories than in defining positions of power.

After reading the student papers, Flora, a professor from Education, is eager to comment. "I think the first one does the best job of responding to the assignment as it stands. The student lays out the three theories that were obviously examined in the course and then argues for democratic pluralism in which the people rule as the superior one.

"Yes, but that would be accepting the theories on their own terms," argues Sam, a French professor. "The United States is a democracy in which the people rule just because we *say* it is. The student who wrote the third paper understands that—theories are just tools, which can themselves be questioned and refined, not mirrors of reality. But Jack, I think your assignment really hides the football here. If you want kids to use and critique both theories and governments, then don't lull them into thinking they can give you an airtight summary of lecture."

"Wait a minute," injects Muriel from the sociology department. "I'd say the last paper is just as likely to be Jack's lecture notes recycled as a paper. Besides, that's a very simplistic analysis of the role of the army and the KGB."

"For just these reasons," says Anna from Comp Lit, "I like the second paper because the student demonstrates she comprehends the course material but can use it to generate her own theory which she then applies to her observations.

"I disagree," says Isabel from English. "She's trying to get away with a move to personal expression that is an unnecessary cop-out. The other three theories allow her to make and refine those observations."

"What I want to know," adds Adam from Computer Science, "is whether Jack—and the rest of us, for that matter—should spell everything out in a writing assignment. Should he say up front that he will evaluate students on the basis of the extent to which they can use and critique the three political theories in their original analysis? As it stands now, why shouldn't all of these papers get A's if Jack was just looking for a thesis, supporting evidence, and good mechanics? There are no points for analysis."

"Why should he change his assignment at all if the third student was able to figure out what to do with it?" asks Rachel from Philosophy. "To unpack all we've said just now would be to turn it into an essay exam in which the student just returns the goods undamaged. The context of the course should make it clear that what Jack wants to see is analysis."

QUESTIONS FOR REFLECTION AND DISCUSSION

1. Just as Steve's faculty group did, consider his writing assignment. Is it clear what tasks are being asked of students?
2. Look carefully at each of the student papers. What does each student think the assignment calls for?
3. Which paper would you rank the highest, next highest, the lowest? Is your ranking because of the assignment or in spite of it?
4. Why do you think Steve gave the third paper the highest grade? Would you give it the highest grade? Why or why not?
5. How might Steve rewrite his assignment so that more students might succeed on this assignment? How might he adjust his criteria so as not to "hide the football" or "give it all away"?
6. Consider the various responses of the brown-bag group. Whose comments do you find most valid or appealing, and why? What might you say in response to those with whom you disagree?

READINGS FOR FURTHER CONSIDERATION

Farris, Christine. "Giving Religion, Taking Gold: Disciplinary Cultures and the Claims of Writing Across the Curriculum." *Cultural Studies in the English Classroom.* Ed. James A. Berlin and Michael J. Vivion. Portsmouth: Boynton/Cook, 1992. 112–22.

Farris, Christine, and Raymond Smith. "Writing-Intensive Courses: Tools for Curricular Change." *Writing Across the Curriculum: A Guide for Developing Programs.* Ed. Susan H. McLeod and Margot Soven. Newbury Park: Sage, 1992. 71–86.

Herrington, Anne. "Writing to Learn: Writing Across the Disciplines." *College English* 43 (April 1981): 379–87.

Prior, Paul, et al. "Research and WAC Evaluation: An In-Progress Reflection." *Assessing Writing Across the Curriculum: Diverse Approaches and Practices.* Ed. Kathleen Blake Yancey and Brian Huot. Greenwich: Ablex, 1997. 185–216.

Smith, Raymond, and Christine Farris. "Adventures in the WAC Assessment Trade: Reconsidering the Link Between Research and Consultation." *Assessing Writing Across the Curriculum: Diverse Approaches and Practices.* Ed. Kathleen Blake Yancey and Brian Huot. Greenwich: Ablex, 1997. 173–84.

9

Pieces Missing
Assignments and Expectations

Joan Mullin

I n operation for fifteen years, the Writing Center at Huron State University has gained a positive reputation for connecting tutorials to classroom instruction. On this campus, the Writing Center and WAC are one and the same; faculty know that their students are not being tutored on only assumed expectations of the discipline. While the center was being created, faculty across the disciplines were interviewed and asked to provide sample assignments and writing guidelines. The goal of the interviews was to ensure that writing consultants would be trained to support ways in which their students are expected to write and think.

When students come into or are sent to the Writing Center, they are likewise aware that many faculty have worked with writing consultants; some faculty have even had consultants linked to their classes. But both students and consultants have sometimes been confused by the gaps between what a professor may write as an assignment and what that professor may say are his or her expectations.

As part of continual training, the Writing Center director often invites professors to consultant in-services in order to learn about the faculty expectations and assessments of writing in their discipline. Stretched out on the comfortable chairs, couches, and pillows that serve to harbor staff meetings, writing consultants have learned to value this seemingly relaxed space as one in which difficult matters can bubble to the surface. Meetings are often tape recorded for the convenience of the occasional staff member who can't attend and also to provide a research base for the development of the center. Today, four professors—in biology, geography, English, and art history—have agreed to bring an assignment they give to their students and explain to the consultants what level of writing they expect, how they expect their students to respond, and how they imagine a writing consultant could best help their students. Excerpts of their recorded conversations appear below, along with the assignments for which they have sought consultation.

SCENE ONE

The biology professor, Dr. Wressler [DW], is a well-known researcher in the field of microbiology, known for his NSF grants and his international reputation in the field. He is considered by students to be an excellent though demanding teacher. He has brought an assignment from his writing-intensive course, Readings in Biology. The junior and senior majors who take this course are expected to read about current topics in recent journals, research the conflicts concerning an issue, and write from various materials throughout the course. Accustomed to working with Dr. Wressler's students, Rebecca Holgarth [RH], the writing consultant, is looking forward to asking him questions about the nature of his assignments. He begins by handing out what Rebecca knows to be a typical assignment from him:

> After reading the leading article on sheep cloning in Scotland, explain the processes undertaken by the researchers, focusing in particular on any steps in the process that seem to be missing. This may be a list initially, but explain in a two to three page paper the procedures involved.

DW: I expect clear, relatively error-free writing from my students—they are juniors and seniors and should be serious about science. They should summarize in stages the cloning process in the article. We've spent a lot of class time the previous week on the use of controls in the research literature in microbiology and the need for attention to primary and secondary experimental environments in this field. You see, I expect students to notice that the article lacks descriptive background in these areas, that information is missing that is important to understanding the whole process.

RH: What are the main problems you see when students do this assignment?

DW: Well, besides the grammar and sentence problems any one student has, they spend too much time describing the processes—they ought to be able to pretty much list them and be done with it.

RH: Do you actually want a list?

DW: No, no, I mean that I don't want a short story.

RH: Oh, good, because that's what I assumed when I worked with your students; I try to tell them that writing in biology is not like finding the central point in a novel.

DW: No, I know—I've worked with you enough to know that, but students still seem to spend too much time on that part, no matter how much I cross out on their papers. And then when it comes to finding the missing sections in the research piece . . . I don't know why they can't find something that, when pointed out to them, even they see as obvious.

RH: I noticed the crossing out on papers when the students come in for revision, and you do point out in the margin "pieces missing???" But, well, there are two things I find: students don't seem to know why certain facts are crossed out and others aren't, and then they seem unsure of what you mean by "missing"—I mean, I never knew you covered it in class the previous week—students never said anything.

DW: See, they just don't make the connection; I go into detail about how important controls are in microbiology, environmental controls, but then when it gets to the cloning piece, they just don't seem to make the connection. I certainly don't want to give away what it is I want them to do! How else would I be able to evaluate what they know? They ought to be able to figure out when I cross something out that I mean for them to eliminate the wordiness. And if there are question marks in the side margin with "Pieces missing" they should figure out that I want more information. Yet their rewrites—well, except for those who come in here regularly—don't show much improvement, even though I know that they are bright students. Look, one student explained for one of the processes that cultures were sealed and stored; then the embryos were implanted in the female. "Well, what happened in between?" I asked in the margin. It's as if suddenly there was a miracle and an embryo appeared. That's not science.

QUESTIONS FOR REFLECTION AND DISCUSSION

1. What philosophy of education is evidenced in this comment by Wressler?

   See, they just don't make the connection; I go into detail about how important controls are in microbiology, environmental controls, but then when it gets to the cloning piece, they just don't seem to make the connection. I certainly don't want to give away what it is I want them to do! How else would I be able to evaluate what they know? They ought to be able to figure out when I cross something out that I mean for them to eliminate the wordiness.

2. What issues of importance to Wressler's teaching are evidenced in this comment by Rebecca?

   But, well, there are two things I find: students don't seem to know why certain facts are crossed out and others aren't, and then they seem unsure of what you mean by "missing"—I mean, I never knew you covered it in class the previous week—students never said anything.

3. What measures might Wressler take to ensure that his students are prepared to do the assignment?

4. What kinds of feedback might help ensure positive responses to revision?

SCENE TWO

Dr. Anchia [DA] is an associate professor of geography, well published in her field, who is teaching a class in industrial geography. She always sends in her assignments before students come to the Writing Center. Today, Tom Sisk, the writing consultant, has Dr. Anchia's latest assignment before him:

> Discuss the similarities and differences between the Mexican maquiladora outlined by Robert B. South in the article "Transnational 'Maquiladora' Location" and James Rubenstein's "Changing Distribution of the American Automobile Industry." Then answer the following: How does location theory operate in the same way on both sides of the border? What elements of the arguments would be pertinent to an American automobile manufacturer's decision to choose either site for relocation?
>
> Use our class discussions about each of these articles and the current issues in modern manufacturing, particularly as they pertain to NAFTA agreements, to place yourself in the position of the manufacturer. Assume that you have an obligation to your product, your shareholders, and the community in which your corporate headquarters is located.

TS: I have to tell you, Dr. Anchia, how much I enjoy working with your students. Your assignments so clearly set a context for the discussion and outline the assumptions students should consider answering.

DA: Yes, I want students to succeed in answering the questions so that they can learn through their writing. They seem best to do that when they are given guidance.

TS: This assignment, in which you referred to the articles students were to use as a basis for their discussion on location theory, really gave us something to refer to when students came in unsure of how to reference major points of contention in the articles. I notice, though, that when students revise their work, you seem to want more information than they give, and sometimes, I'm not sure how much more of a discussion you want, given the three page length you ask for . . . I mean, students seem to have difficulty providing a concise response.

DA: Exactly what I wanted to talk about with you. I want them to discuss the issue, not just ramble on about what they think. They go on and on about the material, but they never hit on the main facts.

TS: The main facts—the central point of each article? It seems they do . . . .

DA: Well, they touch on it but then they go on and on about why they think a population might have moved, why they think the conditions changed, where else the movement might have occurred . . . they stray from the articles and imagine conditions for which there is no evidence.

TS: But as part of the discussion, I mean, you ask them to "discuss" what they think about the articles' propositions.

DA: Right, I ask them to discuss it. That's why I keep writing "DISCUSS" in the margins and emphasize in class that they have to cite the propositions of the research, provide evidence for the discussion.

TS: But looking at this student paper you brought in today, the third paragraph, the student says, " If the manufacturers would move to the mountainous region, avoiding the drought conditions, they would then . . ."

DA: IF—why IF? The articles don't discuss "if"; they don't even address issues of mountains or plains. They are concerned with the concentration of factories near the border rather than in the cities.

TS: Some of those cities mentioned, though, are in mountains, which seem to impact the transportation issues that could arise.

DA: Correct. That could arise. But that is not an issue discussed in the article.

TS: You don't want students to discuss the implications of the conditions on their choices? You want . . .

DA: I want them to discuss—to stick to the information in the articles, to juxtapose the arguments.

TS: But for me, well, to discuss means to take the facts and given them, look at what might be missing, consider ideas that the decision may have to include, that may make me locate on the border rather than in the Midwest.

DA: But establishment of a maquiladora focuses on what is good for the people, as well as for the industry. Location theory accounts for the facts as they are presented in the article—the known.

QUESTIONS FOR REFLECTION AND DISCUSSION

1. What is Tom missing about Anchia's use of "discuss?"
2. What, in Anchia's assessment, are the students and consultants not understanding?
3. How might that be remedied in Anchia's responses? In class?
4. What are the implications of the misunderstanding with regard to language use in assessments and assignments?

SCENE THREE

Dr. Cudòr [DC], an assistant professor of English new to the university, has written a letter of congratulations to the Writing Center consultants in which she says she is "pleased to have the support of the Writing Center to help her students understand how to write well." Since she is new, writing consultants Sarah Bernstein [SB] and Rick Harraldson [RH] are a bit reluctant to bring up a question that has been bothering them as they work with Dr. Cudòr's students: papers that are brought in for revision are covered with corrections of verb case, dangling modifiers, pronoun references; rewriting (in the margins) of complete sentences to make them more complex; and references to "fragments," "run-ons," and "s-v agreement." What particularly confuses them is that the assignments do not stress these surface features, but say instead that students should concentrate on ideas. In the latest assignment, students are told to "say what you want to say about how the characters in the novel expose the colonialist attitudes even as they themselves are unable to articulate their own complicity in those attitudes."

Cudòr begins:

DC: . . . deplorable writing that students exhibit—as if they haven't learned anything in high schools. They can't organize a paper, don't know how to support an idea, ramble on disconnectedly . . . no matter how often I comment on their paper. When they turn in revisions, they've made all the corrections but their papers are still poor arguments for their positions.

SB: One of the things I notice about your students is that they often ask us to help them make the "right correction"—they want to make sure that they understand your handwriting and can copy it correctly into their paper. But they also have difficulty with the theoretical positions they are to understand, in this case, how characters can reflect a colonial position when they can't articulate it. They seem to have problems being inside and outside the theories and yet they come here worried about the grammar.

RH: Yeah, I get a lot of questions about "What does 's-v agreement' mean?"

DC: See, they don't know basic grammar!

SB: Right . . . yet, when I ask them to read their papers out loud, they often catch their own mistakes—even if they don't know what they are called. Yet it seems their articulation is connected to their thinking about . . .

DC: Well, that's why I try to rewrite their sentences in the margins . . . that should give them an idea of what I expect them to say.

RH: The problem seems to be that they don't understand that correcting the grammar won't make their argument strong. When they rewrite a sentence that you wrote, it doesn't always help them think about rewriting the whole paragraph. They really think that all they have to do is make the corrections you suggest and then they're done and should get an A.

DC: Well, that's the problem, they just don't think about the entire argument; all they pay attention to is how it looks on the page. If they would just get their sentences correct, they should be able to see how faulty their logic is.

QUESTIONS FOR REFLECTION AND DISCUSSION

1. What is Cudòr's theory about how students learn to write?

2. What is the conflict between what Cudòr says she wants and how she responds to students' papers?

3. What are the consultants trying to point out to her about learning to write?

4. How might Cudòr's evaluations change?

SCENE FOUR

Dr. Sirkof [DS] is a professor of art history whose classes are filled with slides, narratives, and anecdotes about place and culture. His courses are popular and well attended by students. Consultant Maria Escudero [ME] has noticed that students who work on revisions seem overwhelmed by the personality and expertise of Dr. Sirkof.

ME: Dr. Sirkof, I am so glad you're here today because I love art history and like to work with your students.

DS: Yes, the area is so very interesting—except to the students (ha ha)! No, they try, but they just don't get into enough detail . . . never enough detail. I asked them . . . here . . . let me get the last couple assignments. Look; I asked them to do this:

> (1) Compare the gothic cathedral of England with that of France. Or (2), choose one of the sculptors central to the programs that evolved in the transition from Romanesque to Gothic and explain why he was important.

Sorry—no women sculptors were known at that time (ha ha)!

ME: I remember those; the students then have come to the center with their papers after you graded them. And you do write extensive comments in the margin. On the last paper I worked on, I know there was a lot more you referred to about the Romanesque that you wanted included and then more about the sculpture programs in general, and then you wrote a lot on one page about that little church in the Pyrenees . . .

DS: Ah yes! A beautiful example of medieval conquest and divorce! Did you know that the queen building that little church warred with her ex-husband, the king in the next province, over the land on which it was built? That's not often known . . . they used to steal relics from each other's churches, and . . . [DS continues for four minutes].

ME: I learn so much from reading your students' papers and your comments! I'm overwhelmed by it all—I think maybe your students are too.

DS: For the most part I have good students, but even though I have them write all the time, I still find that they can't seem to distinguish between the finer points of a building, place it in a context, and compare it with another—they come in with an idea of a gothic cathedral and leave with the same idea!

ME: And they should be able to . . .

DS: They should be able to point out details that a person who hasn't taken art history wouldn't necessarily notice.

ME: So in class? . . . It seems they do a lot of writing outside of class.

DS: Well, class is largely spent looking at slides and talking about them; the outside papers are geared toward having them process the information. And yet . . .

ME: And yet they don't seem to carry the insights home with them? You know, we see a lot of papers here that students write from in-class freewrites, where they . . .

DS: I've used those occasionally.

ME: They seem to be great resources for students, where they can play with terms and ideas right there, in class, and formulate questions when they don't even know yet that they have them!

DS: So you're suggesting?

ME: Well, I know I often need time to process information, so I know I'm heading in the right direction. I had a student of yours last week and she so admired your knowledge that she didn't think she knew anything. I kept asking her questions and writing down her answers and she was amazed at what she knew! She was sure she couldn't think of enough to write! Another student came in with a terribly disorganized paper chock full of details and generalities that had little relation to each other—they were like lists in sentences. She was almost paralyzed about writing.

DS: They know they can come to me; I give them lots of ideas!

QUESTIONS FOR REFLECTION AND DISCUSSION

1. Identify the problems students seem to be having when they write for Sirkof. Which are related to the classroom? Which are related to the writing?
2. What could Sirkoff do in the classroom to ensure that his students "distinguish between the finer points of a building, place it in a context, and compare it with another"?
3. How might the assignments given by Sirkof contribute to students' inability to fulfill his expectations?
4. What kind of feedback in and out of class would help students overcome their anxiety about their work?

READINGS FOR FURTHER DISCUSSION

Anderson, Rebecca. "Why Talk About Different Ways to Grade? The Shift from Traditional Assessment to Alternative Assessment." *Changing the Way We Grade Stu-*

dent Performance: Classroom Assessment and the New Learning Paradigm. Ed. Rebecca Anderson and Bruce Speck. San Francisco: Jossey-Bass, 1998. 17–32.

Bean, John. *Engaging Ideas: The Professor's Guide to Integrating Writing, Critical Thinking, and Active Learning in the Classroom.* San Francisco: Jossey-Bass, 1996.

Putney, Richard H. "The Civil War and Its Monuments." *ARTiculating: Teaching Writing in a Visual World.* Ed. Pamela Childers, Eric Hobson, and Joan Mullin. Portsmouth: Boynton/Cook, 1998.

10

Managing Disciplinary Difference

Julie M. Zeleznik, Rebecca E. Burnett, Thomas Polito,
David Roberts, and John Shafer

Mike is sitting in Report & Proposal Writing, an upper-level writing requirement he and all his classmates are taking in conjunction with an upper-level agronomy course, Soil, Fertilizer, and Water Management. On some days, he's really glad to be taking these two courses together—after all, he's getting seven credits for two courses and a lab. For the past three years, most of his classes have had many more students than the sixteen students in these two courses, so right away he knows he's getting a lot more attention from the courses' three instructors: Professor Roberts in English and Professors Schafer and Polito in agronomy. But on other days he resents the attention because it means he always has to be ready to answer questions, something he successfully avoided in his large-lecture classes.

Mike co-enrolled for this pair of classes because of his summer internship experience at a seed company, which sells varieties of corn and soybean seed. There he learned that he needs not only more experience in solving complex farm management problems but also stronger communication skills. So far the classes are going pretty well, though he's having more and more trouble telling the two classes apart. He appreciates that his professors seem to have their act together and really like working with each other. Mike also is glad that they often refer to their work-place experiences in class; on the other hand, these professors sometimes treat class as a work place, expecting that student teams will devote lots of out-of-class time to the joint-course major project. In other words, they expect him to act in a professional manner while at times he'd still prefer to be a student working for a grade. He's not comfortable making recommendations that may influence his real client's potential livelihood.

Mike's three-person team has been spending a lot of time together—a lot more time than he imagined would be necessary when the courses started. They are working as certified crop advisors on their major project, a farm plan (a specialized kind of recommendation report) for Victor Hoven, the owner of a large diversified farm. Mike and his teammates have to write a farm plan for Victor that is fairly complex; the recommendations have to be agronomically sound, economically feasible, socially acceptable, and environmentally responsible.

During their lab in the agronomy course, Mike and his classmates have visited Victor's farm three times this semester: they interviewed Victor to learn more about his farm operation, and they collected soil and manure samples to use for the nutrient recommendation section of their report. Since then they have been organizing and analyzing these data and other information for their farm plan. When they received the results of their soil and manure samples from the state laboratory, they knew Victor would want to know what the results were, so they spent a lot of time—both as a team and in class—discussing how to interpret the data. While the state guidelines for manure-based nutrient applications were clear, they were surprised that the results of the manure analysis weren't easy to interpret. They discovered that each team in the class had a different take on what the recommendations based on the same results should be.

On this Tuesday morning, Mike is sitting in class next to the other two members of his team. While this time slot is scheduled for the English course with Professor Roberts, the two agronomists, Professor Schafer and Professor Polito, sit in the back of the class (and Professor Roberts sits in on the agronomy class and lab).

Today Professor Roberts is reviewing upcoming checkpoints for their major project, the farm plan. Looking at his syllabus, Mike knows that he and his teammates will be giving an oral presentation of their farm plan to Victor at the end of the semester. The presentation sounds like it's supposed to be formal. And although Mike is pretty comfortable talking with farmers—because he grew up on a farm and because he talked to a lot of farmers during his internship—he's not comfortable getting up in front of a group and giving a formal presentation.

Trying hard to take careful notes (after the big deal all three professors made about note taking during the second week of class), Mike is dutifully writing down the key points of what Professor Roberts is saying:

ROBERTS: So, when you're planning your group's oral presentation, two key elements are a slick PowerPoint presentation that captures the key points and engages the audience, and a professional appearance. That means wear your business attire—no jeans or t-shirts.

Mike is thinking he'll have to have his Mom send his suit to school, when he realizes that Professor Polito has interrupted Roberts, which isn't really unusual. But his words catch Mike's attention right away:

POLITO: Dave, I think we might have a problem here.

ROBERTS: Well, let me run through the presentation criteria and . . .

POLITO: I think we should talk about this before we go any further.

ROBERTS: [Sighing with pretended annoyance] All right, Tom. As usual I yield to your superior knowledge.

POLITO: [Laughs, then returns to a serious tone] The usual setting for the farm plan presentations would be at Victor's home with everyone sitting around Victor's kitchen table—no place for a laptop, no place for PowerPoint, no place for a business suit. It's a *conversation* between the crop advisors and the farmer.

SCHAFER: That's right. Each team has an hour to outline its recommendations to Victor and to field his questions about the farm plan since he'll already have reviewed their document. Crop advisors need to know how to manage give and take with a farmer.

ROBERTS: Oops! I hadn't thought about that! Thanks, John. I can see how an *informal* presentation fits the rhetorical situation of this project. But here's a thought: From my experience in industry, the students also need to know how to prepare formal presentations. They need the experience of designing and delivering a PowerPoint presentation. They need to know stuff like how to hand off to a co-presenter without being awkward or fumbling. And they need to develop a professional image.

POLITO: You're right, Dave. Those skills *are* valuable. Before we integrated these courses, we always tried to place the students in a real-world situation we knew they would face, which is sitting around the farmer's kitchen table. And we wouldn't want to just trash that.

SCHAFER: I agree with both of you, as usual [mild laughter from the class]. I can see that having the formal presentation skills would be important, but Dave understands that students also need the skills that we've traditionally emphasized. So what do we do?

ROBERTS: [Smiling] Well, folks, I guess we'll get back to you tomorrow on this one.

And all this right in the middle of class . . . .

QUESTIONS FOR REFLECTION AND DISCUSSION

1. *Assumptions.* What assumptions had Polito, Schafer, and Roberts made about the nature of the oral presentation for this farm plan? Are these assumptions disciplinary or experiential? How do these differences reflect what each discipline typically may teach students about this type of client presentation?

2. *Representation of task.* The three professors spent time during the spring and summer coordinating their syllabi (content and schedule), creating joint assignments, and discussing the pedagogical approaches they will use. Time planning? Hundreds of hours. Yet they made different assumptions about this issue. Being comfortable with their assumptions, they did not think of discussing this during their collaboration. Knowing this, then, how can you avoid similar obstacles as you plan your team-taught courses?

3. *Perspectives.* At mid-semester, during a hallway conversation with his classmates, Mike noted that the three professors worked well together to make the classes flow. For instance, Mike said that it was nice to see the professors

work in a team and that it gave him the motivation to work in his own team. Yet in the end of the semester course evaluations, Mike noted that having three professors was, at times, like working with a three-headed creature—sometimes one head didn't know what the other heads were thinking or planning.

From Mike's perspective (and perhaps the perspectives of other students), what was beneficial or uncomfortable about this unexpected exchange between Polito, Schafer, and Roberts? What do *you* believe was beneficial or uncomfortable about their unexpected exchange? Could Polito, Schafer, and Roberts have anticipated it?

4. *Integration.* Mike commented that the classes are going well, but in some areas they are distinctively different while in other areas he's having a hard time "telling the two classes apart." What are the benefits and downsides for faculty who wish to integrate two very different disciplinary courses? What are the benefits and downsides to students who take these courses?

5. *Timing.* Of course, colleagues who are co-teaching can never anticipate all the different assumptions they will discover. Should they pass over the problems that arise if they discover them in the middle of class and deal with them only after they have a chance to discuss them in private, or should they address these issues as they occur?

6. *Resolution.* At the end of the scenario, Roberts articulated that he envisioned a formal presentation; Polito articulated that he envisioned an informal presentation. If you were in their situation, what would you have done? What do you believe the students end up doing?

READINGS FOR FURTHER CONSIDERATION

Gabelnick, Faith, et al. *Learning Communities: Creating Connections Among Students, Faculty, and Disciplines.* (New Directions in Teaching and Learning no. 14.) San Francisco: Jossey-Bass, 1990.

Huba, Mary, and Jann Freed. *Learner-centered Assessment on College Campuses: Shifting the Focus from Teaching to Learning.* Needham Heights: Allyn & Bacon, 2000.

11

In the Writing-Intensive Univers(ity)

Wendy Bishop

Preetha stares at her computer screen, then at the desk where the first page of her art case study rests, then back to the screen. She gets up with a sigh, straightens her Crandall University T-shirt and walks barefoot to her kitchen table to find the phone. When her mother answers, Preetha lets out her writing anxiety in a long familiar breath. She leans into this moment of family-supported problem-solving.

"Mom, remember when I told you I was going to that traveling art exhibit, 'Master Drawings from the Worcester Art Museum' at the Lowe Museum on campus, as part of my art history course?"

"Of course I do Preetha. Did you enjoy it?"

"Well, of course, Mom. Enjoyment is not the problem. Writing my case study is. Don't tell me again how useful the case study format was to you as a medical student. What's happening here is different. For example, the assignment sheet says: 'Choose the drawing whose subject-matter, style, and relationship to the artist's historical time period and culture interest you the most.'

"But then there was that group work. What I enjoyed, others didn't. What they did, I thought was pretty silly: imagine a crash-test dummy plastic mannequin strapped into its car seat but out of the car, and the whole car/chair thing sitting on a city street corner while people walk by in the crosswalk. The pencil lines were well executed—I've been taught to say that, you see— but the whole thing was dumb. That was someone else's favorite drawing. I found a pretty neat small rural sketch: a farmhouse, flowers along the near fence.

"Our groups were supposed to discuss each member's drawing but we ran out of time so suddenly we were supposed to just 'model' the discussion segment so we could do that for our own project—as if we would— and of course group members voted to practice on the crash-test dummy. It made me angry, though I didn't say so.

"And then, I went back to my drawing and tried to recapture my 'initial impressions'—only they weren't initial anymore. The whole museum visit was a mess. An okay idea but everything out of order. What can you expect with fifty of us art history students and an exhibit of only thirty drawings, some of them small, some of them stupid.

"Anyway, write some impressions, that's easy. But then these impressions had to turn quickly into this very formal thing. Listen: 'Formulate a preliminary thesis in writing, concerning the relationship of the drawing to the artist's work as a whole, the artist's time period, culture, and background (his or her contemporaries and any relevant historical antecedents you can trace).' And on and on—and that's only half of number 3, Mom."

"Preetha, I've never known you to be someone not willing to work hard. Maybe you need to slow down. Read the assignment again. Go back to the museum."

"That's not it, Mom. Of course I'm willing to work hard." Preetha is staring at the papers on the floor beside her desk. She's walked back to her desk and remains standing on two pages of yellow legal notepaper. She toes these aside and finds the thesis paragraph she plans to present to her professor, Dr. Pulliam, on Tuesday as her mom returns in memory to the case study form as she experienced it, way back when.

"Um," Preetha interrupts. "Okay Mom. I even like the case study concept. But I'm rather intimidated by an assignment that has ten steps, some of them with sub-steps, including an observational visit, two class presentations, and what seems like a lot of latitude . . . but . . ."

"But what, Preetha? There's really no but . . . you have good directions, so you just follow them, right?"

"But . . . there is a but, Mom. But we keep running into time problems and the steps get out of order and besides all that, I'm still expected to write like an art historian. I'm not an art historian, Mom. I never will be. I just want to study physical therapy. I can't make the connection from what I'm learning to what I want to learn no matter how many directions I follow. Something is just not right here."

Preetha gathers her night's work into a yellow and white paper pile and watches the computer shut down as she listens to her mother and then hangs up. She has a thesis paragraph. But she's uneasy. Very.

Preetha is a junior transfer student at Crandall, a writing-intensive university. That is to say, three out of her six instructors this term make the claim on their syllabi that they adhere to the university's new policy to encourage writing-intensive classes. These professors seem to go beyond adhering; these three seem to care about writing. Each advertises the writing-rich nature of his or her class: some verbally, some with written statements on their course syllabi. Apparently, they're proud of the way they use writing in their classrooms because they also mentioned having participated in a WAC training seminar held on campus through the Academic Support Center each spring, explaining that during the one-week seminar, faculty on this campus discuss with colleagues how to make writing-intensive assignments and use writing-to-learn strategies in their courses. They have been introduced to ideas of journal keeping and reflective assignment making, and participated in discussions on responding to and evaluating writing.

Not an avid writer, Preetha is at the same time not unwilling to write. Her parents arrived in the United States when Preetha was three, so she's often in the position of "translating" American academic practices to her parents who are education-oriented professionals. Additionally, Preetha attended a high school and a community college that drilled her in *both* the five-paragraph theme and essay test-taking skills as well as introduced her to variations of process pedagogy where she was asked to draft, share drafts with peers, and turn in a revised draft for teacher commentary and grading. As Preetha explains to her mother on the phone during her first week of classes: "I've been there, done that. Whatever type of writing they ask for, I'm pretty sure to have tried it." Because of this, Preetha feels confident she'll be able to do well in the writing-intensive courses.

Confident, that is, until week four of the fifteen-week term when our opening phone call occurs. By this time, Preetha is pretty sure she's arrived in a brave new world of writing instruction. Despite first-week impressions, Preetha's equally sure that *each* of her instructors sees "writing intensive" in a distinctively different way. So different, in fact, she's having trouble "reading" the classes well. The party-line is: writing will always help you learn. In practice, she's not so sure. She's received a C grade on one paper, had one set of journal notes returned with grammatical questions and a request that she do more synthesizing, and missed a required posting of a learning log on the class Web board. In addition, Preetha sometimes doesn't see any more intensity in the writing courses than in her "undesignated" courses.

"Mom," she explains during week five. "They seem to think 'intensive' is something I'm supposed to do but they're not. It all takes place offstage, out of class. I'm supposed to put in more time writing. But I don't see them putting in more time teaching me to write."

"Whatever they say," Preetha's mother replies, "you just be sure you do it."

"But that's part of it too, Mom. When one of them says journals, they really mean what you and I would call reading responses. Not the record I kept when I was a high school exchange student. And when one of them says bring in a draft, they mean bring in a typed and formatted paper ready for them to mark on, not those handwritten legal pads I always used in my high school English classes for my first drafts. At least that's what happens in one class. And then in the next I bring in a typed paper and the teacher says: 'Oh, you didn't have to type that. That's just busywork when you type up an early draft.'"

"Preetha," her father says when she worries him later in the same week by obsessing about her C paper grade. "You be sure to do what your professor says. That's what matters."

Because Preetha is Preetha, she starts to formulate a plan to discuss her problems with all three of her writing-intensive class professors. Preetha intends to do well during her next two years at Crandall, so week six of the term finds her thinking about each course—marshaling her impressions before her conferences which she has arranged for next week:

Dr. Chiricos—who teaches Preetha's Philosophy of Medicine course, an introduction for hopeful pre-med majors—explains her course this way in her syllabus: "This is a writing-intensive course. Writing will thus constitute one of the primary modes of class interaction. There will be four kinds of writing: in-class, journal, short papers, research papers."

Dr. Pulliam, Preetha's art history teacher, assigns a case study that asks students to "choose an object, participate in small-group discussion when viewing the object in the museum, formulate a preliminary thesis in writing, find sources, read and take notes on the sources, formulate a developed thesis, write the paper, present to class, and turn in a revised final draft." (See appendix for the ten-step assignment.)

In biology, Dr. Sobanjos requires "group presentations, in-class exams, learning log entries, and a co-authored class paper."

Preetha realizes she continues to have trouble seeing how journal writing for Dr. Chiricos is like (or unlike) taking notes for Dr. Pulliam's research paper, and she doesn't know where to start when composing with group members in Dr. Sobanjos's class since she is more familiar with the thesis-to-draft practices being advocated in Dr. Pulliam's and Dr. Chiricos' classes. Because of this confusion, she is confirmed in her decision to double-check with each professor to get a better sense of just what "writing intensive" means to each faculty member (and so to her). Preetha figures she'd better see just how committed each faculty member really is to teaching her how to make course meaning through writing and to helping her improve her writing at the same time. It's time to talk.

By now it is week seven of the term and her Monday appointment is with Dr. Chiricos. Preetha winds along some beige linoleum hallways, her shoes tapping loudly, and finds her professor, who moves a stack of books he's been leafing through and marking with blue post-its. She seems to remember that Preetha was coming by to talk today.

"Dr. Chiricos," Preetha begins. "First let me tell you how much I like the topics we're covering. The first unit on medicine and quackery was great, just great. But now that we're looking in the second unit at medical evidence, I'm confused about writing my journal entries. It seemed that the one you modeled for us in class—where we discussed our attitudes toward acupuncture and aromatherapy as a way to consider the difference between science and nonscience—made it clear I could use first person. That I could write as I, Preetha. But talking now about randomized clinical trials, I don't see how to write in that same journal voice."

"Well," says Dr. Chiricos. "That's a good worry to have. Probably you shouldn't. In a way, the first unit was meant to invite nonmajors into the discussions, but now we're getting serious. We have a lot of material to cover and I expect you'll do well to summarize each reading and then try to draw conclusions between them. I'm calling these 'reading journals' because the term seems less alarming. But you're right. First person might not serve you well in these entries."

On Tuesday, Preetha enjoys getting lost in the studio art wing of Diffenbaugh, the new art building, on her way to the art historian's offices on the third floor. She's seen enough self-decorated MFA students in one elevator to be sure she's better dressed for a career in physical therapy. Dr. Pulliam's door is adorned with a collage of fine art postcards from museums around the world. Sent by his friends or students, she thinks, as she gets ready to knock. Or maybe he brought them back himself. Preetha is reminded that she would like to travel before going on for graduate work. Then she's inside the office and opening the conversation.

"Dr. Pulliam," says Preetha, "I really enjoyed the trip to the museum three weeks ago to choose our original art work for our paper. It helped me to get excited about my research paper. However, when I read your description of good writing in art history, I became worried. You make an art historian sound like a creative writer to me. How can I, Preetha, a student, write a paper that does all you ask for . . . and so elegantly? You have my revised thesis now; you'll understand what I mean.

"Preetha," says Dr. Pulliam. "I am aware this is a beginner's class. I care overall that you use your writing to explore connections between the object you've chosen and the available cultural and historical materials of that time period. Until you start reading, writing, digging into your sources, and observing and reobserving your object, you can't come to the deeper understandings and insights that all art historians strive for. In that sense, writing *is* your best tool for beginning. Of course, you need to spend a good amount of time at the library and probably in the company of one of our reference librarians who will help you find crucial secondary sources.

"I'm worried though, Dr. Pulliam. I grew up with lots of books on Indian art, but many of the twentieth-century drawings we looked at don't really 'speak' to me. That makes it all the harder. And then your definition in the syllabus: it still stops me cold: 'Good writing in art history is clear and well-structured, articulates ideas richly, and treats works of art and their context with some specificity without becoming overly descriptive. It is well researched in primary materials and cognizant of current approaches. It is original and insightful. It also often makes links to other disciplines both for their substantive materials and for their (critical) theories.' This isn't me, Dr. Pulliam. I don't see myself as a writer in this definition. At least not yet."

Later the same day, Preetha meets with Dr. Sobanjos. She finds her professor facing a computer, back to the open door. Preetha coughs to get her attention and takes the empty seat as Dr. Sobanjos turns and smiles. Preetha tugs at her best skirt and thinks how good it will feel to get home and slip back into her jeans and catch up on today's work; she's feeling a bit worn out from active inquiry but remains firm in her goals—to clarify her understanding of this writing-intensive disquiet she's been feeling.

"Dr. Sobanjos," begins Preetha. "Could you walk through the assignment sequence with me again? It's cool that our class uses the Web board and that I can talk to my group members on the Internet. And I know you've thought the writing sequence out very well. It's just . . . well, I can't really follow your syllabus. There are so many directions here, I keep getting lost. Can I go over things with you? First, I get confused between the Learning Log entries and the Web board postings. Are these one and the same thing? Do I write two separate types of entries or do I just change one from a personal Learning Log entry and then make it more public, post it on the Web for the class to read?

"Let me see where you are," says Dr. Sobanjos, taking the syllabus out of Preetha's hands. "Hmm, week three—oh, I see. I made a mistake there. By week four, I intend that you stop the private Learning Log entries and start posting your responses directly to the Web. I didn't make that clear when I updated last term's syllabus. Let me make a note to remind the class of that next Tuesday. There, does that help?"

"Well . . . not completely, Dr. Sobanjos. Let me see if I can get the sequence clear. First I was completing personal Learning Logs. Now I'm spending two weeks posting to the Web where my eventual group—and all class members—can read the entries. After reading for a week, we start to try to set up affinity groups: find others wanting to research the same question as we do. Right?"

"Yes . . . more or less. I may have to get in the discussion and guide some group members to each other, but yes." Dr. Sobanjos flips through her own copy of the syllabus and starts to make notes to herself.

"And then it says 'class post answers to presentation Question; presentation experts must check all responses for accuracy and note correction during tomorrow's class,' and that means that the group gets far enough along to post their first presentation and then those 'expert' groups you set up in the first week—that's not the same as the writing group, yes?—those expert groups check and respond to the writing group's posting but the rest of the class doesn't have to?"

"Yes. Um. Oh, yes."

"Oh. I guess I get it. I didn't realize at first that I had an editing group and a writing group. And am I right, too, that later in the term I'll have an evaluation group too? Or am I just mixed up again?

"Well, it's more like this: your group will make an in-class final presentation of your co-authored paper and all the class members will evaluate the presentation, but then small groups will exchange papers with another group and take that group's report—a copy each—home and respond on-text. Here, this should help you sort it out. I'm color coding the activities here on your syllabus with highlighters. Yellow equals the editing group assignments, blue equals the writing group assignments, and that one pink highlight represents the final exchange of papers. But anyway, we'll go over this each day in class. All you have to know for Tuesday is to post what you thought of as your Learning Log material to the whole class. And if you don't mind, remind me at the beginning of the next class and I'll clarify this little confusion for everyone. Thanks for pointing it out, Preetha. See you then."

Appendix: The Case Study Assignment
Dr. Lucinda Pulliam, February 20–*Assignment—A Case Study*
ARH-3050-01   History and Criticism: Art 1

1. Choosing the object: Look carefully at the works in the exhibition, "Master Drawings from the Worcester Art Museum" at the Lowe Museum. Read the wall texts and entries in the exhibition catalogue for the works that interest you. Choose the drawing whose subject-matter, style, and relationship to the artist's historical time period and culture interest you the most, as we'll be looking at selected drawings from eight very different, but highly regarded, 20th-century artists. Make notes on your initial thoughts about the work.

2. Small group discussion, in the museum: In a group of three, explain to your fellow students the features of the drawing's subject, style, and artist's time period or culture that seem significant to you, based on your observations and reading so far. The members of the group should question each other and make suggestions about what they notice in the work. Take notes on the other students' comments and the thoughts that occur to you.

3. Formulate a preliminary thesis in writing, concerning the relationship of the drawing to the artist's work as a whole, the artist's time period, culture, and background (his or her contemporaries and any relevant historical antecedents you can trace). Is it a typical example or does it serve as an exception to what is known or assumed about its creator and his or her time and place in art history? Submit the thesis statement to the teacher, who will return it with comments.

4. Finding sources: Search in the library for books and periodicals on the artist and the national or period style or artistic movement represented by the work. Quickly look over the source works to assess whether they will be helpful. Submit a bibliography to the teacher for suggestions.

5. Read the sources, taking notes on those features of content and style relevant to the drawing. These elements may be similar to those you see in the drawing, or dissimilar. Do the sources agree on these features or are there differences of scholarly opinion? Does the drawing demonstrate accepted views or constitute an exception? Or does it confirm one scholarly opinion and counter another?

6. Formulate a developed thesis, revising or abandoning your preliminary one if necessary. Write a paragraph explaining the thesis and an outline of your paper. Submit to teacher for comments.

7. Give a five-minute presentation of your thesis paragraph in class, illustrated by slides of the drawing.

8. Write the paper. Submit a draft to teacher for comments. Revise.

9. Give a presentation to the class, illustrated with slides.

10. Present your final draft to teacher, revised as necessary.

QUESTIONS FOR REFLECTION AND DISCUSSION

1. Where does Preetha go from here? What should she do in each class and what should she do, in general, as a student who is no doubt about to encounter more writing-intensive courses in upcoming terms at this university?

2. Is Preetha wise to try to draw connections between her writing-intensive classes? Are there other ways she could go about doing so, or is teacher-conference the best method? Or should she, as her parents suggest, just do what each teacher says? What observations do you have about this small view into each teacher's "version" of a writing-intensive classroom? Given the conference visit with Preetha, what might you suggest each teacher do to clarify his or her position on the uses of class writing activities to Preetha and her classmates?

3. Have you experienced any slippage between your ideal and your actual curriculum? What issues does this case raise for your own instruction?

4. How would a different sort of student than Preetha respond to these same instructors? Posit a writer with below-average writing skills; with above-average skills.

5. Given faculty members' one week in-service, what suggestions do you have for further in-service support for those members who are willing to offer writing-intensive classes for their university?

READINGS FOR FURTHER CONSIDERATION

Bishop, Wendy. "Students' Stories and the Variable Gaze of Composition Research." *Writing Ourselves into the Story: Unheard Voices from Composition Studies*. Ed. Susan Hunter and Sheryl Fontaine. Carbondale: Southern Illinois UP, 1993. 197–214.

Ronald, Kate. "Style: The Hidden Agenda in Composition Classes." *The Subject Is Writing: Essays by Teachers and Students*. 2nd ed. Portsmouth: Boynton/Cook Heinemann, 1999. 169–83.

Ronald, Kate, and Jon Volkmer. "Another Competing Theory of Process: The Students.'" *Journal of Advanced Composition* 9 (1989): 81–96.

Tobin, Lad. *Writing Relationships: What Really Happens in the Composition Classroom*. (Particularly chapter 3.) Portsmouth: Boynton/Cook Heinemann, 1993.

12

Spreading the Words
Collaborative Writing in "Killer Lab"

Steven Youra

A t East Hill University, the senior laboratory course in mechanical engineering had a long-time reputation as a tough course. Generations of students simply called it "Killer Lab". The course required long afternoon lab hours and lots of writing. Students conducted a dozen different experiments in fluid dynamics, heat transfer, and thermodynamics, and had to put together a formal report for every one of them, a report that usually went on for fifteen or more pages, plus appendices. With all of that time in the laboratory and all of that grading, the class was also a killer for the professor and TAs who taught it. But Killer Lab changed very little over the years: faculty considered it a necessary rite of passage, alumni remembered it nostalgically as boot camp, and generations of students simply put up with the ordeal.

By the time they were seniors, most students had written standard laboratory reports in previous chemistry and physics courses; by the end of Killer Lab, they learned how to crank them out. At least, they usually got the right information in the right section of the report: Abstract, Introduction, Experimental Methods, Results and Discussion, Conclusions/ Recommendations, and Appendices. For those who hadn't quite mastered the format, a lab manual briefly described what information went into each section.

Although the course required a huge amount of writing, the overall quality of reports did not seem to improve much over the semester. The MechE faculty and TAs who taught the class complained that much of the writing was unclear or wordy and that when students discussed their experimental results, the analysis was often superficial or simply wrong. But with so many reports coming in each week, instructors could not give much attention to each student's specific writing problems. They would carefully review the abstract and consider each graph and equation, then quickly skim the rest of the report, putting a check-mark in the margin next to good numbers or decent analysis. Some instructors would dutifully correct misspellings and occasionally rewrite the most glaring errors in grammar or phrasing. Each section of the report was worth a set amount of points and at the bottom of the last page, the score was tallied in red. Grading these reports was not a pleasant activity.

This fall, Professor Zev Nettles decided that as new course director, he'd make some changes to improve the writing—and, he hoped, the learning associated with that writing, too. He slashed the number of required reports from twelve to five and had the students produce the reports in groups, with their lab partners. On the first day of class, he explained the rationale for this approach:

"In school, so far, you've all had lots of practice working alone and being assessed on your personal performance. In fact, you all got into this university on the basis of your individual achievement—your high class standing, grades, and test scores. But when you're out in the world as a professional, you'll often work and write collaboratively with colleagues on different projects. You'll learn from each other and produce a final product that is much better than anything you could have created by yourself. This class will help you prepare for these collaborative situations: you'll conduct the experiments in teams of three or four and write up your reports as a group. And to ensure that everybody pulls their weight, all group members will get the same grade." Part of the challenge, Zev added, is that each group will need to work out its own strategy for successful collaboration.

Zev was optimistic that this new plan would lead to improved writing and learning. He was also pleased that each instructor would need to read only ten reports, instead of thirty, so that the TAs could pay closer attention to the writing and even require revisions. By cutting the quantity of writing, he hoped to raise the quality.

Amy Horger, a senior in MechE, took another sip of coffee. She looked at her watch: two in the morning, and she still had to write the discussion, introduction, and abstract. Then she would need to assemble all of the appendices, create a title page, and send copies via email to her teammates. Amy would have to push hard to get the report in by the 9 a.m. deadline. There'd be no time for her lab partners to review the final version, but at least they'd each have a copy of this report (after all, their names would appear on the title page).

Before the first lab, Amy's group had decided that each person would take charge of doing one part of the experiment and then one person would integrate the material and write up the report. "This feels a little like cheating," said Juanita, "because each of us is not doing it all. But I guess that's what teamwork is all about—everyone takes on a different chunk of the job. At least that's what I've seen at my co-op company. Most projects are done by a really diverse group of people with different specialties, each person working on a different part."

Amy's team had no trouble dividing labors. Rodney took the lead with this first experiment, in fluid dynamics. He was good with the instruments and equipment. Roberto, a careful, meticulous student, took the data and recorded them in the team's lab notebook, marking down the team's observations and hunches as they worked through the procedures. Juanita, a math whiz who declared herself "verbally challenged," volunteered to crunch the numbers and produce all of the graphs. At the time, Amy seemed satisfied with this arrangement. She was glad to defer her part of the work, especially because she had a big problem set coming up in another course. She knew she was a pretty good writer; she'd always done well in English courses and the manager at her summer internship said that her reports were as good as anything written by his senior engineers.

But now, suffering from an uncharacteristic case of writer's block, she regretted that she had offered to write up the whole report. Maybe her group didn't have the right approach to this team writing thing, after all. Yet she wasn't convinced that any other team had come up with a better strategy, either. She remembered a conversation at the student union after one of Professor Nettles's early lectures. She and some classmates had wandered over to the coffee shop to douse their Killer Lab sorrows in lowfat lattés. As they moaned about the work load, they began to compare notes on how their different teams would approach writing in the course.

Amy listened as Cathy explained her group's plan. "My team has figured it all out. We're going to do some major *parallel processing*," she explained. "Each of us will write up one or two of the report sections. Then we'll merge our separate Word files into a single document. To finish up, we'll just throw our extra data into an appendix and the report will be done. The way I see it, this group thing is going to save us all lots of time because we'll each only need to write about a quarter of a report."

"I dunno," said Rasheed. "I think you might be setting yourselves up for parallel *failure*. It will be too easy for slackers to coast by on their partners' work. And how are you going to have any quality control over the report?"

"I guess I just assume that everyone will put in a decent effort," Cathy explained. "Besides, to be honest, I'm the worst writer on my team, so my group's plan has gotta help me! " She took a long sip. "Anyway, Rasheed, how is your team going to handle the writing?"

"Well, after the first experiment we'll gather everything up—the lab manual, our experimental notebook, computer printouts, the textbook, whatever—and head to a computer lab. We'll just sit around the keyboard together and talk out the words of our report while one of us types it all up. That way, everyone will have input. We'll just hammer out the whole thing in one marathon session and be done with it."

Cathy, a track star, smiled and shook her head. "But Rasheed, a marathon is only twenty-six miles. But I bet that you guys will spend at least twenty-six *hours* on that report," she said. "Real inefficient. Way too much negotiation."

Amy turned to Cathy. "Well, Speedy, I think Rasheed's got a good point. Your group may sprint through the writing, but you're going to hit the wall. You'll end up with a pretty messy jumble, unless you carefully edit and integrate the sections."

"You guys might be right," said Cathy. But I don't see how I'd get every-one to work first on their own draft; then again on everyone else's section; and then once more on the group's full draft."

Amy had come away from that conversation convinced that her group had the right idea . . . until now. Sitting at her computer in the middle of the night, she anxiously looked at her watch again. If writing is really such a critical professional skill, she thought, then why isn't everyone individu-ally accountable for doing it? And if writing is supposed to help us learn the material, then why am I stuck doing all of this learning for my team-mates? "I hate working in a group," she said out loud to herself, "and I *hate* writing lab reports." Then she turned back to the computer screen and con-tinued typing.

QUESTIONS FOR REFLECTION AND DISCUSSION

1. Why does Zev assign laboratory reports? What alternative writing tasks, done individually or in groups, could Zev use to support his teaching goals? Why are conventional laboratory reports so often assigned in engineering and sci-ence courses? Who are the audiences and what are the purposes of this genre? Besides lab reports, what writing genres are typically assigned in technical courses? In other fields? Why?

2. What are the merits and limitations of each team's writing strategy? Should Zev have given his students different instructions or more explicit advice about writing as a team? If so, what should he have said to them or written on an assignment sheet? Should Zev intervene in the group writing process at any stage? If so, how? After the first round of reports is completed, what follow-up exercises or class discussions could Zev devise to help students write better reports? If students have particular trouble discussing their ex-perimental results, how can Zev help them?

3. On what basis should Zev assess these reports? Is it fair to give the same grade to all students on a team? How, if at all, should Zev hold students *in-dividually* (as well as jointly) accountable for writing in this class? Why?

4. The official Accrediting Board for Engineering and Technology (ABET) man-dates that each engineering program must document that its graduates achieve certain "outcomes," including effective communication and team-work. How could Zev's approach to writing help his department to demon-strate these two outcomes? What other strategies for including written or oral communication, in this course or others, would complement Zev's efforts in this class?

READINGS FOR FURTHER CONSIDERATION

Accreditation Board for Engineering and Technology (ABET). "ABET Evaluation Cri-teria." <http://www.abet.org/criteria.htm>

Bazerman, Charles. *Shaping Written Knowledge: The Genre and Activity of the Experi-mental Article in Science.* Madison: U of Wisconsin P, 1988.

————. "Special Issue on Engineering Genre." *IEEE Transactions on Professional Communication* 42.1 (1999).

Bergmann, Linda S. "WAC Meets the Ethos of Engineering: Process, Collaboration, and Disciplinary Practices." *Language & Learning Across the Disciplines* 4:1 (2000): 4–15.

Ede, Lisa, and Andrea Lunsford. *Singular Tests/Plural Authors: Perspectives on Collaborative Writing.* Carbondale: Southrern Illinois Press, 1990.

Herrington, Anne. "Writing in Academic Settings: A Study of the Contexts for Writing in Two College Chemical Engineering Courses." *Research in the Teaching of English* 19.4 (1985): 331–59.

Kalmbach, James R. "The Laboratory Reports of Engineering Students." *Writing Across the Disciplines Research into Practice.* Ed. Art Young and Toby Fulwiler. Upper Montclair: Boynton/Cook, 1986. 176–83.

Lay, Mary M., and William M. Karis. *Collaborative Writing in Industry: Investigations in Theory and Practice.* Amityville: Baywood, 1991.

Waitz, Ian A., and Edward C. Barrett. "Integrated Teaching of Experimental and Communication Skills to Undergraduate Aerospace Engineering Students." *Journal of Engineering Education,* July 1997: 255–62.

Winsor, Dorothy A. *Writing Like an Engineer: A Rhetorical Education.* Mahwah: Erlbaum, 1996.

Youra, Steven, ed. "Communications Across the Engineering Curriculum." Special issue, *Language & Learning Across the Disciplines* 3:2 (1999).

Part 3

Reading Student Work
Scenes of Response and Evaluation

13

Making Learning Visible
What You Can't See Can Change Response

Kathleen Blake Yancey

As a new professor, Rick hadn't found teaching to come very easily at all. True enough, he hadn't learned how to teach as a graduate student, and admittedly, this was his first job. So, he laughed to himself, you might expect a steep, oh, what was it that they called it? Oh yeah, a steep learning curve.

Still. This wasn't what he had expected. These students, for one thing: they weren't like him at all. As an undergraduate, he'd worked two jobs in order to attend a private college where scholarly seminars grounded his study. These seminars, which predicted perfectly the kind of work he'd continue in graduate school, were an oasis of intellectual life, a place where people of well-informed minds came together to grapple with important questions. Rick had lived for those seminars; even now (perhaps especially now), he missed them. At this new place, the urban university where he taught, the students were unlike other students he'd known: they didn't seem to care about their education. Like him, they worked, but that didn't account for the difference, really. It was more, he thought, like they had lives—work and family and church responsibilities. Which might have been fine if school were considered part of their lives. But it seemed to him that for these students, school was last on the list—when it made it to the list at all.

Another problem, Rick thought, was that students didn't seem to bring much context to the material—geographical context, historical context, political context, you name it. What this meant, of course, is that the students had few opportunities to make comparisons, to talk about one event or phenomenon in terms of another—and this too seemed to make intellectual work increasingly unlikely.

Not surprisingly, then, his classes didn't run as he'd hoped. Right now, for instance, he was teaching a general education political science class with about forty students in it. Since it wasn't marked as writing intensive, the students resented the writing assignments, and in response, he had reduced the number to three. But the students wouldn't talk in class, either, and he couldn't understand why. The reading assignments were clear, he thought, and he previewed the questions that would be addressed the next class period. What was also clear, however, was that the students were prepared to wait him out during class. Typically, he'd ask a question, he'd wait for a reply, but no hands would go up, so he'd proceed to answer the question himself. Not that all the questions were alike, either. Sometimes the questions asked for direct summaries of the readings, sometimes for interpretations, sometimes for speculation. The silence, however, was constant.

It was only October, and already he was dreading the next two months.

The first assignment was basically simple, foundational, you could say. Students were to choose from a list of countries and examine forces that affected the country in one of two ways: either the force worked toward coherence within the country, or it worked to fragment the country. He had given the students some examples in class. Ethnic diversity in the United States worked against coherence, while the English language worked toward it. He had told the students that the assignment could be completed in three to five pages.

But he wasn't confident about what he'd find, so he had decided to take some advice offered by a colleague: he was going to ask for some reflection to accompany the assignment. He wasn't at all sure what he'd find in this reflection, but he didn't see that it could hurt. So when he collected the assignments, he asked students to take fifteen minutes to complete the following tasks:

- Believe that this is the best assignment that you've ever written.
- Doubt that this assignment is any good.
- Predict how the professor will read the assignment.
- Tell about what you learned in writing this assignment that doesn't show up in the assignment itself.

The first assignment that he read made him think that perhaps in his review of the class, he had underestimated the students' abilities, after all. Written by a young woman, it told the story of Denmark in exactly the terms he had specified: it was a country that cohered in significant ways. What he learned in the reflection, especially what he couldn't have known, was that the writer's grandmother was Danish and that the author hoped to visit Denmark (and grandmother) the following summer. Well, he thought to himself, I guess motivation does matter. This is sort of interesting.

Feeling optimistic, he opened the second assignment. A mere two and a half pages, it addressed coherence and fragmentation in Canada, but in an incoherent way. It started not as an essay, but as a response to the questions; there was no opening context at all. Worse, as it listed the factors, it seemed to lurch from one to the next without comparing or synthesizing them at all. Wearily, he turned to the reflection. The student had written:

I am trying to *believe* that this is the best paper I've ever written, but it's too short. I know that. I don't know how much the shortness will hurt my grade.

I *doubt* that this paper is any good because I don't think it's long enough. I couldn't seem to understand what you meant by coherence and fragmentation, and I couldn't check the textbook because I haven't bought it yet. I can buy it next week when I get paid.

I *predict* you will be disappointed in this paper. I am, too.

You can see everything I learned in this assignment. I put everything I learned into the paper, and it's still too short. Can you help me?

QUESTIONS FOR REFLECTION AND DISCUSSION

1. Given this student's reflection, how might we respond, and why?
2. More generally, how might reflection alter our response practices?
3. What other kinds of reflective questions might we want to ask?
4. What other kinds of assistance could the writer have been given ahead of time to make it more likely that her assignment is written successfully?
5. What do we make of the silence of the class? Is there a way to explore what, if anything, it means?
6. Is there a connection between the silence of the class and the second student's paper?
7. Rick finds that the first paper is successful and attributes that success in part to motivation. What role does motivation play in students being successful learners? If we think motivation is important, how can we build that into our assignments in appropriate ways?

READINGS FOR FURTHER CONSIDERATION

Smith, Jane, and Kathleen Blake Yancey, eds. *Self-Assessment and Development in Writing: A Collaborative Inquiry*. Cresskill: Hampton, 2000.

Yancey, Kathleen Blake. *Reflection in the Writing Classroom*. Logan: Utah State UP, 1998.

14

Two Papers, Two Views

Joan Graham

Katie Seiko is an English department faculty member who has lots of experience with writing in the disciplines, and her fall term was about to begin. She was going to teach a writing course for students with something important in common: they would all be concurrently taking a psychology department course called Personality Theory. Katie's writing assignments would build, in various ways, on their psychology study context, and most of the students would be sophomores. Since they were likely to have had a little writing experience at the university already, Katie was trying to come up with a quick, accessible, but slightly sophisticated way to introduce key writing issues for discussion during the first week.

Paging through files of assignments and student work from past writing classes linked with psychology, she came to two papers that made a tempting set. Although addressed to the same assignment, the papers were very different—and the contrast seemed interesting and instructive. She hesitated just a little because she normally did not focus discussions on paired samples that might get summarily reduced to "good" and "bad"; in fact, she never did that with samples produced by members of her current class. But she decided to go with this pair because the writers would not be present; the assignment was a type that her new class would soon need to address; and the papers dramatized the importance of taking context and purpose into account when evaluating written work.

The papers were responses to a common kind of assignment in social science disciplines, one that asks students to apply a concept or theory, that is, to use it as a tool with which to analyze a case. The focus in this particular assignment was on the family as a system: in the study of child development, this concept has been important for the last twenty years as research has moved beyond the tradition that concentrated almost exclusively on the mother-child relationship. The psychology textbook discussed at some length the idea of families as systems, pointing out that "mothers never care for children in a vacuum," that sibling relationships affect and are affected by larger family dynamics, that parents influence children but children's characteristics and responses also influence parents—in general, that interconnected behaviors and perspectives shape, and are shaped by, a family system. The related writing assignment asked students to explain some aspect of their own development by employing the family system concept, in effect testing its explanatory power with respect to their own "case." In the first paper Katie chose, the writer attempted to analyze the way teasing functioned in her family; in the second paper, the writer focused on procrastination as a family trait.

At the first day's meeting of her class, Katie explained logistics and general expectations, then turned to the relationship between the writing course and the psychology course which would be expressed in writing assignments. She said that students would be writing as participants in focused inquiries, since psychology, like other disciplines, is a site where particular investigations and arguments are going on.

Both in short assignments and in longer papers, students should think of themselves as writing for the lecturer, the TAs, and the other students taking the Personality Theory course, that is, for a community defined by its concern with psychological issues raised by observations, theories, and research.

Finally, Katie offered the students an illustration, in the form of the family system assignment and two sample papers.[1] To prepare for their second class meeting she asked them to read the papers carefully, make marginal notes on features they thought important, and be prepared to discuss their views about how the papers compared. She assumed that, given the context and the writing purposes she had identified as central for her class, the students would recognize the "teasing" paper, despite its numerous problems, as the more successful.

Here are the two sample papers:

PAPER I

How would such a trivial thing as teasing affect my development? Contributing to homeostasis in my family system, teasing affected the person I am today. While the causes of teasing cannot be pinpointed, they intertwine into the very complex workings of my family. Teasing reflects individual roles, relationships among individuals, and balance within my whole family system.

In the case of teasing, birth order had a great impact on the roles of siblings. I was the youngest, born five years after my sister, Linda. Doug, next in line of birth order, was four years older than Linda and two years younger than the eldest, Brian. Most often, the "ripple effect" occurred, where teasing started at the oldest and progressed down the line. First, my parents teased Brian and Doug when they were young. As they grew up, they picked on my sister and me. As the youngest, I also was taunted by my sister, besides the teasing of everyone else in the family. Consequently, all the burdens of teasing tended to land on me, because I was the smallest and least experienced. I could hardly defend myself. Still, I influenced how teasing worked in the system because of my varying reactions that changed over time. Reflecting positions in birth order, everyone in the family played a part in the ever circulating tease.

So where did this teasing come from? Because of many factors, there is no *particular* cause for teasing. One reason definitely involved modeling. My parents teased each other, the kids, and even the dog. While my parents served as the major source of imitation, my siblings and I also modeled such influences as peers, siblings, other families, common social settings (such as school), and television. Since my parents also witnessed these influences, teasing due to modeling could easily circle through the family.

In addition to modeling, outside influences contributed to teasing in our family by affecting dispositions of family members. For instance, if one of my brothers had just broken up with a girlfriend, he might take his frustration out on me. Instead of just running a finger up my sensitive foot, he might completely constrain me, and then roughly jab, poke, and supposedly tickle me. Sometimes I could not even breathe and therefore lost my only defense: Screaming. In this sense, teasing was used as displacement. After stressful days at school or work, teasing tended to be more abundant and more violent.

Another source for teasing evolved from the indirect rewards of attention gain. Manipulating my brothers, my sister would often annoy them until they would become frustrated and tickle her or call names, etc. Then she would cry until Mom came. She blamed the problem on my brothers. In seeking my mother's empathy, my sister used teasing as a secondary beneficial reward.

In the middle of a complex family system, maintaining family roles served as an important factor in teasing, while teasing reciprocally emphasized individual roles. Like a traditional "nuclear" family, my father was the provider. He worked in an office all day, while my mother stayed home and cared for my three siblings and me. Generally, my mom was the head of the household who handled the majority of familial problems. After a long day at work, Dad would return home to often moan and complain to Mom. Struggling to uphold her role as loving wife, my mom would simply listen without mentioning her own frustrations of the day. Instead, teasing was use as an outlet. In teasing, my mother also upheld her role as the "one who said 'no,'" because no one could easily tease her back without getting her angry. Keeping a rather stable lifestyle, my parents worked hard at maintaining a homeostatic environment for the family. Teasing provided an accepted release to help balance the family lifestyle.

Among siblings, roles in teasing could almost define each's role in the family. Since Brian was physically smaller and not as strong as Doug, he prestiged himself as eldest through his wit. Brian was always quick with sarcastic remarks, clever names, and zany actions. As a result, Brian ensured his security by his mindful individuality. In contrast, Doug mostly used physical dominance to tease. Although he also was intelligent, Doug easily kept his power in the family by mere brute strength. Therefore, Doug tended to apply himself in athletics and enjoyable pastimes rather than concerning himself with more accepted life priorities (like attaining a job that required his college education). Next in line was Linda, the smallest. Because she could hardly fight back, she received the most teasing in the family. Often helpless, Linda grew up with a rather low self-esteem in many areas. But because she had learned to manipulate my brothers for my mother's attention, she gained confidence in her talents. Now, Linda has successfully owned her own nail shop for a year and one half. Finally, there is me. Being the youngest, I received as much or more teasing than my sister did, since her teasing was added into the cycle. I remember as a tactfully ignorant child, I once told my family something like: Sometimes I wish I could have a different family. I was referring to the fact that I did not enjoy so much teasing. In retort, my mother said, "I could always put you up for adoption." Since I still recall this remark, it obviously affected my thoughts. Instead of standing up for myself, I helplessly accepted the teasing (with screaming as my only defense), or learned to enjoy it because of the attention from beloved family members. (The latter occurred when my siblings had moved out, and I missed them.)

While maintaining family positions through teasing, the family system was reflected through reciprocal determinism. In order to gain attention, I sometimes would tickle my brothers' feet until they would clobber me. My tormenting them determined the teasing I received, while their responses determined how I tormented them. With constant bidirectional effects, every member of the family was affected by teasing.

As individual situations intertwined through reciprocal determinism, teasing served as a major component of maintaining family homeostasis. For example, my sister constantly sought means for self esteem. When my brothers picked on her, she was often degraded. As a counterbalance, she picked on me. To maintain this balance, I passively bore her abuse. Since I generally tended to be more confident than Linda, I would have broken the family homeostasis by teasing her back. Our roles would have reversed, only she would have handled my position completely differently. As a result, individual relationships in teasing could easily upset the original family balance.

While working for a balanced system, the family depends on many sub components. Birth order, modeling, outside influences, desire for security, and reciprocal determinism in teasing all contribute to a very complex family system. In many ways, the workings of my family (and therefore my own character) have been affected by teasing.

PAPER II

Families are systems in which all members learn from each other. Not only do children learn to walk and talk from other family members, but they can also learn and acquire their family members' habits. I learned to procrastinate by observing my father, mother, and sister.

On page 51 of our text, *Child Development: It's Nature and Course* by Stroufe, Cooper, and DeHart where family systems are discussed, it states that not only do mothers influence a child, but "others in the family greatly influence the child's development."

Both of my parents have a habit of putting things off. My father makes the perfect "model" of a procrastinator. He is a General Contractor, and yet his own house is falling apart. For as long as I can remember—at least seventeen years—the bathroom floors have been warped and display the trampoline effect—a little girl who came to visit not too long ago even had her mother come back to see the "neat bouncy floor." The floor slopes downhill in one corner (under the counter and sinks) and leaves a hole—about an inch and a half high—between it and the moulding. Every now and then—usually after it has been dark in there for a while—you get to witness slugs in action as they ooze into or out of the hole (pretty creepy!).

The bath tub/shower has an interesting feature or two also. Because the wood under the floor is soft and rotten, you can push the linoleum down with your foot and get your toe stuck in between the floor and bath tub (it's kind of painful, too). My older sister, Kara, and I had another thing to watch out for: the tiles on the shower wall. We were always really careful when we cleaned in there—some of the tiles were loose, and we didn't want them to fall out. But one day while Kara was taking a shower, I heard a loud clacking noise and, "Oh, no . . ." come from the bathroom. I went to see what had happened. Somehow, Kara had stuck her foot through the wall (don't ask how, I don't know). About four or five tiles lay in the tub and what was behind where they used to be? Nothing . . . no dry wall. It had long since crumbled and rotted away.

The master bathroom has all of these features and more. There are holes in the shower through which slugs come in from the cold, the dry wall next to the shower has decayed into a doily, and the ceiling grows a coat of mildew if left unattended.

The roof, too, needs some rather extensive repairs—it is a sorry excuse for shelter from the elements. No, old rotten wood is not saved exclusively for the bathrooms; the roof has it's share, too. There is a sheet of plastic covering it as rain insurance. The soft, moist roof and clear plastic above make an ideal environment for a greenhouse. Moss, grass, and various other weeds and saplings do quite well up there.

Every now and then, the plastic gets too old—it gets brittle and breaks up in the wind—and the ceiling starts leaking again. And then, my father, the Master Carpenter, simply cuts a new piece of "roof" and places it over the old.

Dad always seems to have a reason for not fixing it. "First of all, we need to submit plans to get a permit." We do have rough house plans that would have been ideal about fifteen years ago—they were to make the house much larger than it is—but they are not very practical now, with only Mom and Dad living there. Anyway, a final draft of the plans needs to be drawn up and approved before he can do anything—that makes a good excuse for procrastination. Another favorite of Dad's is that we'll need to have a long stretch of good rainless weather, which rarely happens around here (isn't that handy!).

Mom does her share of procrastinating, too. She doesn't like to exercise. She's not fat, but she does have a couple of excess pounds here and there. A couple of months before my wedding last year, she started saying more that she ought to start exercising—this wasn't anything new, she had said this before (with no action to back it up), but we heard it a little more frequently this time. "I don't want to look like a dumpy Mother of the Bride." As the date drew nearer, she kept *talking*, but not *doing*. And now she's saying that she ought to exercise and slim down a bit before my sister's wedding (this summer) so she can "look good on the dance floor."

Avoiding exercise is not the only form of procrastination that my mom demonstrates. She also puts off cleaning. She rarely cleans, but when she does, you know company is coming soon. She saves all of the piles of books, magazines, and old mail, dirty floors and rugs, dust, and cobwebs for a last minute cleaning frenzy before the guests arrive.

Through my entire childhood and adolescence, I was constantly aware of things being put off and avoided; the state of the house was an every-day reminder, and there were many more little episodes of procrastination from day-to-day. Because of observing this behavior in my parents, I thought it was only natural to do the same. I would always put off cleaning my room—to the point of not being able to see even a square inch of floor because it was so cluttered with junk.

Not only do parents influence children, but "siblings [also] have a direct effect on younger children [as] companions, teachers, and models," (Stroufe et al. 56).

The putting-off-your-homework syndrome was a prominent form of procrastination with Kara. She would save it all until the last minute. I remember when she had to do a book report once in high school. She kept avoiding it until the night before it was due. She hadn't even read the book yet, but somehow she wrote a good report anyway (at least the teacher thought so; he gave her an A).

In college Kara took some independent study credits one quarter and went to India for four months. Her assignment while she was there was to do some paintings. Being the procrastinator she is, she saved all of this work for after she got home—a few days before she was to show th12e instructor. So in a painting panic, she whipped out about fifteen watercolors (to which the instructor said, "Looks like an A to me.")

Kara demonstrated procrastination of her homework quite well, and I picked up that habit in a jiffy. She was an excellent "model" and "teacher" of procrastination.

Another aspect of family systems that comes into play is the bidirectional effect. It states, "the behavior of the parents helps shape the children's responses, but the children's responses also encourage the parent's behavior," (Sroufe et al. 52) and vice versa.

On another night, Kara had a paper due the next day and hadn't started yet. She was to the point of tears because of it. Mom couldn't let her suffer, so she helped Kara write the paper. Mom stayed up the rest of the night to type it, while Kara went to sleep.

Instead of encouraging Kara to stop procrastinating and start her paper sooner, Mom helped with the work at the last minute. In so doing, Kara's habit of procrastination was reinforced, thus creating the bidirectional effect.

Like I have said before, I would also always save my homework until the last possible moment. Mom and Dad never disapproved of this, and their lack of reaction encouraged me to keep up my procrastination. The bidirectional effect took place in this relationship as well.

As I was growing up, evidence of procrastination was seen daily: from lumpy floors and holes in walls, to dripping ceilings, to piles of junk and thick dust and dirt. The procrastinating habits of my family members formed and reinforced my own, and my procrastinating encouraged my family's habits to continue.

Even now I see myself putting things off. When I do, the question always comes up, "Is this how you want your children to behave?" The answer is always, "no." At that moment, I stop avoiding whatever the task was, and I just do it. Hopefully by the time my husband and I have our first baby, the last strings of my habit will be broken, and I'll have a new "let's get things done" attitude to pass on to the next generation.

At the second meeting of Katie's class, the students were eager to explain what they thought of the papers, especially how much they liked the one about procrastination. "Wow, talk about lively details!" one student said. "That one is really interesting and fun to read!" said another. "I could *visualize* the house falling apart—that paper is personal and it's *not boring*!" chimed in a third.

Katie quickly became uneasy as more and more students expressed their enthusiasm for the "procrastination" paper, but she decided to stay in the background. Finally, Gretchen, a shy but determined student, spoke up: "Wait a minute! The paper about teasing is much better organized, and it says a lot more too." Jake wasn't impressed by that idea, though, and neither was Lucy: "It's just going through the motions." "It's just 'doing school,'" joined in Tim. Eventually a few more students defended the "teasing" paper, but when the hour ended, the class was divided, with about one quarter for "teasing" and three quarters for "procrastination."

Katie left the room thinking she had probably made a mistake in risking an unpredictable discussion that raised fundamental issues at the very beginning of her course. She was still preoccupied when she sat down for lunch with her English department colleagues John and Elaine—so of course she told them what had happened. "It was amazing. Most of the students hardly paid any attention to what the papers were supposed to *do!*"

"So what did you tell them?" Elaine asked.

"Nothing much, really. But I don't think I can just drop it. It would help me figure out what to say tomorrow if you'd look over the papers and tell me what strikes *you.*" Katie handed over her extra copies, and John and Elaine read while they drank their coffee.

"Well," John said, "I certainly see why the students liked 'procrastination.' I like it myself, I suppose because it speaks to my interests as an English teacher. I care about writers' voices—I want to cultivate personal, expressive qualities in writing, and that's where the strengths of the 'procrastination' paper lie. The only tedious part is toward the end where the writer tries to use terms from her reading, and I don't understand her example of 'bidirectional effect.' She was probably just trying to be the obedient student, following the assignment there."

"Following the assignment is an important issue!" Elaine interrupted. "I think Katie's students held it against the writer of the 'teasing' paper that she clearly *did* try to do what the assignment asked. She's awkward—you can tell she's using concepts that are new to her—but she really is *using* them. I actually understood the idea of the family as a system better after I read her paper, and I think she understood it better after writing. In fact, I think she may have understood her family better too after analyzing it this way, even though her essay isn't what you'd call 'personal.' Of course, she does miss some great opportunities. Look at the end of that long paragraph—one, two, three—the seventh one. That's the only place where she refers to the pleasurable aspects of being teased, and implies a connection between teasing and family bonds, but she doesn't explore it at all. 'Teasing' isn't smooth or entirely worked out, but I think it would be a very good draft. 'Procrastination' is way off."

John's and Elaine's reactions gave Katie even more to think about, and at the end of the week she went to see Charlie, the discussion leader for that year's sequence of meetings for WAC faculty. Charlie said he would like the group to respond to the papers at the next month's brown bag lunch, and since Katie was eager to hear what her colleagues in other fields would say, the plan was made.

It turned out there was disagreement among the WAC faculty too, although the "teasing" paper got much more support. First, though, Professor Monk from biology praised the diction and syntax of "procrastination," saying that control of words and sentence structure had to come before there was any point in worrying about larger issues of organization and content. An anthropologist, Professor Blaine, disagreed, saying he'd seen plenty of weak, confused arguments written in correct sentences, and occasionally strong, interesting arguments with awkward sentences and grammar mistakes. He was lukewarm about the "teasing" paper, though. "It's inefficient and really stiff—I think the student was just writing what she thought she had to. There's nothing creative there."

Then Professor Coolidge from psychology played what she hoped would be a trump card in the discussion: "Look at the *arguments*! These students are supposed to be figuring out how one kind of behavior leads to another in their families. The 'procrastination' writer brings up just one causal idea: modeling. It's supposed to be the explanation for everything! And she doesn't even say anything about questions like why she and her sister just adopted their parents' ways, when lots of kids *reject* behaviors they see in their parents, deliberately turning away from them! The writer of the 'teasing' paper is actually trying to do a causal analysis. She brings up *several* causes, does a little bit with relations between them, and even suggests more complicated cause-and-effect connections, although she hasn't figured them out yet."

There was a short silence, and then Professor Anker joined his colleague, challenging the idea that in the "teasing" paper there was nothing creative. "I think creativity *was* involved in that student's analysis. Creativity gets expressed in many different ways. Let me tell you about a student we did an exit interview with last spring. This young man said he had learned to love writing when a community college teacher 'provided an ideal environment for self expression' and 'encouraged creative output.' When he began to write as an upper division psychology student here at the university, he felt he could not use what he had learned doing earlier writing, and he was not pleased with his work because it seemed dry and 'uncreative.' Eventually, however, his feeling about his work changed, as he began to understand how imagination and rigor can work together. He said, 'I remember when I first started reading and writing psych papers I thought they were really drab, full of facts but no energy. I know that is not true now.'"

QUESTIONS FOR REFLECTION AND DISCUSSION

1. When Katie's class first reacted to these papers, do you think she should have taken an active part in the discussion? She wanted her new students to express their views freely, which they certainly did—but she also wanted them to think carefully about what they were valuing and why. Should she have told the majority she thought they were simply wrong?

2. For the next meeting of her class, Katie decided to try furthering the discussion of unresolved issues by distributing two lists. One gave the first sentence of each paragraph in the ten-paragraph "teasing" paper; the other gave the first sentence of each paragraph in the twenty-one-paragraph "procrastination" paper. Was this a good idea?

3. Enthusiasts for "procrastination" said that the writer was entertaining, while the writer of "teasing" was just giving "what the teacher wants." Both students and faculty who read the papers this way suggested that the writer of "procrastination" could easily have written something like the "teasing" paper, but chose to do something more engaging. Do you think the writer of "procrastination" *could* have written "teasing"?

4. A sociologist taking part in the WAC program said he always told his students that writing well was important, and his syllabus for every class recommended that students buy and be guided by Strunk and White's *Elements of Style*. "I thought I couldn't go wrong," he said, "if I urged students to use definite, specific, concrete language. But is that 'procrastination' paper what I'm asking for? It's certainly not what I want!" How would you advise the sociologist?

5. Do you think the family system assignment provides a good opportunity for students to do analytical yet creative work?

6. Have you given assignments that were especially successful in providing such an opportunity? Assignments with this intention that failed?

NOTES

1. Many thanks to Martha Koehler, now at the University of Pennsylvania-Greensburg, who provided the family systems assignment and sample student papers for the Interdisciplinary Writing Program files when she was at the University of Washington.

READINGS FOR FURTHER CONSIDERATION

MacDonald, Susan Peck. "Specificity in Context: Some Difficulties for the Inexperienced Writer." *College Composition and Communication* 37 (1986): 195–203.

Odell, Lee. "Context-Specific Ways of Knowing and the Evaluation of Writing." *Writing, Teaching, and Learning in the Disciplines*. Ed. Anne Herrington and Charles Moran. New York: Modern Language Association, 1992. 86–98.

Walvoord, Barbara. *Thinking and Writing in College: A Naturalistic Study of Students in Four Disciplines*. Urbana: National Council of Teachers of English, 1990.

15

The Jonas Incident[1]

Chris M. Anson

"**W**ell, you *say* all this stuff about linking ideas," Jonas Simmons almost shouted, "but what's really behind this is that you just don't like my position. And I'm probably the last honest student in this class."

The rest of the class had already left the room, but Cynthia was nevertheless embarrassed by Jonas's words, uttered in a kind of clenched-teeth bitterness that made her almost afraid to respond. And his confrontation was all the more disconcerting because he had never given Cynthia any reason to believe he would challenge her so forcefully. An articulate student, Jonas had written his first paper in Cynthia's intermediate sociology course on the psychosocial response to highway entrance-ramp stoplights. Using some statistics he had gathered from the highway department, as well as observations and interviews with drivers, he had argued convincingly that the lights had led to alternative behaviors that did little to alleviate the problem of traffic jams and resulted in more aggressive driving.

In spite of his abilities, Jonas had also seemed withdrawn during class sessions, joining groups reluctantly, waiting for others to volunteer to discuss their ideas. He was usually quiet in discussions, but sometimes came forward with a short, carefully worded statement only to fade out again for ten or fifteen minutes. Cynthia had also felt—though she wasn't entirely sure—that there was something just a little off-center about his demeanor; she thought he made odd, subtle facial expressions from time to time as she or other students talked.

As she had gotten to know the class over the past few weeks of the term, Cynthia weighed her comments on Jonas's work carefully, finding herself sometimes torn between thinking her cautiousness was a sellout for not being more confrontational about his sometimes odd ideas, and worrying that something—what, she had no idea—could come from pushing too hard at this rather unusual student.

In her three years of teaching at Powderhorn University, Cynthia had not encountered any students who had presented problems for her. A generally successful teacher, she taught her classes in what some of her peers felt was a pretty standard way, focusing on the learning of the subject, helping students to develop their ideas and find support or evidence for assertions, and allowing students some freedom to choose topics to explore in their papers.

In her committee work and in departmental meetings, she had become more outspoken since her first year, often challenging people's ideas but cautious not to seem abrasive. Now she felt a growing desire to do the same thing in her sociology classes.

For the second assignment in her course, Cynthia had asked the class to choose a recent event that could be understood through the lens of the sociological concepts the class was studying, and then write a commentary on the event from a sociological perspective. Her assignment sheet stressed the need to be "thoughtful," and not to rely on sound bites from the media. In her example, she alluded to a local case in which a woman had been caught plotting to murder her abusive husband. "What's at stake?" she asked rhetorically. "What issues does this event raise about the concept of abuse? Was the woman right, based on the evidence? What is justifiable revenge in our society? How can we *link* this event to sociological concepts and theories?"

In this second assignment, Cynthia formed the students into small groups to give each other some feedback on their rough drafts. Pressured by an overdue book review for an academic journal, she didn't have the time to write up a revision guide with questions that would focus the students' attention on important issues in their papers. Instead, she suggested some things to look for, then set the students to work. She noticed that Jonas was, as usual, the last to join his group, reluctantly moving his chair over and sitting with his peers, three other young men whom Cynthia felt she didn't know very well yet. She noticed that toward the end of the session, with about five minutes to spare, the group began talking about Jonas's paper, but she was busy with another group and didn't hear anything that they said.

When this unit of her course had ended and she sat in her office reading papers, Cynthia was generally impressed with the quality of the students' work. When she reached Jonas's paper, her feelings about his abilities were confirmed. His opening, which used a personal anecdote, was well written and appealing. But as she continued to read, she felt herself bristling, shaking her head, and then boiling with anger. Jonas had written a paper more blatantly racist than anything she had ever seen as a faculty member. She sat, stunned, looking at his work.

THIEVING, THE BLACK COMMUNITY, AND FRAGMENTED VALUES

Jonas Simmons

When I was young, about six or seven, I stole my cousin's flute. It was a beautiful instrument given to him as a gift, much smaller than a regular flute but solid gold with a silver mouthpiece. Finding myself in his room alone, I slipped it into my pocket in a moment of sudden insanity, and left his house.

The values reinforced in my home were strong enough that for days I wrestled with the guilt of my theft. Peter didn't miss the flute. His family was wealthy, and we were on the lesser side of middle-class. He had lots of toys, games, and recreational opportunities. Maybe he thought he just misplaced it. I'm not sure. Still, these thoughts didn't console me at all. After a time, while the flute sat in the bottom drawer of my dresser (which opened with a special knack only I possessed), I decided to return it. I couldn't play it without being heard, and showing it to anyone would have revealed my theft.

But unlike the theft, this time the deceit wasn't so easy. For one thing, it didn't carry the same heart-pounding, terrible glee. It was also harder. I needed a reason to see my cousin, I didn't want to wait until an invitation came along months later, and I needed an opportunity that might never come again, a chance to be alone again in Peter's room. Of course, there was also simple confession, but the idea soon took on an awful complexity that made the deceit tidy by comparison.

The plan eventually worked, and the details are now unimportant in the scope of my claim. What's important here is the magnitude of this event in my memory and my growth. But why was it so important? Not because of "me" in a personal way, but because of the values instilled in me by my parents and community.

Now imagine a young black teenager during the recent local protests over the black kids accused of provoking a brawl at a football game. Caught in a tide of hatred and hostility, he joins a band of his friends and goes on a tirade of looting and destruction in his own community. Why is it that this kid, hardly man enough to shave (if he cared at all about his appearance), would turn against his own kind and rob them, destroying their property while taking pleasure in his actions? The reasons are obvious. His race, once struggling to pass on deeply felt values through its generations, has lost the vision of its own morality. Black mothers in the inner city care more about getting the next dose of crack than raising their kids to become decent citizens. Black men give the youngsters in their community the role model of thugs, thieves, addicts, and pimps. More impassioned by the desire for sleek cars and fancy electronic equipment than the concept of guiding the younger generation toward health of spirit, they begin to care only for themselves and their own conditions. How many looters really felt even a twinge of regret? How many even considered taking back their stolen jewelry, TVs, or leather coats? (Even if they had, their sin had already done their cousins in; the looted stores remained closed and boarded up.)

There may be no solution, at least immediate, to this moral blight. Liberals always blame the system for creating the conditions that lead to such lapses in the black culture's moral center. But history has shown examples again and again of people in the most terrible circumstances rising above their degradation by the energy of moral spirit. Where has it gone? In an essay tracing the black struggle for literacy, a noted historian notes the same loss of values in the black community, only this time toward education. Cut from the same cloth, the urge for learning and morality has largely disappeared from a majority of black "households," replaced by guns, drugs, open sexuality, vulgarity, child abuse, battered women, and a shunning of physical health and well-being.

Our "dominant culture," the "hegemony," should, according to the liberals, blame itself and bail out inner-city blacks for their own communities' loss of a moral center. But this solution does nothing to create changes within. More sensible is a strong message to these communities: no pain, no gain. No focus *by* black people on their own problems, no regaining of the moral center. And no more bailouts.

While some critics may argue that the needs of poor communities make them unable to do "bigger" things, I would argue the opposite. Morality is bigger than even hunger. Can I help those communities? I used to think it was my obligation. Now I wash my conscience of them. They must help themselves, and show the rest of society that they are worthy of the dignity they once deserved.

While reading Jonas's paper, Cynthia wrote no comments on it, feeling almost like it was like a dangerous virus. Then, very deliberately, she opened up her laptop and typed out the following note:

Jonas: I'm afraid I must return your essay without grading it. As you know, I have strong feelings about a number of issues, especially racism, which your paper only promotes. Since I can't judge your essay fairly, I won't judge it at all. Because the issue here is ideological, I will ask that you write another paper on a different topic, and I will give you the rest of the term to do so. Please submit a rough draft to me at least two weeks before the end of the term, so you can revise it for final submission. I will apply the grade on the revised paper to your average. If you choose not to do this, you will receive no credit for this unit.

As soon as she typed in the last word of her note, Cynthia had misgivings about this strategy. Although she had no reason to think that Jonas wouldn't just go off and write a new paper, something about the refusal to grade his work kept nagging at her. She had talked with other teachers who had done this before, but always in connection with the "quality" of their writing—a second chance to clean up the errors. But not about their *ideas*. But, she mused—weren't ideas also quality? Besides, even though Jonas was supposed to benefit from his group's comments, he'd turned in a paper that was not very different from the original. In fact, it was hardly revised. Still, Cynthia felt apprehensive about a comparative analysis of Jonas's rough and final drafts as the main basis for her grade.

A year ago, she wouldn't have given it a second thought: her syllabus had made it clear that the improvement of the writing, based on peer feedback, would weigh heavily in her assessment of each unit. Predictably, many of her students received high grades by virtue of their efforts alone. Several times, her department chair had raised the issue of grade inflation, urging the faculty to toughen up on their standards. For Cynthia, this had led to some shifts in the way she read papers and told students about her evaluations. Her syllabus now included the following revised statement of her criteria:

> I will expect you to *make use* of opportunities in class to work on your papers (such as small-group revision sessions). I will collect rough and final drafts, but will only judge the quality of the final draft, not the extent to which you have improved it. Opportunities for revision are yours to use, not mine to grade. Make use of them, and your final papers will be better.

Glancing at the comments of Jonas's conference partners, Cynthia regretted abandoning her old improvement criteria; back then, she could have easily given Jonas a D for not revising the draft. What else was there? As she scanned her assignment sheet, she suddenly realized that Jonas hadn't referred directly to anything they had been reading in the course. Not one theory, not one concept, was explicitly linked to the event Jonas was describing, except for an uncited reference to an unknown historian. A feeling of vindication washing over her, she penned in at the bottom: "This doesn't fully respond to the assignment—D+." She put the paper aside. She would worry about commenting on it later.

———

As if reading her mind, Jonas continued to challenge the basis of Cynthia's grade. "The fact that I don't mention five theories isn't relevant. It's not what these papers are supposed to do, at least by your own admission," he said, looking off toward the window as if addressing something there. "These are my thoughts about a sociological event, and I doubt that you'll find any errors in the writing."

Cynthia knew she couldn't criticize Jonas's writing on technical grounds or even, for that matter, stylistically. There was no question that Jonas was as decent a writer, from this perspective, as she'd ever had. She had to rely, then, on something rhetorical, but other than the reference issue, all that came to mind, in an objective way, was audience: Jonas hadn't considered his readers. "See," she started hesitantly, "I think what's missing from your paper is a strong acknowledgment of your audience. I mean, let's face it, lots of people would find this piece pretty blatantly racist." Feeling as if she were becoming trapped, she added quickly, "most sociologists are more objective than this."

"No," Jonas challenged, still looking at the window. "*You* found it racist. But *I* imagined an audience of like-minded thinkers. I *hear* these sentiments expressed on a daily basis, even in this class."

"No, not here, Jonas," Cynthia said firmly. "Not once in this class, and you know it."

"You *don't* know it," Jonas retorted. "They're just playing the game. You can't know what I know; you're the teacher. That's why the group didn't give me anything to change. Besides, most of us aren't even sociology majors."

Cynthia felt herself becoming defensive. "I don't care what they think outside my class," she blurted. "In here, no racism. Period."

Jonas, now looking at her directly for the first time, handed Cynthia his paper. He waited until, with a puzzled look, she took it. "I won't take up the issue of freedom of speech," he said very formally. "I ask only that you reconsider my grade objectively, based on the quality of the writing. I know you'll change your mind." For a second, Cynthia felt that she had never met a more displeasing individual. Then Jonas left the room.

Later that day, wondering whether she should consult a member of the administrative staff, Cynthia checked her mailbox to see if there had been any fallout from the Jonas incident. There was only one thing in her box. It was a photocopy of an item one of the members of the faculty-development staff had pinned on the bulletin board next to the mailboxes earlier that week.

SEVEN PRINCIPLES OF GOOD PRACTICE IN UNDERGRADUATE EDUCATION

- Good practice encourages student-faculty contact.
- Good practice encourages cooperation among students.
- Good practice encourages active learning.
- Good practice gives prompt feedback.
- Good practice emphasizes time on task.
- Good practice communicates high expectations.
- Good practice respects diverse talents and ways of learning.
  —AAHE, Education Commission of the States, and the Johnson Foundation

At first, Cynthia thought that perhaps the faculty-development program had decided to give all teachers a copy of the item. Surreptitiously, she pulled out the contents of some of her colleagues' mailboxes to see if a copy of the item was there as well; it wasn't. As she did this, looking around to be sure no one was nearby, she felt a strange sense of confused embarrassment, no doubt a residue of Jonas's focus on morality. As if caught in a little breach of ethic—what, she thought angrily, because of *Jonas's* morality, bred of absolute *racism?*—she thrust back the papers she had pulled out from a colleague's box and stared again at her copy of the item. Why was this here? Then she noticed a tiny asterisk penned next to the last statement on the list.

It had to be Jonas.

QUESTIONS FOR REFLECTION AND DISCUSSION

1. Is Cynthia's course of action (relying on her citation policy to determine Jonas's grade) appropriate? Why or why not?

2. Does Jonas have a right to express his views, even if some might consider them racist? Does Cynthia have a right to "ban" certain ideas or expression from her students' writing or her class?

3. If a small group, like the one Jonas is in, agrees with a writer's views and encourages little revision, is the writer justified in assuming the paper needs little further conceptual work or revision? Why or why not?

4. At lunch in the faculty club with her colleagues, Cynthia recounts the Jonas incident. Respond to the following comments from the resulting dialogue:

ED: Cynthia, my feeling is that you're reacting too personally to Jonas's ideas and not to what you're teaching, which is good essay writing.

SUE: I agree. Teachers who assign writing have a responsibility to make good writers, not good liberals or good conservatives. If I were you, Cynthia, my duty would be to make Jonas the best racist writer I could, by finding better support for his arguments.

PAULA: Wait a minute, Sue. I think as teachers we have a moral obligation to help students to be fair people and good citizens. I'm not sure I agree with your tactics, Cynthia, but I sure do agree with you that Jonas needs to learn about his racism. Isn't this what sociology is about?

SAM: How can you call him racist? He's simply pointing out a problem in the Black community—and doing it pretty well at that. I almost agree with him! I mean, there are even African American scholars out there who are criticizing Black culture for its attitudes. McWhorter's *Losing the Race* comes to mind.

MILES: Look, this guy's paper is about Cynthia, not his own beliefs. He's doing a power play on her, maybe for fun, maybe because he's vindictive or just egomaniacal. And—don't take this wrong, Cynthia—but I think you played right into it. He would never have turned in this paper to me because I'm Black and I'm male. It's just as much an attack on Cynthia's politics and her vulnerability as it is an indictment of the Black community.

NOTE

1. An earlier version of this case appeared in, and has been reprinted with permission of, *Dilemmas in Teaching: Cases for Collaborative Faculty Reflection*. Anson, C. M., L. K. Cafarelli, C. Rutz, and M. Weiss, eds. Madison: Mendota, 1998. ISBN 0-912150-51-3.

READINGS FOR FURTHER CONSIDERATION

Brooke, Robert. *Writing and Sense of Self: Identity Negotiation in Writing Workshops*. Urbana: National Council of Teachers of English, 1991.

Walvoord, Barbara E. Fassler. *Helping Students Write Well: A Guide for Teachers in All Disciplines*. 2nd ed. New York: Modern Language Association, 1986. See especially chapter 3, "Planning to Coach the Writing Process" and chapter 6, "Principles of Effective Response."

16

Esmeralda's Math Class

Sandra Jamieson

In a recent conversation about education with his daughter, who taught in a middle school, Albert was bemoaning the generally poor writing skills he sees in college students. His daughter's response, "Well Dad, what are *you* doing about it?," took him by surprise. Albert had been teaching college math for twenty years, and he'd tried to protest that it wasn't his job to solve his student's writing problems too: It was all he could do to keep students interested in learning math. But in his heart he suspected that it wasn't enough to leave all writing instruction to the English department. A few weeks later he received an invitation to participate in the annual WAC workshops, and (to his daughter's delight) he accepted.

The workshop introduced participants to a number of problems, solutions, and strategies for incorporating writing into classes in different disciplines. Albert was intrigued by the idea of assigning journals, but he was even more interested in developing a written version of Linda Flower and John R. Hayes' spoken protocols he read about in Patricia Bizzell's essay ("Cognition, Convention, and Certainty"). As he explained to his daughter, adapting the idea of writing protocols to the math class would be easy. He could ask his students to write about the process of solving the problem sets as they worked through them.

Seeing his interest, the workshop leader downloaded some Web sites from college math teachers who used letters and responses to encourage students to apply calculus skills to imaginary situations. In one, the students used Newton's Law of Cooling to help a fast food restaurant determine whether the coffee it served could have burned a customer; in another, they used Riemann sums to help a CEO determine how much carpet he needed to replace the orange shag in his new office (http://www2.wheatonma.edu/academic/academicdept/MathCS/faculty/tratliff/writing/home.html). Another series of assignments invited students to solve "cases" such as "The Case of Lead Poisoning" (using coupled differential equations) and "The Case of the Fall from Grace" (using calculations about the motion and timing of a falling body) (http://www.fandm.edu/Departments/Mathematics/writing_in_math/writing_index.html).

Albert was hooked. These assignments invited students to work out what the problem was, use the information provided to solve it, and write a letter to a specific audience explaining the solution mathematically and in prose. The students needed to consider the audience and had to really explain how and why the calculations revealed what they did. In talking through their answers (in writing), students would show him their thought processes, just as they would with writing protocols, but in these assignments they would also be finding a practical use for math. Asking students to write about their answers seemed akin to having a conversation with them about how they reached those answers. They could tell him the way they were thinking, and from this he would be better able to judge whether they really understood the material he was teaching. And asking them to write for a "real" audience would encourage them to practice writing clearly and concisely.

For his workshop project Albert designed a handout for his class in which he explained exactly how he wanted them to write the responses. He based his handout on a checklist by Annalisa Crannell (http://www.fandm.edu /Departments/Mathematics/writing_in_math/checklist.html) and directed them to the Web sites listed above to see sample answers. He also redesigned the assignments for the two sections of Calculus II he would be teaching the next semester.

When he explained his idea to other workshop participants, they pointed out how much additional work this would be, both for him and for the students. They discussed why math students often resist writing, and he decided it would be fairest to reward his students for their effort by making the written part of each assignment an essential part of each grade. He settled on fifty percent.

On the first day of class he enthusiastically explained the assignments, handed out the description, and told the students that if they wanted to do so, they could provide their answers handwritten rather than typed. He was secretly delighted when students started complaining that this class felt like a writing class and protesting that they shouldn't be graded on their writing because the issue here is mathematics. This gave him the chance to launch into his speech about the importance of writing in all walks of life, and to reassert his belief that reading the answers in prose form would help him to understand how his students got to their answers and so help him to teach them more effectively.

Two weeks later he collected the first responses and returned to his office to grade them. He finished the first batch and found himself writing responses that discussed mathematical reasoning *and* the student writing itself (mostly grammar and punctuation). He fired off an email to his daughter telling her that now he *was* doing something about his students' writing. Some of the answers were very creative and overall the students seemed to enjoy the humor of the imaginary situations he had designed; some even added their own in their responses (making up hilarious names for the companies they represented and the mathematicians they had consulted, for example). As he thought about the difference this kind of assignment had made to his ability to engage his students, he sent another email to the person who ran the workshop thanking her for introducing him to this kind of assignment, and copied it to all the other participants.

The next morning as he sat in his office trying to finish up grading the homework before class, he was still feeling enthusiastic. Then he got to Esmeralda's homework. The math was totally accurate, but he could barely read the explanation, which contained odd spelling errors and a rambling and disconnected description of the process she had gone through to get to those answers. Esmeralda was certainly not the stereotypical math student. She came to class fairly scantily dressed and seemed very concerned about her appearance, and she was always surrounded by a group of adoring males. He had noticed that she seemed to prefer the brightest ones in the class, and they certainly paid attention to her—sometimes competing for her attention when they should have been listening to his lectures! He thought she encouraged them too, as she was doing when he described the importance of the written responses and the danger of them lowering grades. She seemed bored in class, yet she had declared as a math major in a department with very few female math majors.

He decided to stop grading for the day and headed off to get a cup of coffee. On the way he ran into a colleague from the workshop, who teased him gently about his newfound enthusiasm for writing. Instead of the chuckle she expected, he sighed and asked her opinion of Esmeralda.

"A brilliant student! She got straight A's in each of my computer science classes—her programs were flawless. That girl has a very bright future."

"Hmm. I just got her first written response and I've never seen anything like it. The math is perfect, but the writing is diabolical."

"Sloppy?"

"No. This goes beyond sloppiness. Her prose is almost incomprehensible and seems to have little to do with the answer. She jumps from point to point with no transitions, and the process she describes makes no sense—it doesn't even seem like a process, the handwriting is a mess, and some of her paragraphs are just one long run-on sentence."

"Well, maybe she ran out of time."

"I hope so. I fear worse. Your assignments are mostly take-home, aren't they? I fear she *isn't* the brilliant mathematician at all. I don't see how she could be so unable to explain the answers if she wrote them herself. I fear someone else is doing her math for her. You know how much attention she always gets from the boys in the class. And I hesitate to mention the way she dresses . . ."

"Albert, that's a serious charge! Maybe you should wait until you've given an in-class test before you jump to any conclusions. I'm sure she just didn't pay attention when you said you'd be grading the writing as well as the math."

Albert agreed that waiting would be the best idea. He had scheduled a test for the next week anyway, and that test required no writing. He gave Esmeralda a C− for the first assignment: F for the writing and A for the math, although he wasn't really comfortable with that resolution to the problem. He never intended the writing to *hurt* anyone's grade. He decided not to hand back any of the written homeworks until he had graded the test as well.

During the in-class test the following week, Esmeralda seemed to be concentrating hard, but she was finished a good fifteen minutes before the end of class and sat looking around and fidgeting. He was surprised and relieved when he graded the test: She got a perfect 100—the only student who did. When Albert returned the in-class tests and the first written assignments, he carefully explained again what he wanted from the written response ready for their second one, due in a week. He stressed the fifty/fifty grade and the importance of proofreading carefully. He handed out the checklist from Crannel's Web site and asked students to proofread their own prose and hand in the completed checklist with their next assignment. Throughout this whole explanation, Esmeralda never met his eye—in fact, she seemed particularly distracted by the young man sitting behind her.

A week later he was again sitting in his office in front of a pile of written responses, but this time he turned to Esmeralda's first. Once again, the math was faultless, but the explanation was even worse than its predecessor. The prose might have been a little better, although it was made up of very simple four- to six-word sentences, and she hadn't clipped the completed checklist to the back as he had requested. He sent her an email message asking her to come and see him as soon as possible.

When Esmeralda arrived she was alone and seemed a little nervous. He motioned for her to sit in the chair by his desk, and as she did so she looked around and seemed fidgety.

"Esmeralda, I'll come right to the point. I don't understand you. You scored 100 on the in-class test. The math on these two homeworks is perfect. But the written explanations are hopeless. You're a native speaker of English, aren't you? What's happening here? When I read your first written homework I thought you must be cheating, but your in-class test score seems to show you aren't. Please tell me what's going on."

Esmeralda said nothing for so long that Albert cleared his throat and passed the second written response to her.

"Look at this. Can you explain yourself, young lady?"

She looked at the test, and then down at her feet. Then she looked him in the face and said:

"The truth is that I'm learning disabled and I can't write the way you want us to. I really tried. I even asked my friends to look at my writing and fix it for you the way you wanted it, but I can't write like you want us to. I'm a math major. It isn't fair if I'm gonna get a C in your class when the math is perfect. I don't think you're being fair at all."

Her tone was somewhere between brazen and desperate, and Albert didn't know what to say. He'd heard about learning disabilities. Something had come round from the dean about giving students extra time on tests if they requested it, and his daughter had told him all about the middle school students on Ritalin. But this seemed like an excuse. Esmeralda was smiling now, and he smelled a rat.

"Perhaps I could come to your office and explain how I did the homework instead of writing it out?" She leaned forward in her chair, revealing much too much cleavage for Albert's comfort.

"I'm afraid that won't be satisfactory at all. First of all, the idea of a written response is that you write it out *with the math* so that I can see what you're thinking as you work through the problems. I want to understand how you work, step by step. And second, as I explained in class, writing is essential in whatever career you enter. You won't get away with writing like this when you go out to work, and I don't think I'm really doing you any favors if I accept this excuse rather than making you learn to write effectively. Now am I? I gather you might be thinking about graduate school, but you'll never make it there with writing like this. You'll have to learn how to do it. Students who grew up speaking another language have to do these assignments too, and I don't hear them complaining or making excuses. They know that they have to learn to write if they want to succeed in this country. I expect they'd prefer to come to my office and just tell me the answers, too. I can't go making exceptions for you when they are working so hard on their English and aren't getting any special exceptions. Now can I?"

He was about to explain that he didn't have time to meet everyone individually to go over their homework with them, but Esmeralda had pushed her chair back and was rushing for the door, tears streaming down her face.

QUESTIONS FOR REFLECTION AND DISCUSSION

1. Should writing assigned in nonwriting classes be graded at all? And if it is, should we grade the writing at equal weight with the content material, as Albert did?

2. Albert tells Esmeralda that he won't make an exception for her because he doesn't make exceptions for students whose first language is not English. Should we penalize second-language speakers for the errors in their written prose, or should we evaluate them by a different standard? If the latter, how might we design such a standard? How would we explain it?

3. Although Albert had reason to be suspicious of Esmeralda's work because of the differences in quality between the math and the writing, to what extent do you think stereotypes about "typical math students" and females who dress and act "provocatively" played into his suspicion?

4. Should Albert have asked Esmeralda to explain her learning disability instead of dismissing it as he did? If so, how might he have approached the situation so that the conference had a less painful outcome?

5. What legal responsibility does Albert have to respond to Esmeralda's learning disability (assuming that such a disability has been documented in the appropriate office)?

READINGS FOR FURTHER CONSIDERATION

Bizzell, Patricia. "Cognition, Convention, and Certainty: What We Need to Know About Writing." *Pre-Text* 3 (1982): 213–44.

Crannell, Annalisa. "Checklist for Your Writing Project" ⟨http://www.fandm.edu/Departments/Mathematics/writing_in_math/checklist.html⟩

———. "How to Grade 300 Mathematical Essays and Survive to Tell the Tale," *PRIMUS* 4.3 (1994): 193–201.

———. "Writing in Mathematics" ⟨http://www.fandm.edu/Departments/Mathematics/writing_in_math/writing index.html⟩

Dance, Rosalie A., and James T. Sandefur. "Hands On Activities for Algebra at College." ⟨http://www.georgetown.edu/projects/handsonmath/⟩

LD Online: The Interactive Guide to Learning Disabilities for Parents, Teachers, and Children. "LD in Depth: Writing" ⟨http://www.ldonline.org/ld_indepth/writing/writing.html⟩

Meier, John, and Thomas Rishel. *Writing in the Teaching and Learning of Mathematics.* MAA Notes Series. New York: Mathematical Association of America, 1998.

Ratliff, Tommy. "Making Group Projects in Calculus Manageable and Creative." *UME Trends,* September 1995. ⟨http://www2.wheatonma.edu/academic/academicdept/MathCS/faculty/tratliff/writing/aux/ume.html⟩

———. "Writing Assignments in Calculus." ⟨http://www2.wheatonma.edu/academic/academicdept/MathCS/faculty/tratliff/writing/home.html⟩

Sterrett, Andrew, ed. *Using Writing to Teach Mathematics.* MAA Notes Series. New York: Mathematical Association of America, 1990.

17

The Finger on the Pulse
Who Teaches Writing?

William Condon

Monday at Enor State University (ESU) begins normally enough, but before the morning is out, two portentous events unfold. First, one of the Writing Center instructors comes in to report that a TA in a psychology course had been rather too blunt in commenting on a paper that a student had brought in for advice about revising. Later, the receptionist remarks that the appointment calendar for the week is beginning to fill up with students from a single course. These two events turn out to be related. By the end of the day, two-thirds of the week's appointment slots are filled—an unusual occurrence only a fourth of the way into the semester—primarily with students from a large first-year psychology course, Psychology as a Natural Science. Two more instructors have reported written comments from psychology TAs, calling the comments "inconsiderate" and "rude."

Tuesday begins in a similar manner, as appointment slots continue to fill with psychology students and instructors continue to report that the comments on the papers are not good examples of responding to students' writing. A few comments are downright offensive. One TA has written, "Didn't you *read* the assignment?!?" Another observed, "It doesn't take a lot of intelligence to follow directions. You didn't even do that. Go to the Writing Center and get this straightened out."

Clearly, some kind of action is needed.

The director of the Writing Center, Clive Mangini, is alarmed that so many students from a single course are showing up—perhaps, thinks Clive, the instructor in this 250-student course has, without checking with him first, simply required all her students to come to the center. And then there is the matter of the commenting style of the TAs—unhelpful, for the most part, and in some cases clearly out of bounds. Clive decides to gather some evidence and contact the instructor.

As events unfold, Clive discovers some useful information. First, his Writing Center instructors inform him that the fifty students who have come in that week have all received a grade of D or F on their assignment. All have been required to come to the center to get advice about revision. Several students have brought the written assignment sheet with them to the Writing Center, and Clive now has a copy. The students were asked to write up the results of a "cola challenge" experiment that had been conducted in class. All the students had the same data, and they had been advised to write in a standard social science research report format: IMRAD (Introduction, Methods, Results, Analysis, Discussion). The assignment sheet contained only a brief statement of the requirements and only a mention of the correct format—and that in the form of a caution to "be sure to follow standard APA style for a research report." Few of the students who were coming into the Writing Center had successfully followed that format. Almost all had written an essay, rather than a research report.

One instructor, Kim, says, "You know, the TAs are trying to help, but they just don't seem to know how."

Helene, an instructor who has taught a writing course that was attached to a different psychology course, remarks, "The students haven't written anything that even looks like a research report. I don't think the TAs know how to reach students whose work is so far outside what the TAs expect."

All the instructors remark that one TA seems to have responded well and productively, making comments that were tactful and that were geared to promote effective revision.

By Thursday, Clive is in the psychology professor's office. Leslie is fully aware of the problems occurring in her course. "One-fifth of my students failed the assignment," she notes, "and they are not happy campers. I've never given an assignment—or even a test—where the *median* grade was a C−."

She is also disturbed at many of the TAs' comments. She says, "They aren't writing teachers; they are psychology students themselves. They don't know how to handle such poor writing. That's why I wanted to send the students who had earned poor grades to the Writing Center."

"I've always taught upper-division courses," she continues. "You know, the writing-intensive ones. I think it's incredibly valuable to have the students write like that, but I always noticed that they didn't seem to know how to write like psychologists do. I was hoping to get an early start with these students, so that the ones who go on to be psych majors will know about how we write before they get to the junior-senior writing-intensive courses."

"Did you go through one of the university's writing-across-the-curriculum workshops?" asks Clive.

"Oh, yeah. I got a lot of good ideas from that. And my TAs in that class also did a workshop of some kind. I guess, in hindsight, they must have learned a lot about responding to writing, because I never had any trouble like this before. And Joe—the TA who's been through that seminar—did fine. He seemed to know how to help the students revise. All I wanted to do was bring some of the good points of the WI courses into this first-year course. But I have 250 students now, not 45. That makes a big difference, I guess.

Clive also finds out that Leslie has three more writing assignments on her syllabus: a second, slightly different kind of research report, a response to a published study about IQ, and a critical analysis of a selection from Stephen Jay Gould's *The Mismeasure of Man*. She is understandably concerned about these assignments. "Frankly," she says, "I can't really see myself using writing assignments in this course again." Clive tries to encourage her, and does manage to persuade her to keep an open mind until he can think of how he and his staff might help her. He collects some samples of successful papers and leaves on a somewhat hopeful note.

When Clive returns to his office, he opens a discussion with his staff. Given the information he's gathered, his colleagues believe that several changes might improve the situation for the students.

"Leslie needs to change the assignments," Helene advises. "They need to provide more guidance. She's used to upper-division students, who know how to figure out a college-level assignment and who already know something about writing in the field."

"Yes," responds Kim, "and most of these first-year students are not and will not be psych majors; they're taking the course for the social science distribution credit. They need more support, more scaffolding, in order to succeed at this specialized format."

"The successful papers," observes Emily, "do at least approximate the right format. I think the TAs just didn't know what to do with papers that didn't at all fit their expectations. These papers didn't get across what I'd call their threshold of expertise. If you drew a circle that represents the TAs' expectations, most of these papers would be outside that circle."

"Yes," responds Jan, "That's why most of their marginal comments were so useless, and why the WAC-trained TA made some very productive and useful comments. And the 'rude' TA was the least experienced of the bunch. He's teaching for the first time."

"What about the rest of the semester?" asks Clive. "What can Leslie do to salvage this? I'd like to see her continue using writing, but if things don't improve from here, she won't."

"Well," begins Marty, "could we meet with her to help redo the assignment sheets? These others don't give any more guidance than the first assignment did."

"Yes, that's right," says Helene. "I also wonder whether she could move a couple of these earlier. The last two call for an essay format—the students learned that in Freshman Comp. That might help—give them a fighting chance to get their grades up, build some confidence. Then give them a better assignment sheet for the other research report."

"That's great, Helene," says Kim. "In fact, I think next time—if there is a next time—she ought to start with something like the Gould essay. And I think she might find an article in the research report format for them to critique. Even better, let it be a *bad* research report. That way they can learn about the format by critiquing a failed study. That ought to help them feel more like experts."

"Something has to give," Marty complains. "This week has been hellish. The students were all angry, both because of their grades and because they were required to come to us for help." All nod their agreement that the fifty papers were uniformly poor, so the appointments were extremely challenging. Finally, they note that week was robbed of the usual variety—by the time the dust had settled, ninety percent of the week's appointments had been filled with angry, frustrated psychology students.

Clive's weekend is occupied, in large part, in mulling over his options.

QUESTIONS FOR REFLECTION AND DISCUSSION

1. What do you see as the major issues you'd want to address in this case?
2. What do you think about the reactions of the Writing Center staff, both at the beginning and the end of this vignette?
3. Have you had experiences similar to this psychology professor's? How did you resolve the problems?
4. What changes might Clive, the Writing Center director, suggest that the psychology professor make? What kinds of assistance might Leslie demand in return?
5. Assume for the moment that you are in a situation like Leslie's. How might you bridge the gap between your area of expertise and Clive's? Do you see points of contact that the two of you might explore?
6. What do you make of the professor's attempt to introduce writing into this large course? What do you think of the assignments? How about the order? The number? Should she continue to use writing in the course? If so, what might she do differently?
7. What might the university do to help the professor and her TAs as they look toward the next iteration of this course? What policy changes might you want the writing center to make to help deal with such situations in the future? What policy changes would you like to see your university's WAC program make in response to a situation like this one?

READINGS FOR FURTHER CONSIDERATION

Condon, William, and Susanmarie Harrington. "Don't Lower the River; Raise the Bridge: Preserving Standards by Improving Students' Performances." *The Dialogic Classroom: Teachers Integrating Computer Technology, Pedagogy and Research*. Ed. Jeffrey Galin and Joan Latchaw. Urbana: National Council of Teachers of English, 1998.

Haswell, Richard, et al. *Beyond Outcomes: Assessment and Instruction Within a University Writing Program*. Westport: Ablex, 2001.

McLeod, Susan, Chris Thaiss, and Eric Miraglia, eds. *WAC for the New Millennium: Strategies for/of Continuing Writing Across the Curriculum Programs*. Urbana: National Council of Teachers of English, 2001.

18

It's All Academic

Deanna P. Dannels

"You're doing good things here, Ed."

"Thanks, Sandy, I'm just glad you can participate. You know these students—there's nothing like bringing in the big guns from industry to get them whipped into shape."

"Yeah, well, it gets me out of the office and into a classroom again—plus, I have to keep tabs on what you academic types are putting into these kids' heads . . ."

Edwin chuckled. "OK, OK—gotta go. Thanks again, Sandy."

Dr. Edwin Walder hung up the phone feeling quite happy. It was nice for him to receive such a boost from his friend in industry. Sandy had been a long-time friend of Edwin from graduate school and was working in a high-power engineering firm in the local area. Edwin's capstone course was always an excellent place for Sandy to recruit future engineers, and Edwin prided himself on preparing students who would be technically proficient and successful in industry.

Edwin had been teaching the capstone senior design course for ten years now—long enough for it to have become pretty routine. The students were certainly working on projects that were important, but they seemed, well, almost disconnected from the "real world." They were learning engineering, alright—that he was sure; but by the time they left his course and graduated, they just didn't seem to have become "professional."

This year, he was bound to change that, starting with his senior capstone course. He was having the students not only work on the design, but engage in activities he knew they would face when they graduated: writing memos, crafting a design report, and talking about their design in front of people. Not only was Edwin having students write more professional documents, but he also instituted a "design day" where they could showcase their work. Each design team would also, on this day, present their final design report in front of an audience. With all his connections in the local area, he had even managed to get a few friends from upper-level management in well-known engineering firms to agree to participate in the day.

Edwin was excited about these new changes—about the connections he was making with folks like Sandy in industry, and about providing students with a better educational experience. He also found himself more energetic and interested in his teaching than he had been in years. He was thrilled about the opportunities that could emerge for his students. His one informal connection with Sandy had often led to future employment for his students, and now, with this design day set up with management from a variety of firms, it was bound to be a huge success for him, and for his students.

With a renewed excitement for teaching and high hopes for improvement in student work, Edwin walked into class on the first day and said, "This quarter, you're going to learn to be professional engineers."

"A design report? This is absurd—this is nothing but an outline. If they turned this in to a manager in industry, they'd be fired."

Edwin was frustrated. It was the end of the quarter and the students were learning some conventions of professional writing in the field, but it had gone much more slowly than he'd expected. For much of the semester, the students had complained about the writing. They didn't seem to have problems with the weekly oral progress reports, but most of them just read their memos aloud. Several students felt that the assignments were taking time away from the design of their projects, making it difficult for them to complete all of the technical work.

Edwin had just received the final design reports from the students. These were documents that were going to be displayed the following morning at "Design Day" for faculty, industry sponsors, and other students to see. As he worked his way through the reports, he was gratified to see at least one that was outstanding. Polished, thorough, and eminently professional, it included design specifications, drawings, computer printouts, and evidence of experiments. He was quite impressed.

The others, though, were mediocre at best. They weren't quite getting the hang of it. One report, according to Edwin's standards, was abysmal. The team had designed a wheelchair assist device for senior citizens, and although Edwin liked the idea, their report showed no evidence of design sophistication. Instead of the requisite ten pages, they had turned in just three. The report failed to present any of the numerical evidence to support the team's design decisions. The writing was sloppy, and the report was littered with grammatical mistakes and typos. Worse, it didn't even come close to covering everything Edwin had specified in the assignment outline. "Oh well, I guess you can't get them all," he mused, shoving the report aside.

On design day the students arrived in suits and ties, ready to present their reports to their classmates, departmental faculty members, and the industry representatives Edwin had invited. Copies of the students' written reports were out for display, and they all seemed excited to showcase their designs.

The cross-country ski pole team was first up to bat. This team had handed in the best-written report—it was detailed, sophisticated, and thorough. Edwin was sure this idea could be funded in industry and even knew of a few firms that would be immediately interested. The leader, Josh, explained to the audience that each team member would present one aspect of the written report. Edwin leaned back in his chair, gratified that the audience would see something really first-rate right away.

As the team members took their turns, he could feel his optimism fade a bit. The team was delivering on its promise, following the written report in structure and organization, but the students just read the report aloud. Their reading was also somewhat uneven and halting; they stumbled over words, made poor transitions, and didn't expand in any way on the report itself. The presentation wasn't horrible, though—just flat. They would brush up on their presentation skills once they got into industry, he mused; he didn't have time to teach that here. Some students are simply better public speakers and this wasn't a communication course, really. They shouldn't be penalized on their engineering for having less speaking talent. They were just a bit rough around the edges. Their design idea was brilliant and marketable. Their written report was stellar.

On the final page of their report, Edwin wrote:

Design: A
Written report: A
Presentation: A

Nice job. Your design idea is one of the best I have seen. You obviously did the work to evidence its need. Dr. Walder

The next presentation was from the wheelchair assist team, creators of the infamous three-page report. Unlike the ski pole team, this group veered off wildly from their written report. They spent the entire time discussing current designs for wheelchair assistance, and how their own design provided useful market innovations. They didn't show any numbers, experiments, or design specifications. Instead, they produced a prototype of the design and recruited a member of the audience, to the amusement of the rest, to practice with it. They ended their presentation with quotes from several senior citizens they interviewed during the customer needs phase. Their closing statement was a call for continued funding for their project based on market appeal and need.

Edwin was impressed with the team's analysis of the market need and he was persuaded that their efforts might just fill this need, but he could see right through their presentation. They were using emotional appeals to cover up the lack of clear design. Sure, they had a good idea, and it seemed like an idea that was marketable, but where were the numbers? Where were the design specifications? The experiments? The prototype seemed to work, but there was no way of justifying that.

On the final page of the written report, Edwin wrote:

Design:	C
Written report:	C−
Presentation	C−

Although I think you have a good design here, you have not done anything to convince me of its validity. I could see that it works, but that is not all this course was about. Your written report did not detail anything except a rough framework. And your presentation was polished, but you should have spent less time marketing your idea and instead illustrated that you know how to do design. Not to overuse the recent cliché, but "show me the numbers."

The next day, Edwin arrived at his office early to several phone messages from faculty who were quite impressed at his success with the course and students. The first one was from Sandy:

Hi there, Edwin. Hey, I just wanted to tell you that what you're doing is great. Those kids really worked this quarter. I'm glad you brought me in on this. I wanted to chat with you about a couple of designs—the wheelchair assist device and the MRI detection device—what great ideas. Let's have lunch; I'd love to hear more about them. I even think I know of someone who would fund that wheelchair assist device. Those kids really peaked my interest. Anyway, nice job, bud. Let's talk soon.

As he was listening to the message, there was a knock at the door. The wheelchair assist team filed into his office, all five of them, with a copy of the design report and grade. Orlando began speaking (in a clearly irritated tone) as Edwin hung up the phone:

"One of the people from industry—I think his name was Sandy—came up to us after the presentation and told us we did a great job. He said ours was the most interesting presentation because we didn't read anything from the written report and if he were in a position, he would fund us. But you gave us a C and we don't think . . ."

Basel, another student on the team, interrupted: "he even thinks we can get it funded—we really sold him. Come on, Dr. Walder, how can you even—"

Clarissa jumped in. "Listen Dr. Walder, what Basel and Orlando mean is that we prepared the presentation like we would in industry. They don't want a full-blown reading of a report; they want to be persuaded of the need. All that other stuff—it's all academic. You wanted us to learn to be professional engineers, right?"

QUESTIONS FOR REFLECTION AND DISCUSSION

1. Should Edwin consider changing the students' grade on the basis of positive feedback from the industry representative?

2. What are some of the difficulties this case raises in trying to balance both academic and professional contexts? How can Edwin validate the students as both students and professionals? Should their written and oral assignments simulate industry and/or the classroom requirements? What if they are different?

3. Is there any way the wheelchair assist group could have constructed a presentation that met both Edwin's needs and what they thought was important for industry?

4. What are the issues this case raises about criteria for assessing oral and written assignments? Should students be graded according to the professor's standards? Should industry representatives have input into the students' written and oral work?

5. How can faculty and students account for multiple audiences in written and oral assignments? How can faculty address issues of disciplinary forms of argument and evidence if those are different in the academic and work-place medium?

6. High quality reports do not necessarily mean high quality presentations, and vice versa. Yet often the two media represent the same idea, in this case, the design itself. What implications does this case have for understanding the relationship between the oral and written medium?

7. What issues does this case raise about the connections between content (the design), delivery, and medium of communication? If the content is good, thorough, and of high quality, does it matter how that content is presented? If students perform well in an oral presentation, is that necessarily equated with high quality content?

READINGS FOR FURTHER CONSIDERATION

Dannels, Deanna P. "Learning to Be Professional: Technical Classroom Discourse and Professional Identity Construction. *Journal of Business and Technical Communication* 14.1 (2000): 5–37.

Freedman, A., and C. Adam. "Learning to Write Professionally: 'Situated Learning' and the Transition from University to Professional Discourse." *Journal of Business and Technical Communication* 10 (1996): 395–427.

Freedman, A., C. Adam, and G. Smart. "Wearing Suits to Class: Simulating Genres and Simulations as Genre." *Written Communication* 11.2 (1994): 193–226.

Part 4

Coaching Writing
Scenes of Ideology and Interaction

19

Rewriting the Culture of Engineering

Thomas Hilgers, Joan Perkins, and Monica Stitt-Bergh

W hen Sylvia Higashi finished her doctoral work in civil engineering, she was offered jobs at several universities. Her experiences as a student in a field long dominated by men had left her with a sense of personal mission: to make science education and engineering studies more congenial to women. She finally decided to accept an appointment at Roosevelt University because she saw Roosevelt's extensive writing-across-the-curriculum program as evidence that its faculty was committed to more than lecture and examination in the classroom.

Eager to experience the innovative side of the Roosevelt curriculum, Dr. Higashi asked the department chair to assign her a writing-intensive class during her first semester. The chairman, responding by email, suggested that she might prefer a traditional lecture-course assignment so that she would have more time to settle in and work to establish research sites. Higashi responded that the twenty-student enrollment cap in the writing-intensive class would help her manage the work load. She also promised to seek practical advice from more experienced hands before the start of the fall semester.

One of the first things Higashi did when she arrived at the Roosevelt campus was to sign up for the full-day workshop offered for teachers by the Roosevelt writing program. She was pleased to find that the workshop instructor, the writing program's director, was a strong advocate of collaboration in the classroom. Higashi took particular note when the director stressed the importance of helping students to develop social skills as well as critical skills as part of the effort to make peer response groups effective. She was eager to translate that advice into practice: from her perspective, emphasis on social-skills development was preferable to the competitiveness she had experienced as a student in engineering classes. And social skills are a must for anyone assigned to a "project team" of the sort that prevails in engineering firms today.

When classes began in September, Higashi was happy to find that her course was fully enrolled. The students, six women and fourteen men, were all juniors in civil engineering. She asked them to write about their experiences in other writing-intensive courses during the first class meeting. She also carefully went over her syllabus and described some of the processes she expected the students to engage in as they worked through four relatively early writing assignments and then a comprehensive team-authored analysis of a particular transportation engineering problem.

After class, Higashi skimmed the students' comments on their earlier WI course experiences. Most students had at least two, and many had three, writing-intensive classes. Most of the comments on experiences with writing in earlier classes were positive. However, one student, Milton Lau, sounded a warning: "I hope you're not going to waste a lot of time talking about writing. Please remember that this is an engineering course." In noting the comment, Higashi decided that she would have to talk about why she was requiring group work in her classroom.

Higashi's first assignment asked students to observe a point at which two traffic corridors intersected and to record and describe instances of conflict. Students were told to select a vehicular intersection or a pedestrian intersection, including among possibilities pedestrian intersections at airports and the local train station. The assignment was given in conjunction with several class discussions and with assigned readings that involved observation techniques and predictive models. A draft of the assignment was due on September 28.

The new assistant professor brought to the September 28 class meeting some suggestions for peer response groups that she had learned at the writing program workshop:

> As you read the draft, mark words, phrases, images that really stick—for whatever reason. Put a straight line alongside parts that are particularly clear. Put a wavy line alongside sections that are difficult for you to follow. At the end of the draft, try to summarize the central point of what you read—in a single sentence. The goal is to let the writer know "what your piece of writing did to me."

Higashi did more: she asked class members to identify key items that an effective draft response to the assignment might include. She jotted several suggestions offered from class members on an overhead and left it illuminated at the side of the classroom. She recommended that students consult the overhead as they discussed the drafts. Finally, she assigned students to groups because she was a little afraid that self-assignment would lead to same-gender groupings.

As the feedback sessions progressed, Higashi observed from the sidelines. Most of the students glanced up at the overhead as they read one another's drafts. The amount of actual talk varied considerably from group to group. She did note, however, that Milton Lau didn't talk at all. Instead, he was busily writing on the drafts he had received from the other two group members. At the end of class, Higashi asked the students to look over their peers' comments and to highlight comments they would use in writing their final draft, due at the next class meeting.

Late that afternoon, Higashi checked her email as a prelude to leaving her office. One message came from Heather Widner, a student in her class.

"Professor Higashi, I'm not sure what to do. One of the people in my feedback group marked up and crossed out almost everything in my report. I've never written this kind of report before so I guess I made a lot of mistakes. I don't know how to use his feedback except to just start again."

Higashi was troubled by the response. Negativity, put-downs—this is what I was trying to avoid, she thought. This is what keeps women feeling that they have to retreat or develop thick skins. "Heather," she quickly wrote, "I'm sure you don't have to begin all over. Focus on what the other person in your group wrote. Read over the assignment sheet and do a self-assessment of your draft's strengths and weaknesses. Then build upon the strengths as you revise. I look forward to reading your report."

Midway through the next class, as Professor Higashi was collecting each student's first and second drafts, she offered a collective comment. "I was impressed during our last meeting at how conscientious you were in giving one another feedback. I know that it may be a little unusual in an engineering class, but I think it's really important to help you to develop the kinds of group skills you're going to need out in the field. One of the things I've always thought about groups is that they work better when members respond to one another constructively rather than negatively. I'll be interested to see if you found the same thing when I look at the kinds of revisions you made between draft one and draft two."

That afternoon, when she returned for her scheduled office hour, Milton Lau was sitting in one of the lobby chairs near her office. "Are you waiting for me, Milton?" He nodded, got up, and stepped into her office behind her.

The conversation began with Higashi's asking Milton about his background. He responded pleasantly, but rather quickly cut her off. "Professor Higashi, I'm here because I want to become an engineer. You're new, and that's fine, and I know you have your right to your own philosophy of education. Your teaching style's okay and all that. But for me this writing exchange stuff is a waste of time. My father isn't paying all that tuition money so I can waste my time being touchy-feely with other people about their first drafts. That's not how it works in the real world. Engineers are paid by the minute, and they're not paid to make each other feel good."

"I understand your concerns, Milton," said Higashi. "Thank you for coming by to share them. Tell me, did you get any useful feedback from the other members of your group?"

"Oh, I don't mind feedback. It's just that I want it to be relevant. I had this professor last semester for a writing-intensive class who had us give feedback all the time. We didn't put our names on papers. We put code numbers. He collected the papers and then gave them back to us and we wrote feedback. He explained it all to us—he said it was like 'peer review' that you do with project proposals and even journal articles. 'Rip it apart,' he told us. 'If they're serious, they'll want a strong critique.' This isn't some English class, Professor Higashi. This is engineering. You've got us trapped now—it's too late to drop the course. I just want to get my money's worth."

QUESTIONS FOR REFLECTION AND DISCUSSION

1. If you were Professor Higashi, how would you respond to Milton?
2. As Lau observed, each field does have conventional procedures for "peer review." Should professors use their field's peer-review conventions when they teach a writing-intensive class?
3. Should Professor Higashi acknowledge Milton's observations to the full class? If so, how might she best do it?
4. Should Higashi, as a result of Milton's comments, change her approach with subsequent assignments? What additional approaches to peer review would you suggest that she consider? Should she consider, in particular, the approach to feedback that Milton experienced in his previous WI class?
5. Is it appropriate for an individual to work to change habits that are typical for members of a particular community or culture? Is it any different for persons who play teaching roles in the culture?
6. Should a teacher explain his or her approaches to instruction? Should students' compliance with instructional protocols be reflected in course expectations? in evaluation procedures?

READINGS FOR FURTHER CONSIDERATION

Dorman, W. Wade, and James M. Pruett. "Engineering Better Writers: Why and How Engineers Can Teach Writing." *Engineering Education* 75 (1985): 656–58.

Herrington, Anne, and Deborah Cadman. "Peer Review and Revising in an Anthropology Course: Lessons for Learning." *College Composition and Communication* 42.2 (1991): 184–99.

Schwom, Barbara, and Penny Hirsch. "Re-envisioning the Writing Requirement: An Interdisciplinary Approach." *Business Communications Quarterly* 62 (1999): 104–08.

20

Who's "Infantalizing"?

Sharon Quiroz

D r. Allison Soderstrom remembered sitting quietly, waiting for Carla to read over the paper. She had had some misgivings about showing a student another student's paper in this setting. In a peer review Carla could have drawn her own conclusions, but in this private office conference Allison could not see how to avoid saying "Do it like he does." At the same time, her past comments had had no effect on Carla's essayistic, confessional style of writing. It was important for this class that students begin to write like political scientists. Carla was smart, often self-assured, but the black lipstick, nose-ring, velvet cape—all this was off-putting even while the young woman seemed to have a perpetual question mark in her eyes.

Carla looked up, without turning to Allison, holding the paper in front of her. "I don't see anything here—this is just the same old academic stuff. Cut and dried."

"It's very much closer to the way political scientists write," Allison had said, taken aback by the criticism. "I'm not saying that you have to write exactly as he does, but no one is going to read a narrative for this kind of information. It takes too long to read a narrative, and to find the information I've asked for. But mostly the narratives you write make *you* the subject, rather than the information we're dealing with."

"That's my style," Carla had replied grimly. She stood up and began gathering her things. "I've always received good grades for the way I write," she said as she opened Allison's office door and pulled the bottom of her cape around her legs.

Allison thought for one moment that she'd quit teaching and dedicate herself to research, or packing groceries. She thought of her friend Jean who had "a passion for teaching." What would Jean do? Well, Jean would never insist on writing in the professional style. Allison had been meeting with a group of progressivist teachers on campus, mostly feminists like herself, thinking hard about how to implement new pedagogies into her classroom. She was slightly suspicious of claims that seemed to amount to the notion that students would teach themselves if left alone. For one thing, she had long thought that the biggest problem with some progressive educators among her friends was the assumption that, left to their own devices, students would infallibly find the same truths their parents had found. They seemed to expect students to reinvent history and physics all over again, as if such things were just lying around waiting for sharp-eyed students to spot them. Wrestling with that, she had taken time to read the great John Dewey's important books: *Experience and Education; How We Think;* and *Mind and Society.* But her reading of Dewey inclined her to think that his methods were intended to lead to the knowledge already encoded in social formations that she thought likely to stay in place for a good while yet. Dewey's approach seemed to her to offer quite a lot of guidance—it was just packaged differently. She smiled when a radical friend criticized Dewey for just that.

In support of her own position, she always remembered how Jean, who was dedicated to student-centered education, had even suggested that Dewey's classrooms were not so perfectly student centered as those of people like herself, trained in the Peace Corp. Allison took some comfort in that. So she had worked hard all semester in this junior level political science class to reconcile such oppositions: to give students a specific project, materials they would need and space they would need, and turn their learning over to them. Still, they had to come to terms with the practice of the discipline. She tried to embed that in the task and the learning materials. The primary task had been for each to gather information about his or her own hometown, compare what they were finding with the findings of others in the group, and arrive at a socioeconomic description of the place. She wanted students to move from a personal viewpoint to a public one.

To some extent, she rather agreed with Carla about the style in Scott's paper. He was trained in debate, and he polished off every paper in a clear voice; well-organized, well-developed paragraphs; counter-arguments—all you could want, except it was just this side of slick. "Why," she asked herself once again, "is it the conservative white males who know how to write?" Scott was a self-possessed young man, who commanded everyone's attention in the class, and articulately defended the most conservative positions. Allison thought Jean really was unsympathetic to white males, and she didn't want to see herself that way.

So what about Carla? The task Allison had set herself was to use progressive pedagogy in the service of disciplined study. But Carla seemed to read Allison's politics as permission to write undisciplined, self-indulgent prose. Allison approved that for early drafts, but Carla refused to use a more public style when the time came to work on the formal paper.

No other students were waiting to see her, and Allison glanced again at a copy of Carla's paper.

> When I think of my hometown the thing that comes to mind is the farmer's market. It seems to sum up the meaning of Ann Arbor: a small town in the midwest with a very sophisticated population. To me, nothing is more delightful than wandering through the Farmer's Market on a beautiful Saturday morning in the fall. In my mind's eye, I can approach the aisle nearest the building—the section that has mostly flowers and crafts. I can see tomatoe cans, without their labels, full of astors,

or coxcombe, or marigolds. Or on the left—the herb seller. Even in fall they sell herbs (did you know there are at least five kinds of mint? With fun names—chocolate mint, grapefruit mint, orange mint—and they really do have those added flavors!) So you wander along, towards the man who sells salad greens at exorbitant prices because his salad greens include edible flowers. You aren't wandering alone, of course. You have to slip and slide through the crowd—the young professors with babies on their backs or in strollers, old ladies with walkers, couples with big potted plants. I always remember the middle-aged professors, in the beards, the worn jeans, the shapeless sweaters, discussing the latest politics in front of a stall heaped with apples and pears, cider, tomatoes, potatoes, green beans, and soon, pumpkins.

There was little question that she and Scott Williams were miles apart on this assignment. She looked again at Scott's essay, and then at her assignment sheet.

The Federal Penitentiary dominates all else in Clarkston. Whether one investigates the economy, the social structure, the schools, the politics, or any other aspect, all eventually hinges on the presence of the Federal Penitentiary. The town is actually quite pretty, spread along a river. But the most inviting public space is the expanse of grass and gardens, framed by a tall stone gate that announces the Federal Penitentiary.

Clarkston was originally established in 1860, settled by three families from Indiana who moved further west in search of land. It grew slowly after the turn of the century, until the Federal Penitentiary was built in 1935 (Anderson, p. 2). At first the influx of workers employed in building the prison, and later the new citizens who came to staff the prison caused the building of new businesses on main street. Even during the Depression and after that the war, the town flourished, since the main business was not farming, but the more stable hand of the government supported prison (p. 12).

Today, any day, a look at the local newspaper demonstrates the role of the Federal Penitentiary, even if you don't know the story behind the names. If you are from Clarkston, you will recognize that the mayor, for instance, is the son of the chief warden who ran the penitentiary longer than any other person.

Assignment: The purpose of this assignment is to give you practice in using tools from political science to analyze the social, economic, and political forces in your hometown. For the first half of the term you will be asked to comment every week on reports in your local newspaper. In the second half of the term you are to draft an essay describing the social and political characteristics of your hometown. This draft will be graded. It will be reviewed by members of your group, as well as by the instructor. The final assignment is to revise the essay, and submit it for a final grade.

Instructions for writing the essay:

This essay should answer the question, what are the social, economic, and political characteristics of your hometown? You should reference models or methods we have read about either in the textbook or supplemental materials. The essay should be appropriate for a journal in political science.

The introduction should:

- introduce the essay: identify the town and the issues that will be addressed in the essay;
- summarize one or two of the most important factors you believe determine the quality of life in your home town;
- indicate the approach you will use.

Carla was icily polite in the few classes left before the term ended. And Allison couldn't think what to do. Classes were not very uncomfortable because most of the students were fairly enthusiastic. Scott had no reason not to be his usual poised self, perhaps a bit above the fray.

This April morning she handed out the regular class evaluation forms. And besides that, she handed out a very short questionnaire: What did you like best? What did you like least? Allison looked hopefully at the groups of students clustered in those wretched desk seats. Mostly she had read that students give high evaluations to courses that are student centered. But she had also read otherwise, especially for writing-intensive courses. Had she succeeded in making enough students feel safe and free, and responsible for their own learning? She herself had often felt at a loss in the classroom, though she had carefully prepared each task, provided guidelines, and handed out worksheets, and students appeared to be doing the work. She couldn't think of anything to do, and had often spent the time pacing in the hallway, fighting the urge to go in there and tell them. She made arrangements for one of the students in the class to gather the official evaluations and drop them off with the department secretary. Another agreed to collect Allison's own questionnaire and put it in her mailbox.

When Allison read the comments later she was annoyed to find them positive, but not much less perfunctory than the official evaluations. But one jumped out at her: "Your teaching style," it said, "is infantilizing."

Scott Williams. Her mind jumped to that self-assured young man. He already belonged to the world of the university—even as a junior, he knew the rules of the game. At some level, he knew how to own his own education. For instance, he was quite capable of objecting to an idea or a grade on the grounds that "the professor just wanted to impose her ideas on you."

But a moment later she thought of Carla again. Carla, who had somewhere gotten the idea that confessional writing is more sophisticated than academic prose. Yes, that criticism could come from Carla. But, Allison asked herself, who are the students that profit from these progressive techniques? What kind of student does this progressive feminist pedagogy construct?

QUESTIONS FOR REFLECTION AND DISCUSSION

1. Should instructors in upper-level courses in the disciplines insist on disciplinary writing?
2. Do you agree with Allison's reading of the two styles?
3. Does the fact that the assignment invites students to use their own experience strike you as potentially confusing for students?
4. Carla's essay could easily be rewritten to make the university central to her hometown, as Scott's makes the penitentiary central to his. Would that be worth doing?
5. What are some other ways Allison might have worked with Carla?

READINGS FOR FURTHER CONSIDERATION

Bazerman, Charles. "From Cultural Criticism to Disciplinary Participation: Living with Powerful Words." *Writing, Teaching, and Learning in the Disciplines.* New York: Modern Language Association, 1992.

Kathlene, Lyn. "(Re)Learning Gender Through Expressive Writing and Critical Reflection: Electronic Discussion Groups as Idea Mediators Among Students." *Language and Learning Across the Disciplines* 3(1998): 5–24.

Maher, Frances A., and Mary Kay Thompson Tetreault. *The Feminist Classroom.* New York: Basic, 1994.

21

Shobhna's Pronouncements

Chris M. Anson

"**N**o way!" Jody Sash almost shouted. "I don't know about dumb politicians, but unless you write with correct English and speak that way, forget about anything more than—" she paused, searching for an example"—anything more than a job flipping burgers or collecting garbage."

Shobhna Patel knew that the discussion in her food science and nutrition class had gotten close to being out of control, but she'd learned in her three years of teaching at Hapsburg State to let things go a bit before reigning them in. Students had to express their feelings, dump ideas out on the table. Her job was to sort out all the emotional statements into piles that could be examined more cooly, once the passions had died down.

Now in their third week of the semester, the students seemed to be on track, and the previous meetings had moved ahead pretty much on schedule. The students had just finished a full rough draft of the first paper, an analysis of a provocative article on food-handling regulations for industrial kitchens, and had come to class ready to debrief the small-group revision conferences Shobhna had arranged during the previous class.

Before moving into a presentation on strategies for improving structure, Shobhna asked the class to recount their experiences in the small groups. How had they gone? she asked. What feedback did you get that was helpful in rethinking your drafts?

At first the discussion seemed productive. Bruce Cohen told how his group had helped him to find his main point, which seemed lost in a tangle of ideas. Ratasha Smith praised her group for helping her with detail. Jon Preston added a positive comment about becoming more aware of his audience.

As Shobhna shifted their attention toward remaining problems and uncertainties, Jacob Rothemich tentatively raised his hand. "I guess I want to hear what you suggest about, like, when someone uses a style that's not, you know, standard," he said, glancing about at the other students.

"I'm not sure I understand your question, Jacob," Shobhna replied. "Do you mean an unusual or avant-garde style?"

Jacob folded his arms. "No, I guess I'm talking about a different way of speaking, you know, what do you call that . . ." He glanced around the room again.

"You mean a dialect?" Kelly Ballard said from the back row.

"Yeah, dialect," Jacob said. "You know, some people just talk different and I'm wondering if you think that's OK or what."

Shobhna had become familiar enough with the class to know that Jacob was not aiming his comments at her. Born and raised in Bombay, Shobhna had attended schools that followed the British educational model and had learned impeccable English—better, one of her colleagues had once jokingly told her, than the language of most Americans. Thoroughly versed in formal grammar, precise in diction, and well aware of American stylistic conventions even though she preferred to use a more British register, Shobhna had easily gained the respect of her students as a good communicator in her field. Now they were seeking her advice.

Jacob's comments were still too vague for Shobhna to formulate a response, and even though the hour was moving on and the class had not started her planned activity, she decided to pursue his thoughts a bit further. "What do you mean by talking in a dialect, Jacob?" Shobhna asked, cocking her head to one side. "Are you referring to the use of dialogue in someone's paper?"

Shifting his weight in the uncomfortable metal chair, Jacob again glanced around. Several students were looking at him intently. "Well," he began, "not so much dialogue. I mean dialect. Stuff that sounds the way you . . . some people, the way some people speak." As if anticipating Shobhna's next probing question, he added rapidly, "you know, jive stuff or, I mean, slang, city stuff."

Ratasha, Jerome, and James, three of the African American students in the class, glanced at each other as if to compare their collective reactions. With an expression of interest, Shobhna pushed further. "Do you mean Ebonics, Jacob, the language of many African Americans—what is sometimes still called Black English vernacular?"

"Yeah, I guess so," Jacob replied. "But you know, stuff like that in general. Sloppy English and incorrect grammar and things."

Shobhna realized that Jacob had, in his own uncertain way, opened up some complicated issues about language and writing. As the class fidgeted under the weight of Jacob's words, Shobhna thought about her options. She could shut this down and move into her lesson, maybe promising to come back to the dialect issue later, as the students honed their papers and thought about style. After all, Jacob had initially put it under that topic. Or she could dive in for a while and entertain some further reflection on the subject. The class, for its part, seemed emotionally mixed: some students appeared ready to add their own views, while others stared down at their desks as if embarrassed by the topic.

After what felt like a long pause, which she knew was just another second or two, Shobhna took a breath, raised her eyebrows as she always did when about to make a pronouncement, and began.

"Let's not confuse two communicative media," she said, turning and writing on the board, in large letters, "WRITING" and "SPEAKING."

"Writing—" she said, gesticulating toward the word, "—writing requires you to conform to many conventions of grammar, punctuation, diction or word choice, and style. Speaking, on the other hand, allows much more flexibility." She paused to write a sentence on the board: *Ain't nobody really think the FDA a follow up on this law.* Then below it: *There is no one who really thinks the FDA will follow up on this law.* "OK," Shobhna said, turning back to the class. "Not much question about which sentence gets more credibility, right?"

Almost as soon as Shobhna had finished, Ratasha Smith pounced on her conclusion. "You just said writing and speaking are different things," she said, her voice tense. "What you put up there is speech written down. I sometimes talk like that with my friends but I don't write that way. The example is totally unfair."

Kendale Jones raised his hand but began before Shobhna could call on him. "I agree with Ratasha," he said in his heavy rural Georgian accent, "but not for the same reasons. I mean, I agree that the example looks like speech written down, but I don't agree with you that speech and writing are different, so the example doesn't make any difference." Sensing the confusion of the other students, he went on: "Y'all know that we gotta do oral presentations in this class. So what's the difference between writing that kind of junk and saying it? You might could try, but no one will listen to you."

"So you're saying it's because you're white," Jerome said almost under his breath.

"Huh?" Kendale replied, glancing at Jerome. "I'm saying—"

Stan Koehler interrupted. "I'm from Michigan," he said, looking at Kendale, "and if you came up to my town of Flint and tried to sell something, you know, cars or something, everyone would . . . I mean, you might be a nice guy and all, but your southern accent and that 'might could' stuff would really mess things up for you. People might be suspicious or something."

"Yeah," Andrea Totillo said. "I had this friend from Kentucky and she moved up to Long Island, where I'm from, and people just thought she was cute—you know, they didn't hate her or nothing but she didn't get much respect."

"Difference is," Ratasha said, "her accent is probably more accepted because, you know, she's white. So she just cute. She might have the same amount of language difference but black people are more prejudiced against because we're black."

Paula McPherson, who had been watching the discussion as if she were at a tennis match, spoke up. "Isn't it who has the most people?" she asked half rhetorically. "I'm from Iowa and we don't have an accent. They say people in the Midwest talk like the news broadcasters because everyone can understand us no matter where they're from. Shouldn't everyone try to talk like the greatest number of people?"

Vergia Brown shot Paula a fierce look. "So we gotta conform to people in Iowa's standards?"

"Yeah," joined in Kelly Ballard. "And what do you do with people from England and Australia and stuff? Should they speak like people in Iowa? That's so totally bogus."

Immediately defensive, Paula retorted: "I didn't mean that. Aren't we talking about America? Who's in the majority?"

"Well, Hispanics, soon," threw in Jim Flower.

"America is people from all over," said Phil Aaron. "Look at Professor Patel. Her English is perfect. It's not where you're from but how well you know the rules."

"That's what I meant originally," Jacob said. "Aren't we supposed to help each other to fix all that bad English stuff or what? Otherwise what's the point?"

"The point is," Ratasha said, turning to face Jacob, "that some people speak a different language. It's the language of our homes and communities. It's who we are. Why do you want us to become people we're not? We're not asking Kendale to sell out on his Georgia heritage or Bruce to stop talking like people in Michigan."

Before Shobhna could bring the discussion back on track, she noticed that Trent Harroldson, an unusually quiet student, had been patiently holding up his hand. "Yes, Trent," she said, making a signal to stop others from jumping in.

"OK," Trent began slowly. "I'm also from New York and a lot of my friends talk like people in Brooklyn. Everyone in New York knows that smart people don't talk like people from Brooklyn. So if you want to get ahead, you've got to change your speech. Writing and speaking really are the same, Professor Patel," he said, looking at Shobhna. "In fact, maybe speaking is even more important because most of the time you've got to make an impression in person before you do in writing."

"How do you explain politicians, then?" asked Ted Forn. "How did they become successful? There's this governor who says stuff like 'The people of this state done real good in my budget' and uses words like 'irregardless.' It's not what you say, it's who you are."

"Yeah, right," added Ratasha. "Notice they're usually white. It's about power."

"No way!" Jody Sash almost shouted. "I don't know about dumb politicians, but unless you write with correct English . . ."

Later that day, as Shobhna reflected on the heated exchange that had taken place in her ten o'clock class, she wondered what she might do to bring some perspective to the question of language variation. Her class was, she admitted, quite diverse regionally, socially, and economically. Was her job to iron out all their individual differences, make them into clones? Was style her only recourse for variety? Was she supposed to be a role model of linguistic assimilation, with her privileged upbringing in a wealthy Indian family and her excellent schooling? And this thing about speaking—she'd always separated it from writing, "allowing" for regional differences in speech but arguing for conformity and standards in written text. But wasn't Bruce Koehler right—even without the "might coulds," Kendale would lose at least some credibility in Michigan. Or would he? And what about her—had she gotten by on impeccable grammar? Had she really gotten by? How much better did she have to be as an immigrant, compared with her American colleagues?

Her head spinning with these questions, she sat down to figure out what to tell her ten o'clock food science and nutrition class on Friday about speaking, writing, and variation.

QUESTIONS FOR REFLECTION AND DISCUSSION

1. What should Shobhna tell her class about language variation and dialects in written documents?

2. In her comments and example, Shobhna implies that it's more dangerous to use dialect variations in writing than in speaking. Kendale Jones doesn't agree. Is there a difference between the two modes of communication?

3. If you are or will be incorporating both writing and speaking into your courses, should students be given clear expectations for dialect variation in their formal written assignments and formal presentations? Are those expectations the same for informal writing and speaking activities?

4. What counts as "deviations from the standard" in your classes or in your institution? If Ebonics is "unacceptable," are other dialect differences as unacceptable—such as regional northern features if you teach in the South or vice versa? How *do* you define a "standard," especially for speaking? Is it based on your own region or someone else's?

5. In a class where writing and speaking are used primarily to help students to learn and work with the subject matter, should nonstandard features of writing or speaking play a role at all? Why or why not?

READINGS FOR FURTHER CONSIDERATION

College Composition and Communication Online. "Students' Right to Their Own Language" ⟨http://www.ncte.org/ccc/12/sub/state1.html⟩

College Composition and Communication Online. Statement on Ebonics. ⟨http://www.ncte.org/ccc/12/sub/state7.html⟩

Elbow, Peter. "Inviting the Mother Tongue: Beyond 'Mistakes,' 'Bad English,' and 'Wrong Language.'" *JAC: A Journal of Composition Theory* 19.3 (Summer 1999): 359–88.

Townsend, Jane S., and Candace Harper. "What Future Teachers Know and Don't Know About Language Diversity." *The Professional Educator* 20.1 (1997) ⟨http://www.auburn.edu/academic/education/tpi/fall97/fall97.htm⟩

22

It's Not Working

Carol Rutz

"Martha?" The voice on the phone sounded tight and anxious.

"Yes, this is Martha," answered Martha Sanderson, WAC director at Unity University, a small, liberal arts college in the Midwest.

"Oh, I'm so glad I caught you."

"Well, yes. Here I am. And, uh, who's calling?"

"I need—oh, this is Laura Welsh. I'm in such a state that I just sort of assumed you'd know by magic who's yammering at you over the phone. Sorry. How unprofessional of me. I'm really sorry."

"It's OK, Laura. Something's got you derailed—what's up?" Martha pictured Laura in her basement office a few buildings away and wondered what could possibly have upset her so much. Their previous conversations had been lively (and even silly) but never with this weird, hysterical edge. Martha had enjoyed Laura's sense of humor and her uninhibited laugh, but none of their interactions had prepared Martha for what she was hearing. The person bleating on the other end of the phone line sounded like an imitation Laura—or else a traumatized Laura.

"This is going to sound really stupid. But I'm losing control of my first-year seminar, and I don't what to do. I just got out of class, and I was lucky to get back to my office before bursting into tears. It was so awful today. The students—" Laura broke off, and Martha heard the telephone's being muffled.

"Sorry." Laura gulped and took a deep breath. "Look, could I come to your office and chat?"

"Of course," Martha replied. "I'm here for at least another hour. I'll put on some tea."

"Thanks," breathed Laura, "but skip the tea. Makes me cranky, and that's the last thing I need today. I'll be right there."

Martha replaced the receiver and thought about Laura. This was Laura's first semester at Unity U, and her first semester of teaching. Well, that wasn't completely accurate. From all reports, Laura had been a sterling scholar in African American studies at a major university, and she had landed several prestigious fellowships, including a Fulbright, which she spent studying and teaching in Nigeria. By the time she finished her doctorate, she had taught recitation sections in her home department and complete courses at a university in Nigeria, and she had also taught composition in an interdisciplinary program at her doctoral university. Actually, compared with the typical new faculty member at Unity U, Laura was far more experienced in the classroom. Furthermore, as she confided to Martha during orientation activities, one of the reasons she accepted Unity U's offer was the chance to teach in the WAC program.

Unity's devotion to its first-year seminar program was well known. The program, which consisted of interdisciplinary, semester-long seminars, required a significant amount of writing, and students who completed first-year seminars then elected at least two other writing-intensive courses during their four-year careers. Martha worked closely with the WAC faculty, most of whom taught first-year seminars regularly, and she was confident that Laura's enthusiastic attitude toward her seminar would guarantee an excellent first semester for both Laura and her students.

Something had changed in the past four weeks. The strong investment Laura had made in the seminar was not paying off, for some reason. Martha composed herself by sipping tea and preparing to hear Laura's story. A few minutes later, she heard rapid footsteps on the stairs followed by more measured footfalls on the hall carpet. Laura arrived at her door, briefcase in hand.

Martha smiled. "Please sit down, Laura. I know tea isn't the right therapy today, but would you like coffee or something else?"

"Oh, no, thank you," sighed Laura, as she settled into a chair near Martha's desk. She fingered a leaf on a robust rubber plant and seemed lost in thought. Martha waited. After a moment, Laura hoisted her briefcase into her lap and dug for a folder.

"Here we go. I thought it might be helpful to show you my syllabus. The course is called Slavery in the U.S.: Stories and Politics, and the readings include a variety of primary sources such as abolition treatises, slave narratives, bills of sale, manumission agreements, and other artifacts dealing with people as property. I even have some wills written by slaveholders and free Blacks—they're really interesting."

"Wow." Martha leaned closer to skim Laura's syllabus. "Sounds like a course that would teach me a lot. Are the readings troubling to the students?"

"No, I don't think so—at least not in the way you might expect. They seem pretty sophisticated, and some of them have read excerpts of the well-known slave narratives—Frederick Douglass's is the most common—in high school. The class is pretty well mixed in terms of race and geographical origin, and they've been willing to test some of their family and regional assumptions. So I can't complain about their attitude toward the material. For the most part, they seem engaged. They have ideas about all of this, and they're willing to put those ideas out there. Trouble is, they won't cooperate with the writing part of the course."

"Won't cooperate? What do you mean? Do they hand in assignments late? Or do a lousy job?"

"Sure, there's some of that. But fundamentally, they just don't buy into the structure of the course as I've laid it out." Laura flipped pages to a handout on pastel blue paper. "Here, let me show you how I've set this up."

Handing the blue page to Martha, Laura pursed her lips for a moment. "I think the basic problem—well, this is my tortured analysis, anyway—I think I've just miscalculated."

"Miscalculated? How so?"

"When I was teaching writing back in grad school, I took a course in composition theory. One of the things that really impressed me was the idea that students take writing assignments more seriously if they are writing for a 'real' audience, an audience beyond the teacher."

"Makes sense. Lots of people here at Unity assign students to write letters to the editor or position papers that could conceivably be published, or mock grant proposals. You're on solid ground." Martha offered an encouraging smile.

Laura winced. "Yeah, well, here's the deal. I worked up this really exciting workshop approach that requires a lot of group work. So far, so good—I know. And it went over just fine at Granville State, but—I better finish describing the course before I go on. Students actually belong to two different groups within the class. One serves as an editorial board for a publication that the students define. They have to get my approval on that definition, of course; I don't let them do anything too bizarre. Then they solicit submissions for their publication from the class. Each person on the editorial board is also submitting papers, of course, but to at least one of the other boards. At the end of the class, the boards actually lay out and duplicate copies of their magazines, and everyone gets copies."

"I think I get it," said Martha, skimming Laura's handout. "You have what—four or five boards?"

"In this class, it's only three. The seminar has fifteen students, so I thought three boards of five would work out pretty well. One group has organized an 1850s-style abolitionist magazine, another group has one called *Civil Rights,* and the third group has this rather loose concept—*The Melting Pot*—which seems to be advocating integration through reproductive freedom. I approved that last one because I wanted some contrast among the publications."

"Interesting. Then they belong to other groups as well?"

"Yes. Everyone is in a peer review group that reads drafts before they are submitted to the relevant editorial board. In those groups, the emphasis is on global revision: organization, structure, argument, sources, and so on. In the past, this has helped the weaker students get their writing into decent shape before they risk the editorial board's feedback, which tends to take the form of fine-tuning all features of the writing. And my past students have come to understand the distinction between helping one another make a good submission on the one hand, and working with an author to polish a piece for publication on the other. It's a nice way to take classroom writing up a notch and allow students to develop critical reading skills and editorial stances as well as improve their writing."

Martha frowned. "It sounds a little complicated to me. I admit I have absolutely no experience with a model like that, but—"

Somewhat frostily, Laura replied, "Look. I'm not here to defend this particular methodology, because I know from experience that it works, OK? These students are perverting a wonderful classroom technique, and I'm just furious with them."

Martha straightened in her chair. "Perverting? The students are perverting your techniques? That's pretty damning—"

Laura broke in, "Martha, that's just it! It's collapsing on me, and I feel like a fool. They love the readings, as I told you, and I think they would be fine with compare-and-contrast essays or the kind of close reading they learn to do in literature classes, but they just don't understand how to think about these magazines as a serious public forum. They're toying with me—they're being downright nasty!"

"What are they doing? Can you show me an example?"

"Oh, sure. I certainly can." Laura reached into her briefcase for another folder and extracted a sheaf of papers. "Check this out. This student is supposedly submitting an article to the civil rights magazine. The title is 'Dog Catcher Trapped,' and it goes into the woes of the poor, misunderstood animal control officer."

Martha unsuccessfully suppressed a chuckle. "Oh, boy. Is the student trying for satire?"

"If he is," replied Laura dryly, "it's a secret from his peer group. They offer him comments on ways to expand his examples and suggest that he find some cartoons that caricature dogcatchers to better prove that discrimination against them is a serious problem. But this isn't the only odd one." Laura flipped through the pile. "For every thoughtful paper on Malcolm X or miscegenation, I get something like 'Declare Peace on Drugs' or 'Animal Rights—What Are We Waiting For?' It's making me nuts."

Martha reached for the pile of papers. "Laura, how is this any different from what we see all the time—students who sort of miss the boat on an assignment? Isn't this why we have revision? To help a student like your dog catcher guy get on track? I'm sure you're talking in class about political correctness and how it differs from discrimination. Rather than 'perversion,' isn't this paper one of those classic teachable moments?"

Laura sighed. "That's exactly what I thought. How can a pseudo issue like this—and these others—compare with the readings for the course? What do they think they're doing? So today, I tried giving them an article on PC speech and asking them to define the differences. They did, in a pretty competent way. But there was this eerie sense of rote compliance."

Laura clasped her hands on top of her head and took a deep breath. "In fact—I just hate to admit this—I had this chilly feeling that they found a very specific, PC way to get around *me* and shut me up. I felt completely manipulated and worse—ridiculed. I came close to just screaming at them and nailing them on their smugness—their cutesy, intellectual games."

Laura swallowed hard, shrugged, and began to tug on the rubber plant again. "That's what I mean by miscalculation on my part. They like the material, but they want to deal with it at a distance. I want them to take it seriously within the structure of the course. They just won't. I thought real audiences and two levels of revision would improve their engagement, but it hasn't. Just the opposite, if anything. And now we're approaching mid-term, and I have a course heading for the biggest dang iceberg since the Titanic. What do I do? I don't have any lifeboats to lower."

Martha's eyes returned to the blue handout, and she placed the pile of student papers next to it. She reached for her cold tea and considered Laura and her painful situation.

"Laura," she began, "what are you willing to change in this course?"

Laura flushed and grabbed her papers, stuffing them into her briefcase. "I'm sorry to have bothered you, Martha. If I'm the problem, I guess I'll just have to figure this out for myself. So long."

Martha rose to her feet and followed Laura to the door, speechless.

QUESTIONS FOR REFLECTION AND DISCUSSION

1. Why did Laura call Martha for help? What was she hoping to hear?
2. Do you see flaws in Laura's pedagogy that would account for students' behavior? Could you suggest some minor adjustments? Major adjustments?
3. What role does course design play in the success or failure of a given course? What are the factors that affect students' cooperation, whether absent, grudging, or enthusiastic?
4. Laura is a new tenure-track faculty member. What are the professional issues at stake for her? How does this first-year seminar fit into her enculturation into a small university with a WAC program?

READINGS FOR FURTHER CONSIDERATION

Elbow, Peter. *Writing with Power*. New York: Oxford UP, 1981.

Fulwiler, Toby, and Art Young. *Programs That Work: Models and Methods for Writing Across the Curriculum*. Portsmouth: Boynton/Cook, 1990.

Lindemann, Erika, and Gary Tate. *An Introduction to Composition Studies*. New York: Oxford UP, 1991.

North, Stephen M. *The Making of Knowledge in Composition: Portrait of an Emerging Field*. Portsmouth: Boynton/Cook, 1987.

23

Requiring Revision, Juggling the Work Load

Joan Perkins, Monica Stitt-Bergh, and Thomas Hilgers

B arbara Gianelli is an adjunct hire in a large state university system with
multiple campuses. While Barbara has recently received a PhD from
the same university that employs her, so far she has been unable to
find a tenure-track position in her field, geography. Barbara has signed con-
tracts that require her to teach classes and maintain office hours at three different campuses to support herself and begin paying off student loans while
she continues to look for a better paying and more professionally reward-
ing position.

As she plans her syllabi, Barbara decides to teach her introductory geography courses as writing-intensive sections. Barbara had been dissatisfied
with the quality of the student writing she had received in the courses she
taught as a teaching assistant, and she is hopeful that the university's
writing-intensive program will provide some kind of magic solution. Barbara makes her decision out of conviction: she believes in the benefits of
learning to write in specific disciplines. She also hopes that her dedication
and willingness to put in extra hours to help her students learn how to write
better will impress the administrators who will be interviewing her.

Barbara is deeply committed to teaching as a profession, but as the semester begins she finds herself struggling with fatigue and depression as
she tries to balance her obligations to her students with the physical demands of teaching, commuting between campuses, and devoting hours
every week to filling out long and complicated job applications. She receives
notice of a workshop offered for instructors of writing-intensive courses, but
she can't find the time to attend. Instead, she glances over the packet of materials she receives from the writing program administrator and focuses on
what appear to be important characteristics of the WI courses offered at her
university: a hefty number of pages of required writing and an emphasis on
process.

In line with what she believes are WI goals and objectives, Barbara re-
vises the syllabus she developed as a TA to require that essays show substantive revision between drafts. She assigns her first paper for the semester: a short analysis of regional issues in the state's economic geography.
After she explains the assignment in class, she reads aloud the paragraph in
her course description and requirements that addresses revision. Papers that

do not show substantive development between the first and final drafts, she explains, will not receive grades higher than a C. A timid hand goes up in the front row. "What is 'substantive development'?" a student asks. Barbara thinks about it for a moment before responding. "Changes in content," she explains. "Changes in structure. New insights about the material. I want to see that you've put more thought into the paper, and that your final draft is more complete and better written because of it." Barbara goes home feeling that she is meeting the requirements for WI instruction.

However, as the drafts of the first paper pour in, Barbara realizes that there is no way she can find the necessary hours it will take to analyze the drafts and supply directive comments on how to revise them. In desperation, she calls a friend who works as a TA in the English department for advice. No problem, her friend assures her. It is pedagogically sound to assign the responsibility for draft evaluation to the students themselves. Put the students into groups of four, the English department TA advises Barbara, and have them offer suggestions to each other.

Barbara follows her friend's advice. At the next class session, she asks the students to get into groups of four and to provide suggestions on how to revise each others' papers. "You have a total of forty minutes remaining," she tells them. "This should give you enough time to read each paper aloud and then allow for five minutes of discussion." Comments on other students' papers, she explains, should be constructive and not derogatory.

Barbara is encouraged when after a few minutes of relative silence she suddenly hears the room buzzing with talk and laughter. She is not sure whether she should participate in these draft-sharing sessions, but finally decides to give it a try and sits down with a group of four students who appear to be engaged in a lively discussion. Immediately, the students stop talking. After sitting with them for a few minutes, she asks how they're doing and retreats as soon as one of the students mumbles, "Fine."

Although she is not quite as confident as before, Barbara is still hopeful that she has found a way of getting students helpful feedback without having to work nonstop to do it. But two days later when Barbara sits down to read the final drafts, she is disappointed to note that there is no major change in content or structure in any of the drafts handed in. In fact, many of the students have simply printed out a second copy of the first draft without even changing the due date for the original draft in the upper left-hand corner. Barbara is both annoyed and alarmed. Can she give the entire class C's? If she doesn't, is there any chance the students will take the process requirement seriously?

Barbara decides not to grade or comment on the papers, returning them instead with checks indicating that students have received credit for completing the assignment. When she assigns the next paper, Barbara gives the class a stern warning: she is not changing her assessment criteria, and the students' grade on the paper will count for two assignments instead of one. She has an uneasy night, wondering if she is at fault and if not, what has gone wrong. Is this simply a responsibility issue? If so, then perhaps all she has to do is hold the line on the requirement and the grading system. But what if she is asking too much of the students, and has somehow failed to prepare them to do what she is asking of them?

The morning the final drafts of the second paper are due, Barbara arrives for her office hours to find that there is a student sitting on the floor in front of the door waiting for her. The student is one Barbara both likes and admires. Shannon is always punctual and has yet to use any of her three excused absences for the semester. She is attentive in class and takes notes diligently, though she has yet to ask a question or make an observation in class. As Barbara invites Shannon to take the seat next to her desk, she notes that the student looks weary. There are circles under her eyes and her hand shakes as she pulls her draft out of a dog-eared "Hello Kitty" binder.

Shannon tells Barbara that she was up late struggling to create a "substantive" revision. She has, she tells Barbara, never failed to hand in an assignment on time in all four years of high school, and she tries to follow her professors' instructions carefully. She is afraid, however, that what she has done will not meet with Barbara's approval. She has written in the revisions on her rough draft, and she wants Barbara to look them over and let her know whether she is successfully completing the project as assigned. As she finishes speaking, Shannon begins to choke up and tears collect on her lower eyelashes. She hands Barbara her draft.

Skimming it rapidly, Barbara notes that Sharon's revisions consist of crossing out four or five words per page and writing synonyms above them in purple ink. The words she has chosen do not enhance the meaning of her sentences. For a moment, Barbara's depression almost overwhelms her. "Please, Miss Gianelli," says Shannon tragically. "Can't you just tell me what it is you want me to do?" Skimming Shannon's paper rapidly, Barbara pulls herself together and comes up with some "substantive" suggestions.

Shannon's class meets directly after Barbara's office hours. Barbara is worried after her encounter with Shannon, but determined to maintain control of the class and to meet the WI course requirements as she understands them. Barbara walks into class smiling and says "Hi" brightly to any student willing to make eye contact. As she crosses to her desk, a tall figure rises from the back of the room. It's Connie, a starter on the university's Division One women's volleyball team. As Barbara lays out her teaching materials, Connie looms ominously over her. She places a copy of her rough draft on the center of the desk so that it faces in Barbara's direction. "I'm not revising this," Connie says emphatically. "And it's a good paper, so I don't want any C on it either. I work really hard on my first drafts, and when I'm done with them they're finished already. I called my mother in Virginia Beach when I was writing this, and she told me exactly what to do. I called my brother at USC, and he helped me edit it over the phone. I put more work into my first draft than most people do into two or three, and I'm not changing a word. It's fine just the way it is!" Connie stalks back to her seat, where she stretches out her long legs so that it is impossible for the other students still filing into the classroom to pass in front of her. Shaken,

Barbara takes a deep breath and invites her students to read their final revisions out loud to the rest of the class.

QUESTIONS FOR REFLECTION AND DISCUSSION

1. Are Barbara's strategies likely to result in the kind of revisions she says she wants? Why or why not?
2. Barbara appears to want revision purely for the sake of revision. Is this a viable teaching objective?
3. When Barbara attempts to participate in a draft feedback session, the group stops speaking. Should Barbara continue to try to sit in on these feedback sessions? If so, what approach should she take?
4. How should Barbara handle Shannon's request for directive feedback? Is it fair for an instructor to require revision without providing directive feedback?
5. If Connie does in fact revise extensively during the first stage of the drafting process, is it reasonable to require her to write multiple drafts?
6. What advice would you give instructors who require revision?

READINGS FOR FURTHER CONSIDERATION

Dittmer, Alan. "Guidelines for Writing Assignments in the Content Areas." *English Journal* 75 (April 1986): 59–63.

Elbow, Peter. "The Teacherless Writing Class." *Writing Without Teachers*. London: Oxford UP, 1973, 76–116.

Gadda, George, and Faye Peitzman. "Evaluation Techniques." *The Shortest Distance to Learning: A Guidebook to Writing Across the Curriculum*. Ed. Joan McGuire Simmons. Los Angeles: Los Angeles Community College District and UCLA Office of Academic Interinstitutional Programs, 1983.

Healy, Dave, and Murray Jensen. "Using Feedback Groups and an Editorial Board in a WAC Classroom." *Teaching English in Two-Year College* 23 (February 1996): 57–63.

Tsujimoto. Joseph I. "Re-Visioning the Whole." *English Journal* 73 (September 1984): 52–55.

24

"You Have No Right"

Rebecca Moore Howard

"You have no right to mark up my paper! You're not a writing teacher!"

Suhail Abdul is an assistant professor of mathematics. This is his first year at an elite northeastern liberal arts college. When he was hired, he was told that all faculty participate in the college's writing-across-the-curriculum program. When he received his teaching assignment, he found himself teaching two sections of calculus and one section of "first-year seminar."

Every incoming student, he has learned, takes a first-year seminar in the fall term. Seminars are taught by instructors from all departments, who design their own course, based in their home discipline. But all seminars share a commitment to writing. In July, before he arrives on campus, Professor Abdul is sent a two-paragraph rationale for the course:

> First-year seminars introduce students to the work of an academic discipline. These seminars are not comprehensive surveys but are special topics courses, investigating a particular problem in the discipline; the connection of that discipline to one or more other disciplines; or the premises of the discipline.
>
> Each seminar will engage a substantial commitment to writing instruction: students will be assigned at least fifteen pages of formal graded writing during the term. All students at this college can benefit from improving their writing skills. Students learn writing best in the contexts—the disciplines—in which it occurs. The best teachers of discipline-specific writing are practitioners in those disciplines.

Professor Abdul is somewhat taken aback by this challenge. In what sorts of writing can he engage first-year mathematics students? After careful consideration—and a talk with his new department head—he decides to teach his first-year seminar on the history of mathematics. He includes in his syllabus not only the description of his particular seminar but also the rationale for first-year seminars. As he plans his course, he designs four writing assignments: three summaries of assigned sources, and one research paper in the history of mathematics.

When he first explains the assignment, the students shift a bit in their seats, and as the class discusses it, he begins to realize that they think summarizing is beneath them. One student remarks, "I haven't had to do a summary since eighth grade!" But when Professor Abdul explains that summary writing, done well, is a high-level intellectual workout, requiring deep comprehension of the source, they look less disgruntled.

Now, as he reads the summaries, he is impressed: The students have obviously worked hard on them, and with only a few exceptions, they have succeeded. Out of twenty students, three earn C's and the rest earn A's or B's. In his written responses to the summaries, Professor Abdul tries to help each student improve his or her writing. Some would benefit from organizing their paragraphs more carefully; others need to state the author's thesis clearly at the beginning of the summary; some need to bring more specificity to their writing. He writes a brief paragraph in response to each summary, and in it, he explains what the writer has done well and how he or she could improve.

When he hands back the papers, he notes that the students read his comments eagerly. He is somewhat uneasy, however, about the way in which a couple of students are laughing as they share his comments with each other.

When he assigns the second summary, he says that he will up the ante. On this paper, he not only wants a clear summary of the source material, but he also wants the summaries to reproduce the balance of the source's argument: when the source spends sixty percent of its time talking about a particular subject, he wants the summary to allocate sixty percent of its time to that same subject.

When he grades these summaries, he sees that the students are having a harder time. Apparently he has taken them into unfamiliar territory, offering them a challenge that they have not previously encountered. He decides he should spend more time in class on techniques for summary writing (a skill that was important to his own education at a British university). Again he writes careful responses to the papers, explaining what went well and also offering suggestions for improvement. The grades range from A to D, with six students earning a C this time.

When he hands back this set of papers, he sees no amusement on the part of his students. They are silent as they read his comments, except for one young man who mutters a few angry words to the fellow sitting next to him.

At office hours the next day, that young man, Brad Jensen, appears at Professor Abdul's door. "I'd like to talk to you about this paper," Jensen says. In his hand is the summary, which has apparently been crumpled up and then smoothed out.

Suhail Abdul has had no previous experience with assigning and grading essays of any kind, but he has had experience with grade complaints. Experience has taught him that listening to students carefully and explaining his own point of view without being defensive usually results in mutual understanding. Sometimes he changes the grade, persuaded by the student's argument; more often, the grade stands, but the student leaves knowing why he or she received it. Professor Abdul is therefore unruffled. He invites Brad Jensen to take a seat, and then says, cordially, "What can I do to help you?"

Jensen is silent for a moment, apparently struggling with words. Then he blurts out, "You have no right to mark up my paper! You're not a writing teacher!"

Nonplussed, Suhail Abdul stares at him for a moment, gathering his thoughts. Then he begins explaining the principles of first-year seminars at this college. He flips quickly through the stack of papers on his desk and finds the syllabus. Pushing it across the desk to Brad Jensen, Professor Abdul explains why writing matters to this seminar.

"But that doesn't justify your grading my English," Jensen quickly replies. "If you want to assign papers and comment on their content, that's fine. But only an English teacher has the right to talk about how I organize my paragraphs."

QUESTIONS FOR REFLECTION AND DISCUSSION

1. Should Suhail Abdul's college have designed the first-year seminars differently? If so, how?

2. Should Professor Abdul have designed his syllabus differently, and if so, how?

3. What are the possible meanings of Brad Jensen's statement, "[O]nly an English teacher has the right to talk about how I organize my paragraphs"?

4. What sorts of schooling experiences might have led Brad Jensen to register these objections? In what ways might Suhail Abdul's first-year seminar be challenging those experiences? To what extent should Professor Abdul's teaching or grading practices take such possible conflicts into account?

5. Should Professor Abdul, who is not a native speaker of English but who speaks flawless (albeit accented) British English, consider the possibility of cultural bias in Jensen's objections? If so, how should he respond?

6. If Professor Abdul decides to stand by his teaching and grading practices, how should he respond to Brad Jensen? Or should Abdul change his teaching and grading practices? If so, what changes should he make? And how should he explain them to his class?

READINGS FOR FURTHER CONSIDERATION

Beason, Larry. "Feedback and Revision in Writing Across the Curriculum Classes." *Research in the Teaching of English* 27.4 (December 1993): 395–422.

Hilgers, Thomas L., et al. "Doing More Than 'Thinning Out the Herd': How Eighty-Two College Seniors Perceived Writing-Intensive Classes." *Research in the Teaching of English* 29.1 (February 1995): 59–87.

Howard, Rebecca Moore, and Sandra Jamieson. *The Bedford Guide to Teaching Writing in the Disciplines: An Instructor's Desk Reference.* Boston: Bedford Books of St. Martin's Press, 1995. See especially chapters 6 ("Designing Writing Assignments"), 7 ("Assigning Research Papers"), and 11 ("Grading Student Writing").

McCarthy, Lucille. "A Stranger in Strange Lands: A College Student Writing Across the Curriculum." *Research in the Teaching of English* 21 (October 1987): 233–65.

Sterrett, Andrew, ed. *Using Writing to Teach Mathematics.* Washington: Mathematical Association of America, 1990.

Part 5

Cybertext
Scenes of Writing and New Technologies

25

Through the Back Door into Cyberspace

Dona J. Hickey and Donna Reiss

The flyer announced "Introduction to Instructional Technology: Tips and Techniques for Teaching. Free Hands-on Workshops for Faculty. Lunch Included." Fifteen faculty from the humanities, social sciences, and natural sciences gathered for a summer workshop in a networked computer lab on campus at Statesville University. They were drawn to this series because the leaders, Pat and Chris, were visiting scholars and teachers themselves as well as members of academic departments at a nearby university. Hopeful that instruction would therefore be clear of technojargon and easy to follow, the Statesville faculty imagined walking away with new technology skills they could immediately apply in their classes.

These teachers regularly used email, mined the Web for research, and participated in at least one email listserv; however, they had not yet incorporated computers into their teaching. They hoped to learn how to guide their students in using the Internet for writing research papers—ensuring the integrity of Web sites as scholarly resources—and how to manage the stream of email messages from students who missed a class or had trouble with an assignment. They expected to learn how to put syllabi and some of their handouts on the Web so that students could find some easy answers on their own. And they especially wanted to offer the kinds of slide presentations they saw at conferences. The workshop leaders, Pat and Chris, had in mind the group's hopes and expectations as well as goals for encouraging active and interactive learning with new technologies.

"Welcome to our workshop," Pat began. "I'd like us all to take about fifteen minutes to write a short introduction to our workshop colleagues. Then we'll look at an outline of the workshop program." Using a strategy familiar in writing/communicating-across-the-curriculum (WAC/CAC) workshops, Pat and Chris asked participants to write informally as a way to focus and articulate their thinking. Writing and sharing introductions would also help develop a sense of community among participants. Pat and Chris projected the following instructions from the workshop display computer to a screen at the front of the room:

> In one or two sentences, tell us your name, the courses you usually teach, and your area of research interest.

> Write a few sentences about your own personal and professional use of computers as well as your use of computers with your classes.
> Write a few sentences about what you hope to learn during this program.

However, instead of asking participants to write on index cards or on paper in a familiar writing-across-the-curriculum approach to opening workshops, Pat and Chris asked faculty to type their introductions into the wordprocessors of the computers and to save them as files. Because they all knew how to type and to save word processed files, the faculty felt comfortable with the first quarter hour of the workshop and felt reassured that they would be "doing" and not just "listening" for the duration.

"We'll use these files again soon," Chris explained. "And we'll explore some of the ways the tools that you already know—tools like email and word processors—can be valuable for helping your students learn what you teach by emphasizing communication online." Later, Pat and Chris would walk participants through copying and pasting these introductions into a threaded Web discussion forum so that the entire group could read and respond to each other's experience and expectations. At that point, each introduction would be framed as a letter, "Dear Colleagues," and signed. This epistolary approach is a familiar WAC/CAC strategy for building learning communities that transfers successfully to the use of electronic communication.

Chris then projected an outline of the week's activities on the screen:

- Composing casual email and Web discussions for discovery, discussion, and critical thinking; composing more formal academic compositions in electronic media
- Evaluating both Web and print resources for research projects and composing Web-based collaborative projects with text, hypertext, and multimedia

Jack Sims, professor of history, leaned over and whispered to his colleague in biology, Bud Philips, "I thought we'd be learning how to improve our slide presentations with sound and pictures." Having conducted many such workshops over the past several years, and as if anticipating the historian's concerns, Pat said, "Many of you would probably like to learn to use PowerPoint. But presentation software alone won't make your lectures more lively."

"However," Chris added, "you can make the class discussions that accompany your lectures more lively by using electronic discussion software before and after class. That way you'll encourage students to think about the topics you consider important and to connect concepts by writing to each other about them. You and your students also can construct PowerPoint presentations in the classroom to encourage collaborative learning.

"Suppose you were teaching a historical concept such as feudalism," Chris went on. "You might ask students to illustrate with examples from their reading and from the Internet, and in an email exchange, discuss the concept in light of their examples."

Pat joined in: "A group of students might then collect and select the best examples, write summaries, organize them, and present PowerPoint slides to the class at the next session. You could work with students, learning PowerPoint from them while they're learning from you, and with each other, how to synthesize and evaluate applications of a theory."

The history and biology professors conferred briefly. Then, speaking for both, Bud Philips, the biology professor, waved his hand in the air. "We already receive a lot of student email. These electronic discussions only add to our work load and time commitment outside of class. Even if we're willing to assign the activity, how do we manage the reading, and more importantly, the grading?"

Jocelyn James, an associate professor in the English department, nodded at her colleague's comments. "Although we do see some of the learning advantages of email exchanges or other such asynchronous discussion programs that you've mentioned, we still hoped to have some instruction in presentation formats like PowerPoint. I don't want to depend on my students to instruct me." She looked around at the gently nodding faces of the other participants. "I'm the teacher, after all, and students expect me to know more than they do."

Chris kept silent and looked for other comments. In part, she was trying to buy some time to frame a response; but in some ways the problems were larger, extending beyond the workshop at hand—false expectations about the purpose of this technology workshop, maybe. To maintain goodwill and to meet the perceived needs of faculty, Chris wondered if she and Pat could shift to a preview and practice session on PowerPoint. But there was something more, Chris mused, something about how rooted Jocelyn's comment seemed to be in her own professorial authority and expertise. The session Chris and Pat had planned assumed a movement toward a more student-centered classroom, demanding a more flexible role from the teacher. Moving from "sage on the stage" to "guide by the side" was a difficult challenge for some faculty; they were facing an entirely new and complicated way of interacting. How could Chris and Pat begin exploring that transition with this group of PowerPoint-eager faculty?

Recognizing the importance of addressing some of the faculty's concerns, Chris framed some implications of Jocelyn's comments in writing and projected those onto a screen for the whole group to consider. She then asked them to address the questions collaboratively in teams of three, each team considering one set of questions. They wrote responses in a threaded Web discussion forum that allowed everybody to read and respond to each other's writing on the issues, extending the discussion with further questions or ideas. Last, each team reported orally to the whole group, synthesizing the discussion, and opening it up for all to consider. And Pat, with just the eensiest smile, typed summary notes of the ongoing discussion and organized them as slides on the spot. Finally, Pat asked faculty to reflect on the exercise that they had just completed, considering its potential usefulness in their own classrooms.

"Student groups or even a whole class might discuss an issue," sociology professor Stan Gruper suggested. "They could identify key points, organize them into an outline, select clip art or even audio and video for multisensory communication, and deliver their own minilecture to expand on my lecture. Students might even develop lectures for certain class concepts, and I could use their presentations as models for future classes."

The history professor, Jack Sims, beamed as Chris and Pat finally showed faculty how to develop short presentations on campus issues such as parking fees, faculty photocopying privileges, and interlibrary loan policies. When the group learned how to incorporate video clips of traffic jams to support their argument that current parking arrangements were unsatisfactory, Jack applauded.

"This is fun," said the physics teacher, Sean Adams.

"But fun isn't the point," reminded Craig Stone, the geology professor. "Coverage is the point. Knowledge is the point. Our students need to learn all the essential course content, and we barely have time to cover volcanoes."

Agreeing that coverage is crucial, Chris added, "but not coverage alone. What will students do with your course content? Might they remember it longer and understand it better if they have not only written to you about it but written to their classmates?"

Pat reminded the group of their own engagement with the workshop exercise: "Your collaborative presentation slide show was informative and amusing, the oral presentation entertaining, the exploration of the campus parking problems detailed and skillfully argued, and the solutions implementable. Even presentation software can be a powerful aid to effective communication of learning and critical thinking."

Nonetheless, the faculty at Statesville University wrestled with doubts as they designed composing activities that could be adapted to assignments in their disciplines. They arranged email groups for students to conduct research and report their results. They located interactive Web sites for their disciplines and created Web resource lists. They moved beyond basic Web research assignments and constructed WebQuest projects based on the model by Bernie Dodge of San Diego State University (http://edweb.sdsu.edu/webquest/webquest.html).

Faculty not only considered how these assignments could guide students to conduct original Web research in support of collaborative problem-solving and individual writing projects on disciplinary issues, but also developed experience in reading and evaluating hypertext. While assigning field research, Web research, print research, and teamwork that would lead to student Web publications, faculty could help students illustrate their exploration and understanding. Pat and Chris foresaw a transformation from participants' earlier skepticism to faith in the potential of technology as an aid to writing-to-learn.

But at the end of the week, when faculty gathered to evaluate the workshop, the leaders discovered that doubts lingered. "Ideally, I'd like to bring everything we learned here into my classroom, but I've only begun to think about integrating the technology, and I fear chaos," lamented Penelope Homer, the classics professor.

"I know the feeling," said Craig Stone, "and the experience. Last semester, I put my syllabus on the web, supplemented class discussion with a threaded Web discussion forum, and accepted hypermedia presentations and hypertext as well as traditional essays. But pedagogically, I wasn't fully ready to take the plunge. At times, the technology seemed to overwhelm the course content, and priorities were lost in the zing of electricity." After Craig's confession, Penelope was more discouraged. "That's all I need for my efforts—student confusion about what matters most in their learning—and the possibility of bad classroom evaluations."

Chris reminded the faculty of their work that week: "Faculty have come to this workshop at varying stages of technological skills, right? And many academic disciplines are represented in this room. Some technology may seem appropriate to a course and some may not, just as some pedagogical practices make immediate sense, and others may not. The usefulness of either a technological skill or classroom exercise depends on the course, the teacher, and the student. That discovery takes time because the goal is meaningful integration of technology, not just the addition of technology."

Stan Gruper added, "The world does business by email; millions of messages and threaded discussions speed through cyberspace every day. The Internet has made reading a matter of text, visuals, and sound. We cannot really ignore this change in society and education."

QUESTIONS FOR REFLECTION AND DISCUSSION

1. Incorporating technology in the classroom often demands that teachers and students learn together. What do teachers imagine losing in a setting such as learning PowerPoint or Web-based programs along with their students? To what extent are teachers right or wrong?

2. When teachers gather to discuss integrating write-to-learn activities, these issues often arise: covering content and finding time to respond to student writing. How does technology further complicate these problems? How might technology be used to lessen these problems?

3. How fluid is a teacher's role in the classroom, with or without technology? In what ways does the teacher's role shift, and in what ways is the teacher's role static? Under what circumstances might students forget who the "teacher" is? When is this perception a problem?

4. What are the differences between teacher authority and teacher expertise? How do those differences relate to integrating technology and pedagogy in your discipline?

5. What are some of the difficulties teachers face when they are cast in the role of learners themselves, particularly within a workshop focused on pedagogy? How might teachers meet the challenges of change or consider alternative approaches to teaching without feeling that their own expertise is being questioned or denigrated?

READINGS FOR FURTHER CONSIDERATION

Academic Writing: Interdisciplinary Perspectives on Communication Across the Curriculum ⟨http://aw.colostate.edu⟩

Anderson, Daniel. "Project-based Literary Instruction: The Women of the Romantic Period Hypertext." *Learning Literature in an Era of Change, Innovations in Teaching*. Ed. Dona Hickey and Donna Reiss. Sterling: Stylus, 2000. 127–36.

Hickey, Dona, and Donna Reiss. "Cybersimulations: Low-Tech Variations of High-Tech Applications for Learning Communities" ⟨http://onlinelearning.tc.cc.va.us/faculty/tcreisd/resource/cybrsims.htm⟩

Reiss, Donna. "Epistolary Pedagogy and Electronic Mail." *Learning Literature in an Era of Change, Innovations in Teaching*. Ed. Dona Hickey and Donna Reiss. Sterling: Stylus, 2000. 18–30.

———. "Discussion Tips for Interactive Electronic Communication ⟨http://www.wordsworth2.net/resource/conftips.htm⟩

Reiss, Donna, Dickie Selfe, and Art Young, eds. *Electronic Communication Across the Curriculum*. Urbana: National Council of Teachers of English, 1998.

WebQuest. ⟨http://edweb.sdsu.edu/webquest/webquest.html⟩

26

Connecting Students with Professionals

Dickie Selfe

D r. Susan Stransberg was a conscientious forestry professor at a large midwestern university and had been using Internet technologies in her class for some time. In her senior research practicum this term, for instance, she put her syllabus and assignments on the Web. She had her students hand in labs and interim research reports as attachments via email. In addition, her students were becoming adept at searching the Web for useful forestry sites, annotating them, and posting those annotations to the class Web site.

This was all well and good, but she had been at a workshop during the summer where the emphasis had been on "Bringing the World into your Classroom" via conferencing technologies. As a result, Dr. Stansberg was trying to imagine other ways of connecting her students with the real working world of forestry professionals, both corporate and academic. One idea she had been considering was to invite academic and professional foresters into her class using some sort of digital or satellite technology. Now, after a long week of conferencing with students, she had other reasons to bring in these professionals.

Student groups had been working on research projects due at the end of the term, and she had just finished talking with these teams. Those review sessions had left her with two nagging concerns. Though they had been collaborating for most of the term, the students—many of whom were going to graduate and move on to field jobs and/or graduate work—still didn't seem to understand how important collaboration would be to their work as foresters. Nor, she speculated, did they take constructive criticism well.

She had the feeling that students considered the teamwork assigned in her class just another hurdle to get over. There was little evidence that they understood it as an integral and necessary component of their future working lives. They apparently couldn't imagine how specialized people became as they worked in the field and how dependent they would each become on the expertise of others as they carried out large-scale corporate and academic projects.

As usual, several teams had members who were not pulling their weight. But in these cases the other group members looked immediately to Susan to mediate work-load difficulties without ever sitting down to talk with each other. The diligent students on these teams were asking privately if they could opt out of the groups altogether and try finishing the final research report on their own—an option rarely available in the working world or in graduate school. In some cases, individuals had shown her email exchanges that were reminiscent of junior high and high school squabbling, a remarkable insensitivity to tone and attitude in their messages.

In addition, she suspected that their resistance to constructive criticism from her and their classmates was a function of time pressure and the enormous effort they had already made to carry out realistic research projects this term. Susan had seen these student groups working long, hard hours in the labs and in the field to collect data, analyze it, and construct reports that represented their findings. Even with five weeks in the term, any comment that suggested major rethinking of the study or alternative interpretations of their data came as a threat. These students still did not realize what an important, even essential moment this type of reflection was to long-term research projects. Instead, there seemed to be a persistent feeling that hard work in and of itself was enough to warrant success and the accompanying good grade.

In a nutshell, these students didn't have a very realistic picture of the working world they were about to enter. She could lecture on these topics herself, and she probably would. But now Susan was also thinking more seriously about ways to connect her forestry majors with researchers and professionals in other parts of the country and world. She wanted these seniors to get used to talking with professionals about working conditions (collaboration in particular) and about both the students' and professionals' current research projects.

That night she dashed off a letter of inquiry (via email) to some of the many colleagues she had worked with in the past and was working with currently. In it she described her concerns about her students as they neared graduation. By the next morning she had already received several responses. Though a few colleagues were unavailable, she was gratified to see how many had encountered the same problems at their institutions. They were very willing to participate if they could fit the activity into their busy schedules. As a result, she decided to set up two "events" in order to address her concerns about students' attitudes toward collaboration and constructive feedback.

In the first event, students would be given a chance hear about the kinds of projects the professionals were undertaking: she would ask her friends to concentrate on describing how often and with whom they collaborated. She hoped to dispel the myth of the individual professional working in isolation on self-contained projects. In the second event, the students would present their research projects informally and get feedback from these distant professionals on the project itself and the potential for future research. She was hoping they would then see that, if a researcher was lucky, one research project led to another or perhaps many others. This activity might also dispel the notion that arbitrary deadlines, like the end of the semester, were important but should not circumscribe a research agenda. Students could then take the comments from her, their classmates, and the professionals and write their final drafts, including a section on the potential for long-term research projects.

The question that Susan was struggling with now had to do with the combination of conferencing technologies that would be most effective for these two events. In the first event, she wanted the professionals to have time to describe the working relationships essential to their projects but also time for students to ask questions about how professionals managed collaborations with difficult people. She did not, however, want it to become a gripe session.

She liked the idea of students presenting and discussing their work. She knew that the distant professionals would be sympathetic and provide productive feedback, but she also had some concerns about student reactions to suggestions.

Susan had to arrange these sessions pretty quickly so that her students and, more importantly, her colleagues could arrange their schedules. Her concerns about the technologies were many:

What kinds of technologies were available to her colleagues?

Interactive TV (ITV) sessions would be interesting but rather expensive, and that cost would come out of her research grant funding! Still, they might be more powerful than online sessions.

She could use several other Internet venues for the exchanges as well:

- postings to the WWW
- synchronous chat software
- threaded WWW discussion forums
- email and email discussion lists

Or she could use some combination of these technologies. What to do?

QUESTIONS FOR REFLECTION AND DISCUSSION

1. What do you think of Susan's attempt to fill the "professional gap" in her student's education?
2. What kind of preparatory work would she need to do with her students and with her colleagues?
3. What technology or technologies would you recommend for each event?
4. Imagine a sequence of activities that lead up to and away from the "events" that Susan is planning. Describe your sequence of activities.

READINGS FOR FURTHER CONSIDERATION

Condon, William. "Virtual Space, Real Participation: Dimensions and Dynamics of a Virtual Classroom." *The Online Writing Classroom*. Ed. Susanmarie Harrington, Rebecca Rickly, and Michael Day. Cresskill: Hampton, 2000. 45–61.

Harris, Lesie, Robert Smith, and Terry Craig. "Fostering Diversity in the Writing Classroom: Using Wide-Area Networks to Promote Interracial Dialogue." *The Online Writing Classroom.* Ed. Susanmarie Harrington, Rebecca Rickly, and Michael Day. Cresskill: Hampton, 2000. 159–86.

Krause, Steven D. "Why Should I Use the Web? Four Drawbacks and Four Benefits to Using the World Wide Web as a Pedagogical Tool for Writing Classes." *The Online Writing Classroom.* Ed. Susanmarie Harrington, Rebecca Rickly, and Michael Day. Cresskill: Hampton, 2000. 105–23.

Matthews-DeNatale, Gail. "Teach Us How to Play: The Role of Play in Technology Education." *The Online Writing Classroom.* Ed. Susanmarie Harrington, Rebecca Rickly, and Michael Day. Cresskill: Hampton, 2000. 63–80.

27

Sondra Gets Hyper

Chris M. Anson and Ian G. Anson

S ondra Krutchnet had always included a research paper in her Introduction to Cultural Anthropology, of one kind or another. The I-Search
paper. The traditional library research paper. The short documented
paper. The Inquiry Contract paper. Whatever its form, she liked to think that
it taught students how to collect information from sources beyond themselves, examine and critique it, synthesize it, and then weave it into a term
paper that was uniquely theirs.

She also had some specific requirements for the paper. It had to have a
thesis, for one thing. It had to include at least eight to ten sources in the bibliography, which compelled students to keep digging for information even
when they thought they'd read everything there was to know about the topic
(and that happened a lot). It had to be at least ten pages long. Yes, a tough
bill—but, she reasoned, entirely doable as a long-term project in one semester, with time along the way to give progress reports to the class. While
she always talked her way through a large assignment like this during class,
she also felt it important for students to have something written down, so
she handed out a sheet describing the assignment.

> Research Paper: This is an opportunity for you to explore something cultural
> (more on this in class) through some sustained library research. What can you
> find out about a particular cultural practice? I do not want to restrict you too
> much as to the form of the paper—you may include both primary and sec-
> ondary data, for example, and you may wish to structure the paper in a way
> that best captures the essence of your topic, such as from a "large" view to a
> microlevel view, or from the perspective of insiders in a culture or group to
> the perspective of outsiders. Try to be *focused*, however; don't choose a really
> general topic, but one you can explore well in about ten pages. Be sure that
> the paper has a thesis of some sort, or an introduction that makes it clear what
> you're presenting, and a series of clearly organized sections or parts. Include
> at least 8–10 references. You may wish to attach an appendix if there are data
> that would be awkward to include in the body of the paper, and you may also
> include photocopies of pictures or diagrams if these help.

At the end of the semester, Sondra had just collected all the final research
papers from her class of thirty-five students in Anthropology 101. It was a
huge mound of stuff to read, she mused, looking at the pile of papers on
her desk. She was determined to grade them quickly so she could have more

time over the break to catch up on other things. That wouldn't be so hard, she thought—the assignment was pretty clear, and she had read so many in the past that another batch wouldn't be all that surprising.

As she gathered her things, she realized that someone had stayed behind in the room. It was Trevor Lotts, a quiet student who had gotten off to a slow start in her class but had picked up speed considerably over the term. "What can I do for you, Trevor?" Sondra asked, filling a canvas bag with the research papers.

"Well, it's about my paper," Trevor said hesitantly. "You see, I don't have it."

"Uh-oh," Sondra said, grimacing. "What's the problem—dog ate it?" It was a risky comment, but she was too tired right now to care much about being "student friendly," as her campus's faculty-development director might put it.

"No," Trevor said quickly, shifting his weight and glancing around. "See, it's not . . . I mean, I *did* it and all. It's just not *here*, I mean, it's . . . I can't actually turn it in."

Sondra had a feeling he was warming up for a lame excuse. "So you did it but you didn't do it."

"Well, you see, Dr. Krutchnet," Trevor went on, "it's done, and you can *get* it, but you have to go to my Web site. See, it's a paper . . . I did it as a Web paper. It's on the Web. All of it."

Sondra looked at Trevor incredulously. "On the Web? How could it be on the Web? I watched you working on it all term in here."

"Oh, I did a lot of the work here," Trevor said, glancing around nervously. "I kept working on pieces of it, but I put it all on the Web. Here's the address." And he handed Sondra a file card with a URL on it.

With some skepticism, Sondra finally agreed to look at Trevor's paper on the Web and meet with him the next day to discuss it. She knew that Trevor was pretty "up" on new technology: she'd seen him use a wireless Internet connection with his laptop in the hall outside class, and one day his binder had fallen open, spilling all sorts of high-tech catalogs on the floor. Although she wasn't a Luddite about technology, she realized that she hadn't really taken a strong interest in some of the advances that her colleagues seemed to be talking about almost daily.

Later that afternoon, she was sitting in her office when Jane Arlt, a friend in the Department of Chemistry, wandered by. "You look troubled," Jane said after the two had greeted each other.

"I was just about to check out this URL that one of my cultural anthro students gave me. It's his research paper in my class; he's done it on the Web."

Jane smiled. "Interesting. Have you seen these before?"

"Never," Sondra said. "I've used the Web for all sorts of things in my class, but I've never had a student turn in an electronic paper. I mean, I don't accept papers in email form, but this guy says the paper is at his own Web site."

"Let's check it out," Jane said, obviously intrigued.

Sondra pulled a chair over to her computer and Jane sat down. In a minute, Sondra had typed in the URL on her Web browser. The first screen was Trevor's home page (Figure 27-1), which showed a picture of him and a menu of categories. Sondra hesitated, looking at the screen.

"Here, try 'School Projects,'" Jane said. Sondra clicked on the highlighted words, and the next screen showed a list of ten items, including one called "Anthropology Research Paper."

Clicking on that soon yielded a short introductory paragraph describing Trevor's topic—the history of Asian foot binding—followed by another menu. Another click, and a page appeared on the screen with large, bold letters: "BOUND FEET." Below the letters were four bulleted items, each highlighted in blue: "Background and Objectives," "Vocabulary," "Activity," and "Bibliography" (see Figure 27-2).

"Woah," Sondra said, taking in the information. "This is wild."

Figure 27-1 Trevor's home page

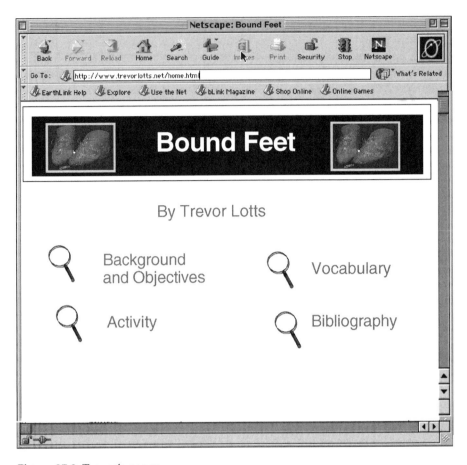

Figure 27-2 Trevor's paper

Jane took the mouse and clicked on "Objectives." This soon yielded a series of questions presumably designed to pique the viewer's interest (Figure 27-3). Although it wasn't quite in the form of a "FAQ" page, Sondra felt that it had the same goal—a kind of checklist of basic information. Each topic area had a link to another page, which contained more detailed information about the topic, usually in no more than two or three additional paragraphs, some containing additional hyperlinks to definitions or brief bits of text. After Jane had gone to a few more links, Sondra felt lost in the midst of the report, unable to remember where they had come from and where they were going.

"What about this?" Sondra asked, pointing at an item, "Image: Footbinding," which appeared at the bottom of one of the pages.

"Probably a picture," Jane said, opening the screen. As predicted, a picture of tiny, pointed feet appeared—feet that had been bound for years. As the screen filled, the image began turning in a clockwise direction, showing

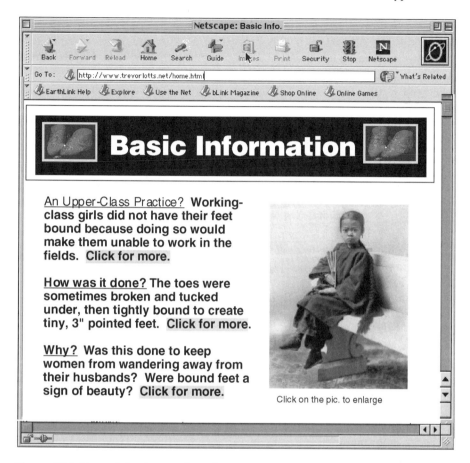

Figure 27-3 Trevor's background section

the feet from different angles. A strain of sad, flutelike music came from the computer's speakers. "Sounds almost like an Irish lament," Jane said, passing the cursor over another set of options at the bottom of the page.

Sondra looked at the image. "My God, Jane, I have absolutely no idea how to judge this. Is this a good research paper, do you think?"

Jane stared at the screen. "Beats me," she replied. "The screens are pretty impressive. But remember that students can copy the background for screens from anywhere; it's a free code, as long as there isn't any copyrighted text on it. So we can't really tell whether he's created his own code for any screen or just copied it. But it all depends on what you're looking for."

Sondra frowned. "I don't understand. You think he may have just taken someone's Web site?"

"I'm talking about the actual screens," Jane replied. "You see how this page is divided, with a blue border on the left, and this interesting beige background on the main part with the text over it, and here, these other buttons to click on? That format could have come from anywhere, from any other site. It's all just code. Then see this background here"—she clicked again—"these faint, luminescent slippers behind the text? Maybe he did this, maybe he didn't. It's kind of neat, though, don't you think?"

"Well, I guess I don't care about the screens," Sondra said, frowning. "It's his *research*. His *words*, that's what really matters."

Jane chuckled. "That helps a bit: you don't have to worry about assessing how well he puts together color or images, as long as you're not overly dazzled by the page designs. 'Course, we can't be sure even the text is his."

"But that's not my concern," Sondra replied, then hesitated. "Well, it *is* a concern, but plagiarism is universal, not just in cyberspace. My problem is, I'm wondering how well the paper hangs together when it's split up this way into so many pages and multiple links."

"Exactly," Jane said, opening up another page of Trevor's Web site. "That's what you have to decide. Maybe you should start by just exploring the entire multimedia paper he's created. Just keep clicking and absorbing. I mean, look at this—"

"But in what *order*?" Sondra interrupted, taking the mouse from Jane. "I can't *read* student research papers this way. I don't read them in boxes like this."

Jane watched as a series of X-rays appeared showing the bone structures of bound feet and normal feet. "Well, just explore. The thing here is that *you're* the creator, in a sense, of your own reading. He's less in charge. He's not leading you through the paper, you're leading yourself."

Sondra's thoughts seemed to swirl in a fog. "But it's his *responsibility* to put together a logical, coherent paper, to make crucial decisions about how to move from one idea to the next. Where's the thesis? How can I judge *his* decisions if *I'm* the one deciding where to go next? I'd be practically grading myself!"

"Better get used to it," Jane said, smiling.

QUESTIONS FOR REFLECTION AND DISCUSSION

1. Should Sondra accept Trevor's multimedia Web paper? Why or why not? What seems fair to you in this situation? What are the consequences for Trevor?

2. If she accepts the paper, on what basis could she assess its quality? What should she "look for" in Trevor's paper? Does its form matter? Why or why not?

3. How can Sondra be sure that Trevor's work is not copied from other electronic sources? What *part* of his work should she be concerned that he hasn't plagiarized: the text? the images? the screens? all of it? none of it?

4. Do teachers have the right to deny students the opportunity to submit writing that takes newer, multimedia and electronic forms? Why or why not? At what point do teachers have a responsibility to begin allowing work that takes unconventional, less linear forms, such as multimedia presentations?

5. Sondra has access to a lot of Trevor's other academic work (and personal information as well) at his Web page. Is it ethical for her to look at that other work when making a judgment about his anthropology paper? Why or why not? Do portfolios of student writing raise the same ethical question?

6. What issues of writing assessment does this case raise for you in a broader sense?

READINGS FOR FURTHER CONSIDERATION

Alliance for Computers and Writing. http://english.ttu.edu/ACW/default.asp⟩

Anson, Chris M. "Distant Voices: Teaching and Writing in a Culture of Technology." *College English* 61.3 (1999): 63–74 ⟨http://www.ncte.org/ce/jan99/anson.html⟩.

Selfe, Cynthia. "Lest We Think the Revolution Is a Revolution: Images of Technology and the Nature of Change." *Passions, Pedagogies, and 21st Century Technologies.* Ed. G. Hawisher and C. Selfe. Logan: Utah State UP, 1999. 292–322.

28

Lost in the MOO

David A. Jolliffe

For Angela Warburton, Introduction to Public Policy Analysis was a challenging course to teach, primarily because the class lacked what she called "atmosphere." Angela, a third-year assistant professor at a mid-sized state university, had done her doctoral work at a large research university in the South where most of the graduate students were about her age, late 20's and early 30's, and were almost always in residence. In Angela's graduate program, there was a strong sense of community: classmates met regularly in the student lounge or at local watering holes, where discussions of the salient issues they were reading about in their courses naturally wove in and out of conversations. Intellectual controversies spilled out into hallways and cropped up at picnics. It was a heady place.

Angela discovered a very different scene when she took the job at her current institution. The university was located in a major midwestern city, and there was literally no sense of community associated with the school. Angela's students were enrolled in a Master of Arts in Public Service program, one designed for professionals in not-for-profit and governmental organizations. Introduction to Public Policy Analysis was a required course in the program. It almost always enrolled twenty-five or so. The students were what the university euphemistically called "older than average"—most were in their late 30's, but some were in their 40's and 50's and many had families. They lived at locations scattered within a 60-mile radius of the university. Almost all of them had full-time jobs. Their classes met one night a week, from 6:45 to 10 p.m., so they could work a full day, drive to the campus just in time to get to class, participate in the three-hour-plus session, then head home. By and large, they were good students. They came to class well prepared to discuss the assignments, and they acquitted themselves nobly on examinations and papers, frequently drawing insightful connections between the theoretical texts they were reading and their experiences at work.

But Angela couldn't help feeling that something was missing from the class. Two things bothered her. First, she felt as though the students didn't know one another, and as a result they weren't taking advantage of the wide range of "real-world" expertise many of them were bringing to the course. Second, she had a vague perception that the students were not inclined to "own" the issues they were discussing in the readings. They read the texts, came to class, listened to her lectures, asked decent questions, and did their work. But there seemed to be very little intellectual spark in them—no one really lit up over specific issues, no arguments were carried out into the hall-ways, no conversations seemed to thrive beyond the classroom walls. When Angela read the final examinations from her first class, she decided that she had to do something to get her students talking to one another.

She came up with this "something" during the summer before she began teaching again in the fall. She was ninety-nine percent certain that all the students had email accounts, so email would be the platform for conversa-tions and virtual community. Angela wrote a series of six challenging "re-sponse" questions—open-ended probes about the central ideas of a reading, its use of evidence, its style, its applications, and so on—that students could use to talk about any of the course texts. On her syllabus for the course this time, she included this requirement: every week someone would write and post to the email discussion list a two-page paper written in response to *one* of these questions. Four additional people would write a one-page "response-to-the-response paper," supporting, challenging, or otherwise adapting its central claim and explaining why.

The idea worked like a charm. After having solicited email addresses on the first night of class, Angela set up the discussion list the following morn-ing. By the next night, the first student assigned to do so had submitted her response paper, and within two nights after that, the four second-tier re-sponders had weighed in with well-conceived counters to, and adaptations of, the original response paper.

"Yes! People are talking," Angela thought as she prepared for the second week's class session. And she was right. The class discussion on night two picked up right where the email conversation had left off. The students were not only well read and well prepared, but they seemed much more thor-oughly engaged with the issues. They raised their hands with questions and concerns. They spoke directly, forcefully yet politely, to one another. Angela was leading the session, but she was clearly one among many knowledge producers. As she sent them off on a break halfway through the session, An-gela heard vigorous, sometimes even heated conversations continue out in the hallway around the coffee vending machine.

The classroom energy created by the email conversations continued ses-sion after session, and Angela was quite pleased with the atmosphere she had orchestrated. By the beginning of the eighth week, however, she felt the need to take the experience to the next level. The email response and re-sponse-to-the-response papers were getting the five writers each week talk-ing to one another, but there still wasn't enough of the sense of community, the intellectual "buzz" that Angela wanted for the class. She described the class atmosphere and the efforts she was making to improve it to Don Britain, an old friend from graduate school who was now teaching at a large, pri-vate university that encouraged faculty members to incorporate technology very thoroughly in their teaching.

"The problem is that the email discussion isn't really a discussion," Don told her. "One student writes a paper and four others respond. It's too static. It's too asynchronous. What you want to do is take them to a MOO."

A MOO, as Don explained it to Angela, was a "multiple-user utility," an online site where students could go, using their regular email accounts, and find synchronous, "real-time" conversation possibilities. As luck would have it, Don had created a public policy MOO and was opening it for business the following Tuesday night, the very night that Angela's class met. "What the heck," Angela thought, "I might as well try it."

The next Tuesday evening, Angela met the students at the door of the regular classroom and announced that they were going to convene in the computer classroom down the hallway. The students dutifully shuffled down to the space, new to most of them since they didn't spend much time on campus, and installed themselves behind the machines. At the front computer, Angela explained that they were going to connect to the public policy MOO and have "a real-time class online" for the next hour and a half, just as an experiment. She gave careful instructions about how to connect to the MOO and, with some effort on the part of students who felt uncomfortable on any computer other than their own, got everyone into the central "meeting room" of the utility.

Once all the students had announced their "presence" with a sentence or two of greeting to the class, Angela moved to get the class started by posing a question from the week's readings. The "silence" in the MOO space was deafening. She could hear students muttering to one another: "How do I get my cursor to move?" "Do we have to tell the computer we want to answer?" "I think I'm in a different room." After about fifteen minutes of largely abortive attempts to get students responding to one another's comments online, someone in the class decided to move to emoticons.

"Here's what I think of the MOO," the student wrote: :(This opened the floodgates. "Why in heaven's name are we doing this?" one student cried out after glancing up from her screen. "My question exactly," another moaned. "The class was going so well, but this is awful!"

QUESTIONS FOR REFLECTION AND DISCUSSION

1. What do you think of Angela's plans to use technology to create what she considered a better classroom "atmosphere?" Did she do too much? Too little?

2. Angela's decision to move the class to the computer lab and teach them to operate in the MOO clearly backfired on her. Why? What would you say Angela's next steps with the MOO project should be?

3 What do you think of Don Britain's assessment of the email discussion list? What might Angela have done to make it more interactive?

READINGS FOR FURTHER CONSIDERATION

Bonk, Curtis Jay, and Kira S. King, eds. *Electronic Collaborators: Learner-Centered Pedagogies for Literacy, Apprenticeship, and Discourse.* Mahwah: Erlbaum, 1998.

Reiss, Donna, Dickie Selfe, and Art Young, eds. *Electronic Communication Across the Curriculum.* Urbana: National Council of Teachers of English, 1998.

Roueche, John E., and Suanne D. Roueche, *Between a Rock and a Hard Place: The At-Risk Student in the Open-Door College.* Washington: American Association of Community Colleges.

Sherry, Lorraine, Shelley H. Billig, and Fern Tavalin. "Good Online Conversation: Building on Research to Inform Practice." *Journal of Interactive Learning Research* 11 (2000): 85–127.

29

Anonymity, Botulism, and Counterfeit Russians

Stephen B. Wiley

"DOES ANYONE HAVE AN IOTA ABOUT HOW TO RESPOND TO SOMEONE WITHOUT YOUR NAME POPPING UP IN BROADWAY LIGHTS!!??" read the message in the online discussion forum. The all-caps style was the textual equivalent of shouting, but just to make his frustration clear, the student had added double exclamation marks at the end. It was his third attempt at posting anonymously to the Web forum, and once again it had failed: above his comments, in tall capital letters, were his first and last names—HILL, BRADLEY—followed by his campus login ID. His cover was blown, his "real-world" identity exposed—again—to the other seven classmates in his online discussion section.

Later that Friday, David Summers, an assistant professor in the history department, checked his email one last time before going home. He found Brad's exasperated message about the online activity. "I spent an hour trying to figure this out," wrote Brad. "In the end I just gave up. Why do we have to use software that doesn't work?" Two other students who had had trouble with anonymous posting had also sent messages. The first student, like Brad Hill, was complaining about the technical hassles of the computer assignments. The email was brief and the tone reasonable. But Wendy Argus, an outspoken communication major, had sent a two-page, single-spaced tirade, arguing that anonymous online communication was a waste of time, had no professional application for her as a future PR director, and was deceitful. Summers sighed, shut down his computer, and headed home. He knew he would be spending another Saturday in the office.

Summers had been working hard to develop the computer-mediated communication assignments in his course on the history of technology, but, with all the software glitches and student complaints (and some raised eyebrows from colleagues and technical support staff), he was beginning to question the wisdom of assigning online writing exercises and discussion sessions. The course was designed to teach students about "the social shaping of technology" and the technological shaping of the social world. It fulfilled the university's science and technology requirement, so quite a few students enrolled from other departments, making for a broad range of expectations, learning styles, and prior experience. In keeping with the university's communicating-across-the-curriculum initiative, the course also sought "to develop practical skills for the competent communicator." Summers expected the students to master a relatively long list of those skills: Internet-based research; critical analysis of online information sources; various genres of computer-based writing (some formal and others very informal); and fluency in a range of computer-mediated communication tools, including email, Web forums, chat programs, and virtual worlds.

For the new semester, Summers had decided to teach those practical skills through a series of "Online Events" that would take the place of the regular face-to-face class meetings on Fridays. In the first such event, the students were asked to join an asynchronous, Web-based, threaded discussion forum that—theoretically, anyway—would allow them to post messages and reply without identifying themselves. Summers wanted them to experience and experiment with anonymous and pseudonymous communication in online discussion groups of seven or eight students each. He hoped that by grappling with the malleability of identity in a virtual environment, the students would begin to see the constructedness of all identities and develop a more critical understanding of communication in general. He believed that exposure to new forms of communication also shook up students' assumptions about technology and helped them see the possibilities and limitations of different technological environments. This had intrinsic value, he felt, in addition to the more instrumental value of mastering new computer literacies and developing agility in new media contexts.

———

On Saturday morning, Summers got up early and headed to the office while his wife and children were still asleep. When he arrived, he set his coffee on the desk, booted up the computer, and began to read the students' forum postings from the day before. He wanted to see what had gone wrong with the first online event.

As part of its online education initiative, the university had adopted WebCT, an integrated, Web-based course management package, and Summers had chosen to use this platform for the course. The package incorporated Web-based content created by the instructor, a calendar program, online testing and survey tools, electronic homework submission, progress tracking for the teacher and self-tracking for students, and a range of communication tools. These included chat rooms, private email, threaded discussion forums, and a networked whiteboard module.

The entire package was designed to allow for anonymous and non-anonymous communication among students while giving the faculty member and graders detailed statistics on each student's use of the various tools. For example, a "Student Tracking" page showed the instructor how many times the student had posted and replied to messages in the WebCT Forum, as well as which content pages they had visited and the dates and times of their first and last visits to the site. Theoretically, this would allow the instructor to assign grades based on a student's participation in the course

> **NICE TO MEET ALL OF YA!!**
> 252. Anonymous (Fri, Aug. 25, 13:52)
>
> **REPLY TO NICE TO MEET ALL OF YA**
> 266. Anonymous (Fri, Aug. 25, 13:54)

Figure 29-1 Anonymous posting

while it retained the student's option to communicate anonymously or nonanonymously.

However, as he read through the forum postings, Summers began to see that this didn't work in practice. Students could only retain anonymity when posting an original message. If they were responding to a message posted by another student, there was no option to post the response anonymously; their first and last names automatically appeared along with the message. The students' comments revealed their surprise and irritation when they discovered, like Brad Hill, that their supposedly anonymous replies in fact were not.

As he reviewed the forums, Summers saw that some of the students had found a workaround: instead of selecting "reply" when responding to another student, they had posted a new, anonymous message, indicating in the subject line that they were responding to an earlier post (Figure 29-1).

This solution was smart but rather unsatisfactory, Summers reflected. Replies were dissociated from the original posting and the thread of the discussion was quickly lost. He read on and saw that most students, in fact, had chosen to forego anonymity for the sake of preserving the thread of the discussion. When they wanted to respond to another student's posting, they clicked "reply" and allowed their real names to appear above their own message; the replies then appeared under the original message, in temporal and topical hierarchy (Figure 29-2).

Proud to have identified a bug in the software and eager to solve the problem, Summers fired off an email to the Learning Technologies Center, the office that administered the WebCT course software for the campus. He described the problem the students had encountered and asked the technical support staff to suggest a workaround. To his surprise, a reply from the di-

> **HI!**
> 11. Anonymous (Thu, Aug. 24, 01:21)
>   158. IAN LARSON (ilars) (Fri, Aug. 25, 13:40)
>   191. SAM HART (shart) (Fri, Aug. 25, 13:44)
>   200. ANNA LYONS (alyons) (Fri, Aug. 25, 13:46)
>   244. THOMAS O'HEARN (tohearn) (Fri, Aug. 25, 13:51)

Figure 29-2 Non-anonymous replies to an anonymous posting

rector of the LTC appeared in his inbox about five minutes later. Clearly, he wasn't the only one working on Saturday.

In her message, the director acknowledged the "limitation" of the software but went on to ask what purpose anonymity served in Summers's course activities. She was surprised that a faculty member would make a fuss over the anonymity option in the WebCT forums, and she seemed to imply that anonymous discussion lacked educational value, and was even somehow frivolous. "If you believe that anonymous discussion forums are a pedagogically significant activity, we'll do our best to support what you're trying to do," she wrote. "But I'm not sure I see the point, given that the overall purpose of the software is to assist faculty in teaching students and evaluating them." Summers felt his adrenalin rise as he read the email and decided to wait until later to reply. He knew from experience that he needed time to cool off before he composed his response.

Summers returned to the students' forum postings and read on. As he skimmed over the text, a message in Section 6 caught his eye. Posting anonymously, a student described herself as a rather colorful individual who, among other things, grew botulism in her refrigerator (Figure 29-3). Here, finally, was someone experimenting with a constructed identity. The author of the posting exposed the joke right away in the same message, however (Figure 29-4), obviously eager to make it clear who she really was. In Section 8, Summers came across a student who went further, posing as a Russian student "still in the process of learning English better" (Figure 29-5). Following the posting were two sincere replies by other students who had

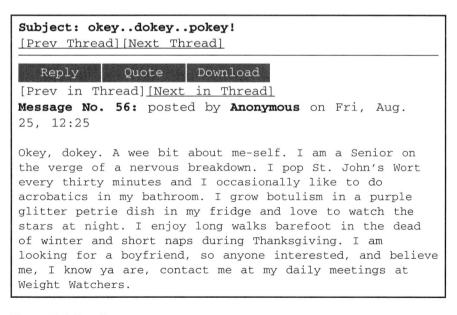

Figure 29-3 Botulism woman

TOTALLY KIDDING!!!

Really, I am a senior. This is my last semester of drama at
this prestigious institution of glamour. I love, no really
love, to write about anything that tickles my fancy.
  I am currently writing a book called "Conversations with
Mo, Larry, and Curly." Look for it in your nearest
bookstore soon. It's a tale about how men and women make
relationships so difficult when in reality it should be
soooo simple. Anyway, I am spawned from the city of
Fayetteville. High fives appreciated, thank you. . . .And
my goal for my future is to grace the cover of People
magazine as the century's hottest new screenplay writer!!
And you better believe I am gonna sleep my way to the top!
Just kidding, I plan on running them over. . .with my
talent of course! Geeez, what kind of person do ya think I
am? Naaaaah, puleeze don't answer that!! See ya. . .

Figure 29-4 Botulism woman, continued

Subject: well, I'm here now
[Prev Thread][Next Thread]

    Reply   Quote   Download

[Prev in Thread][Next in Thread]
Message No. 138: posted by **Anonymous** on Fri, Aug.
25, 13:38

it is i, charlie538. i assume we are not supposed to tell
actual names, but i will tell you a little about myself.
i was born in Yaroslavl, Russia. i am 20 years old, and
have lived here in the U.S. for a little over two years.
i am a public and interpersonal comm. major, and am still
in the process of learning english better. there are so
many problems in russia to do with orphanages (i am sure
you have heard many of them on the news programs here),
and i hope with a better education, i will be able to
return to russia to take some sort of executive position
to help these children. i am not aware of what our
teacher wants us to write, so i will start with this. i
wait to hear what you all have to say about yourselves.
it interests me much to hear about americans, and what
they want to do in the future.

charlie538

Figure 29-5 The "Russian" student introduces "himself"

taken it seriously (Figures 29-6 and 29-7) and wanted to make this "Russian" student feel welcome in the United States. The student had then posted a new message, confessing to her deception and apologizing for lying (Figure 29-8). Interestingly, her new message was also posted anonymously, although she had signed her real name at the end.

Summers finished reading over the forum postings and went to lunch with his colleague, T. J. Baker. Between bites of bagel, he was telling her about the students' encounter with anonymous communication. He was happy that a few of the students had experimented with an invented identity. Baker chuckled. Unlike Summers, she had spent a significant amount of time in MOOs and other virtual worlds, and she found the students' tentative experimental forays and quick retreats somewhat amusing. In most computer-mediated social spaces, she explained, participants don't assume there is a direct link between virtual identity and "real-world" identity. "On the contrary," she said, "in most of these spaces, the whole point is to invent a new self and deploy it in social interactions with other invented selves."

Summers realized that his students, who were for the most part neophytes in the world of online communication, had approached the activity from a completely different perspective. They had experienced anonymity and the invention of an online self as deceptive and even shameful. "They just don't have much experience in virtual worlds," Baker pointed out, "so they privilege 'authentic,' 'honest' self-representation. They see their online self as a transparent expression of their offline identity." If the students' thinking and writing were being shaped by dominant norms of reality, authenticity, and self-representation, Summers thought, there were clear and significant limitations on the kinds of writing they were able to produce in the online forum.

```
Message No. 163: [Branch from no. 138] posted by
EMILY BENSON (ebens) on Fri, Aug. 25, 13:41
Subject: Re: well, i'm here now

hello, it's nice to have you in the USA! Do you like it
so far. My relatives are russian and I love to hear them
speak, my name is emily and I am from Hampton VA. I am a
public relations major, but am still very undecided. I
hate computers and hope this class will help me to get
over my fear.
_____

[Prev Thread][Next Thread] [Prev in Thread] [Next in Thread]
```

Figure 29-6 First reply

Message No. 197: [Branch from no. 138] posted by
LARA MILLS (lmills) on Fri, Aug. 25, 13:45
Subject: Re: well, i'm here now

This summer, I was lucky enough to meet 3 Russian girls
that had just been adopted by a family in my neighborhood.
The woman that adopted them was telling me about all of the
problems with the orphanages over there and why she adopted
the girls. I thought that it was the most noble thing in
the world to adopt these 3 girls, who were not young (12,
14 and 15), did not speak a lick of english and having a
child of her own. I taught one of the girls, Sveta, in
swim lessons and was so touched by her appreciation of
everything that she had here in the US compared to what she
had in Russia. Well, I think that your aspirations to help
these children is a very nobel cause and I really hope that
you will be able to touch many lives

Figure 29-7 Second reply

Reply   Quote   Download
[Prev in Thread][Next in Thread]
Message No. 246: posted by **Anonymous** on Fri, Aug.
25, 13:51

i feel kinda guilty. everyone else is not even using the
anon. posting. well, the teach wanted us to play around
with this, but i feel bad that i told an untruth, even
though he wanted us to if we thought it would be fun. so,
the truth be told. i am 19, and was born here in the U.S.
i am not from russia, but have been there the past 3
summers. i am in love with the russian people; their
culture, language, etc. i do, however, wish to go to russia
eventually and help out with russian orphanages (i already
do that some, but in the former USSR). i am a public and
interpersonal comm major, and am adding russian studies as
a 2nd major soon. again, i am sorry for lying. i thought
that was what we were supposed to do. but please talk to
me about russia if you want. i do know a lot about it, and
have MANY russian friends (including russian orphans).

for now, caio.

Michelle

Figure 29-8 Confession

After lunch, Summers went back to his office to work on grading the online event. As he reviewed the summary statistics on the forum postings, he realized that there were two new problems with WebCT. Although the "Student Tracking" tool indicated which students had logged in and posted messages, it did not show which forum they had posted to, so he could not determine if they had actually participated in their discussion section. Furthermore, anonymous postings were not included in the summary statistics, so if a student had completed the assignment anonymously, Summers could not tell if the student had done it at all.

The students themselves were clearly concerned about this grading problem as well—more so than with the problem of preserving anonymity per se. If the link between their offline, "real-world" identity and their virtual self was severed, how would they get credit for their participation? They were using the forum itself to voice these concerns. One student wrote:

> It's me again. I just wanted to see how everyone is liking the class and all of this computer stuff. It is very confusing to me! Dr. Summers how do you know who's message is whose with them showing it anonymously? I just want to make sure I get credit for doing the assignment. Good luck to everyone trying to figure this stuff out!!

In another exchange on the same issue, one student helped another:

> First student: Hey! Does anyone know how Dr. Summers is going to know who posted what, for grading purposes?

> Second student: He has got a different program that reveals who was online at this very moment

"Well, that's what I thought," mumbled Summers to himself. His patience with the software was beginning to wear thin. The logistics of the online events were complicated enough, but the problem seemed to be even deeper. Summers's experimental online communication assignments seemed to clash with the design of the software itself, with the pedagogical model that informed the university's online education initiative, and with the students' own assumptions about identity, communication, and learning.

Despite the setbacks, Summers decided to forge ahead with his experimental Friday sessions, pushing the issue of identity to a new extreme. In class the following Monday, he announced an overhaul of the Online Events setup: he and the students would bypass the WebCT identification procedure altogether by creating "avatars." Instead of providing the Learning Technologies Center with the students' real names and Social Security numbers, Summers would turn in a list of pseudonyms created by the students, along with an ID number that was not related to their official university ID number. He would retain a list of these pseudonyms and made-up ID numbers, linking them back to the students' real names at the end of the semester for grading purposes. Not only would this allow students to communicate online without others knowing their "real-world" identity; it actually encouraged them to be creative in developing a pseudonymous identity—a virtual avatar who would participate in the online activities "on their behalf."

HIS 200:
HISTORY OF COMMUNICATION & INFORMATION TECHNOLOGIES
ONLINE EVENT #3
DEFINING A VIRTUAL IDENTITY

Your task for this week's Online Event is to create an avatar: a virtual person (or other being) who will participate in the rest of the semester's Online Events on your behalf.

Your avatar's connection to you will be unknown to both your classmates and me, at least until the end of the semester. However, he or she (or it) will be graded for his/her/its participation in the Online Events, and that is the grade that will be factored into your final course grade. In other words, you are responsible for your virtual avatar's actions and performance in this portion of the course. This should allow us to balance creativity and freedom of expression, on the one hand, and ethical online interaction, on the other.

I do encourage you to be creative (but reasonably tasteful) when you define your avatar. You may pick a real-world person or fictional character; a famous person or someone known only to you. For example, you could be Janet Reno, Bob Dylan, The Undertaker, Stimpy, your own mother, or the ghost of your great uncle Mort. It might be more fun to make up an identity from scratch (Hank Flogmorton, the invisible, ill-tempered crossing guard) or from some combination of known and/or unknown people or characters (Paul Bunyan Lecter, the giant, highly intelligent, cannibalistic lumberjack). To take this to the extreme, you could be an inanimate object (the Campus Bell Tower, Tiger Woods's nine-iron, "the human fork"), a body part (Van Gogh's ear), or a geographical location (Neptune, Lake Erie). Or, you could just be yourself, but with a different name.

Step-by-Step Instructions

1. Give your avatar a first name and last name.
2. Write a brief description of your avatar (4–5 sentences should do it). Be creative and have fun with this.
3. Login to WebCT using the identity of your avatar and go into the forum area of your section's site.

4. In the forum called "Online Event #4," post a message introducing yourself (as your avatar) to the section. Include the description you wrote of your avatar in step 3 above. Please do not reveal your real-world identity to your section members or to others in class.

    IMPORTANT: do not check the "post anonymously" option, since you are already using a pseudonymous identity. The first and last names that you created for your avatar (not your real name) are what will appear after you post. If you post anonymously, I will not be able to track your avatar's participation, and he/she/it will not get credit.

5. While you are in your section's forum, read others' introductions and respond to at least one.

After class, Summers sent an email to the LTC director to explain the new setup and to request that new WebCT course sections be added for the avatars, alongside the existing section that used the students' real names. Although he did not feel he had to justify his teaching methods to her, Summers found himself writing a small essay in defense of the avatar assignment:

I plan to disarticulate the students' online identities from their real-world identities completely, though temporarily (until the end of the semester). This will allow for a full-fledged experiment in the construction of virtual identity and the formation of online communities, discussion groups, and project teams based on those constructed "selves." My intention is to expose students to the new communicative possibilities, as well as the limitations, that computer-mediated communication represents.

Identity is always socially constructed, as Erving Goffman and many others have argued. But computer-mediated communication makes this process more explicit and more malleable by removing physical appearance, dress, and tone of voice from the symbolic interactions in which identity is constructed. The remaining forms of expression—text and, in some cases, graphics, are no less socially constructed, but they create the potential for greater user control over presentation of self.

New forms of mediated communication create new opportunities as well as new obstacles. In order for students to become effective communicators and citizens in the new media environment, they must master new literacies, practice and become comfortable with new tools, and develop an ethic of engaged, critical, civil, community-minded discourse.

My hope is that, by working with these new forms of communication first-hand, the students will experience and understand the constructedness of identity. This will eventually allow them to approach online communication more critically and creatively and see communication, in general, as a process of social self-construction. This understanding, as well as their practical experience with new computer-mediated communication tools, will help them master new literacies; develop greater social awareness and self-understanding; become more agile, strategic, and effective in the new media environment; and become engaged and ethical citizens, using new technologies to create and participate in community.

Summers sent the email, shut down his computer, and locked the office. He didn't want to deal with the LTC director's response that afternoon, or with any more student email messages about the course.

———————

Summers found his colleague, Jim Fuentes, and they went to have a beer at the Players' lounge. The dim lights of the lounge and the casual laughter of the other patrons—few of whom appeared to be faculty or students—made for a welcome change of scene after a hectic week on campus. The tables were carved with decades of graffiti, and Summers ran his hands over the smooth grooves of the letters as he told Jim about the ups and downs of the online events.

"I guess this is what it's like to be on the bleeding edge of technological innovation," Summers remarked wryly. "You pay the price for being an early adopter of these online tools."

Fuentes smiled. He was skeptical about the value of the new technologies, and he tended to see Summers's problems as evidence that these untried gizmos weren't worth the work required to incorporate them into teaching. Summers was in fact a skeptic himself, but was always eager to try out interesting new software tools. He found himself making the counter-argument. "For the most part, computers *do* bring progress," he said. "For example, there is no doubt in my mind that our student records software has made student advising easier and more efficient." Summers and Fuentes had both been hired two years earlier, just as the Web-based software was being implemented, and just in time to catch a glimpse of the previous system, which involved endless searching through degree requirements and course listings printed in 8-point font in the undergraduate catalog and then filling out unreadable carbon-copy forms in triplicate.

"True," admitted Fuentes. "And the speed and ease of circulating departmental memos is another advantage—at least to our new chair, who is more prolific in that arena than we could ever have hoped." Summers laughed.

"There's nothing inherently wrong with the technology," Summers began again. "It's just that all of these logistical, cultural, ethical, and policy issues come up *after* we have taken the plunge, with our students, into the new software. We don't have the time, or the support, to work out the bugs ahead of time." He told Fuentes about the student who had tried, without success, to participate anonymously in the online discussion forum, and had later fired off an angry email. He told him about the Learning Technologies Center staff and their skepticism about his use of the anonymous feature. He explained his latest effort to make an end-run around the software by having the students create avatars and start all over with WebCT. "If it weren't for my own intellectual fascination with these problems," he said,

"I would have pulled the plug on my computer—and my experiments with online teaching and learning—a long, long time ago."

"Like I said, it's not worth the effort," said Jim as they finished their beers. "Wait until they have the technical bugs worked out before you make your students use the new stuff. They're just getting frustrated because they're expected to use a tool that doesn't really work."

"But what about the LTC people?" asked Summers. "And what about other faculty and the administration? How am I supposed to pull this off if they don't consider it a legitimate academic activity?"

Fuentes was characteristically blunt. "Is it?" he asked. "What are you trying to achieve with this anyway?" Summers was quiet, thinking. Fuentes continued. "Look. You're putting all this energy into something that isn't ready, technologically. You're making the students do something that they can't wrap their minds around, and the LTC staff doesn't understand the pedagogical purpose. You should be working on your publications. Is all this really worth it?"

Summers didn't have a good answer. He felt that what he was doing was worthwhile and could be a valuable experience for the students, but perhaps the costs of pulling it off did outweigh the benefits. They paid the bill and headed for the door. "Maybe you're right," he said. "But it's too late now. I've got to get them through this semester at least." As he walked to his car, Summers wondered how that was going to happen.

QUESTIONS FOR REFLECTION AND DISCUSSION

1. Was Summers's solution to the anonymity problem a good one? Why or why not? What else might he have done?

2. What role, if any, should anonymous or pseudonymous writing and communication play in university teaching?

3. Should students be permitted complete anonymity (or pseudonymity) in course-related writing and discussion, or should there always be some way of identifying the "offline" author of anonymous online communication?

4. If there is no way of linking online and offline identity in such situations, how can anonymous communication be used for teaching, learning, and evaluation?

5. If there *is* to be a connection between online and offline identity, who should be able to reveal that connection, and under what circumstances? Should the faculty member always know who is who, online and off? Should university administrators or technical support staff have access to that information?

6. Summers was having trouble balancing the radical potential of anonymous communication and invented identities with his responsibilities, as a faculty member, to manage students' "classroom" behavior, hold students accountable for their participation, and evaluate their performance in a course. He was also confronting the contradiction between a new kind of expressive freedom—an important new form of identity, subjectivity, and communication created by the online environment—and the university's age-old institutional interest in monitoring and controlling identity. Given these tensions,

what degree of anonymity should Summers allow? When, if ever, should an instructor have access to the "real-world" identity of an anonymous or pseudonymous author? Is there a place, in university coursework, for completely anonymous communication over which the instructor has no control and for which the student has no accountability? By contrast, should university administrators and computing services staff have access to students' real-world identities, or is it sufficient that the faculty member does?

7. What expectations or rules should instructors establish for anonymous or pseudonymous communication—for example, when an anonymous student posts a racial slur or sexually harasses another online discussion participant? What should the consequences be when those rules are broken, and how can they be enforced if the perpetrator is truly anonymous?

READINGS FOR FURTHER CONSIDERATION

Day, Michael J. "Fear and Loathing in Paradise: Making Use of Dissensus, Disorientation, and Discouragement on the MOO." Excerpt from a talk presented at "The Virtual Classroom: Writing Across the Internet" (Berkeley, California, March 16, 1996) ⟨http://english.ttu.edu/kairos/1.2/coverweb/dis.html⟩

Fanderclai, Tari Lin. "MUDs in Education: New Environments, New Pedagogies." *Computer-Mediated Communication Magazine* 2.1 (January 1, 1995) ⟨http://www.ibiblio.org/cmc/mag/1995/jan/fanderclai.html⟩

Holeton, Richard. "The Semi-virtual Composition Classroom: A Model for Techno-Amphibians." *Technology Source (Case Studies)*, September 1997 ⟨http://horizon.unc.edu/TS/cases/1997-09.asp⟩

Kairos: A Journal for Teachers of Writing in Webbed Environments ⟨http://english.ttu.edu/kairos/⟩

Newbold, W. Webster. "Transactional Writing Instruction on the World Wide Web." *Kairos* 4.1 (Fall 1999) ⟨http://english.ttu.edu/kairos/4.1/binder.html?features/newbold/bridgenw.html⟩

Part 6

Fences and Neighbors
Scenes of Cross-disciplinary Work and Faculty Collaboration

30

Whatever Things Are True
A Scenario in Four Acts

Richard Haswell

ACT I

> The paper will not be rated so much on accuracy of knowledge involved as upon organization of thought and effectiveness of expression.
>
> "Entrance Exam in Subject A (English)," University of California Bulletin, 1905

The squabble begins in the most formal corner of the Truman Reading Room, beneath the gaze of Sir Francis Bacon. The portrait is not a late seventeenth-century oil but rendered in the style. Students sometimes assume that the dark-robed man is Professor Sophus Truman, in whose honor the room was named. Most of the faculty are not fooled, however, remembering that Truman made his scholarly reputation with an exacting and unreadable biography of Bacon. Professor Truman has since retired from the English department, alas, leaving Professor Bradley Phintz to deal with the event in the corner.

It is, after all, Phintz's job. As director of the university's WAC program, he runs the junior writing examination. Students submit portfolios of their academic writings when they become juniors, faculty readers from all around campus assign a few students to an upper-division course in composition when their portfolios do not meet writing standards, and Phintz arbitrates—under Bacon's cryptic gaze—times when the faculty can't agree on the standards.

The squabble is one of those times. The student under question was fortunate in getting Jeff Salazar for a first reader. Jeff teaches two sections of basic writing and co-directs the Writing Center while turning chapters of his dissertation on "Problematicizing Post-Structuralist Theories of Authorship" into journal submissions. He returned the student's portfolio to the "Second Reader" bin with a rating of "Pass." Unfortunately for the student, the portfolio was picked up by Professor Dorothy Craigmont. Craigmont is dean of outreach in the School of Nursing. Years ago she volunteered for the first junior portfolio reading, has never missed one since, and always refuses the stipend that is paid to readers. She is known, at least to nursing majors, to hold fierce standards of good writing. At the moment she is holding this portfolio by the edges, like an X-ray just developed.

"How can you pass this writing?" she is saying to Jeff. They are, as required by the examination reading protocol, "negotiating."

" It's not great, but it's competent. The student can put sentences together. Mechanically, it's flawless—well, a few things, minor stuff, commas, a few misspellings. The essays read like essays, they're organized, the writing's clear, you can follow the ideas easily, I can follow them easily." Jeff trails off, looking at Professor Craigmont with breath held. He knows her a bit. For her part, she gives Jeff a motherly look, as if he were an imbecile, possibly harmless.

"That's not the point. The point is that a lot of this stuff is simply untrue. Look at this." She shows him the second paragraph of a paper that— as it turns out—Phintz will see again, more times than he would like. The paper is called "The Ethics of Pollution," submitted for the course Philosophy 101. It's in Helvetica and the letters are very close together.

> The first problem that pollution can cause is illnesses such as asthma, that make it hard to breathe. The pollutives that we breathe in are not good for our respiratory system either. Our body needs clean air to function right. Unfortunately we will never have totally clean air to breathe in, and it seems like our bodies are becoming accustomed to the pollutives. I think pollution is contributing to the mainstay of viruses in the air. Pollution is a bed for the viruses to grow and proliferate in until we can no longer deal with them effectively. I am firmly convinced that if we had cleaner air, we would not be sick as much.

"Quite a bit of that is just false information. Pollution doesn't 'cause' asthma. Bodies don't become 'accustomed' to pollution. Viruses don't 'grow' in air pollution like in a Petri dish."

Jeff is now looking at the passage, not at Craigmont. "OK. But still that's not badly written. It flows pretty well. 'Mainstay' is good, don't you think, for a junior?" He stops suddenly, knowing without looking up that this last isn't going to sit right with Craigmont.

Dorothy Craigmont came up the hard way. For eight years she nursed full-time at a rural hospital while earning her PhD in nursing from Duke. She knows what it means to read a patient's file.

"Since when," she says, "is passing on lies good writing?"

"Well," says Jeff. He is cornered and starting to dig in. "They're her ideas."

Phintz has some options. He can join the discussion. He can tell the two to keep "negotiating" until they have agreed on a decision. He can turn the portfolio over to a third reader. In his mind's eye, he sees the "More Coursework" bin, which at this point in the reading seems to have an unusually small stack of portfolios in it. He notices that the portfolio writer's name is Ashley Lee Fairchild. Absurdly, he has an image of a docile twenty-year-old girl eating popcorn and watching TV in a suburban rec room.

"I'll look it over," he says, and takes the portfolio.

ACT II

> Some businesses sell cars. Some sell hamburgers. Some sell laughter. We sell the truth.
>
> Editorial writer, *San Antonio Express-News*, 17 Oct. 1999

Bradley Phintz is surprised three times over when Ashley Fairchild shows up at his office. Usually students who have been assigned more course work because of a poor showing on their junior portfolio don't question the decision. If they do, hardly ever do they think to get their portfolio from department storage and bring it with them. Finally, Ashley doesn't look very docile—or twenty years old, for that matter. She looks closer to thirty and she is wearing a stained maternity blouse that already has been through at least one pregnancy. Ashley looks Phintz right in the eye.

"I don't understand why this didn't pass." She sets her portfolio folder on Phintz's desk between them.

"Oh, yes. Miss Fairchild. There were several problems. You know, your arguments could be stronger, organization . . ." Ashley is looking at Phintz, unblinking, with an expression that he finds totally indecipherable. "But all the readers—there were three of us, them, three of them—agreed that you need some work on"—Phintz is having trouble finding the right way to put it—"you sometimes get your information not quite right."

"I don't know what you mean."

"You know, your facts are sometimes inaccurate. Here, I'll show you." Phintz locates the paragraph that Craigmont singled out. "Like your statement here about asthma." He is trying to remember what the dean of nursing had said. "Asthma really isn't defined as an illness. Your statement just isn't factually true."

"But that's the way my teacher told me to write it."

"Your teacher? Well, maybe your philosophy teacher wasn't up on the facts about pollution and disease. But you have to be. You're the writer."

"Not my philosophy teacher, my writing teacher. I rewrote this paragraph for him. This is the way he wanted it."

"OK, but that was Freshman Composition. The standards are a lot higher for this examination. They're junior standards." Phintz is getting his feet underneath him.

"Freshman Composition?" Ashley sounds angry. "No, it's Advanced Composition. English 401." She's looking at Phintz. "Professor Weatherby is my teacher."

"How can you be taking that course? That's the capstone course, for seniors. That's a course that passing the junior exam qualifies you to take." He looks again at the paper. "And this was written for Philosophy 101."

"I'm graduating at the end of this semester. At least I've got to graduate. My husband is finishing up. He has a job out in California." Ashley pauses.

"I know I should have taken the examination last year, well, two years ago. I also used the paper for philosophy this semester." She pauses again. "I needed the three hours of humanities."

Phintz sees the fine lines at the corners of Ashley's eyes and he suddenly realizes that she is physically exhausted, and scared. She takes a breath and begins fishing in the portfolio.

"Look, here's my first draft. Here's what Professor Weatherby told me to do. That's what I did."

Phintz reads the paragraph and sees Weatherby's emendations in ink.

> Many people suffer from illness such as asthma that make it hard for them to breath. Pollutives in the air make breathing just as hard. The pollutives that we breath in are not good for our respiratory system. Our body needs clean air to function right. Unfortunately we will never have totally clean air to breath in, so it seems like our bodies are becoming accustomed to the pollutives. I think the pollution is contributing to the mainstay of viruses in the air. The pollution is a bed for the viruses to lay in until we catch them. I am firmly convinced that if we had cleaner air, we would not be sick as much.

Weatherby has circled the first word and written "transition," circled "illness" and written "illnesses," circled "breath" every time and written "breathe," crossed out "The" at the beginning of the second sentence and added "either" at the end of it, circled "so" and written "COMMA SPLICE," circled "lay in until we catch them" and written "grow and proliferate in until we can no longer deal with them effectively."

Phintz looks at his window. Thank God, he thinks, that I have an office with a window that looks out into some trees.

"I'll tell you what I recommend that we do, Mrs. Fairchild."

ACT III

> What is truth? said jesting Pilate; and would not stay for an answer.
>
> Francis Bacon, "Of Truth"

Samuel Weatherby is sitting where Ashley had sat two weeks earlier. He is staring out of Phintz's window, but Phintz can tell that his real focus is on the student paper he is holding loosely in his hand. It is the first time Weatherby has been in Phintz's WAC office since Phintz left the English department six years ago. Phintz can tell it is Ashley's paper, from the Helvetica font.

"Miss Fairchild tells me that you're letting her retake the junior exam."

"Mrs. Yes. She's rewriting some of her papers in her portfolio."

"So I have found out. One of them is an essay she is writing for me this semester." Weatherby pushes the paper across the desk, open to the second paragraph. One more time in his life, Phintz thinks that for a person who has published an essay on "Class Hegemony and Hand Imagery in D. H. Lawrence," Weatherby has the most nondescript fingers.

"I was especially, what should I say, intrigued with the changes she made in her last draft." Phintz and Weatherby are both looking at Ashley's second paragraph, but not with the same expression. "She said you helped her out a bit, Bradley."

> The first problem that pollution can cause is illness. Carbon monoxide released from pollutants in the air combines with the pigment hemoglobin in the blood, displacing the oxygen that hemoglobin normally transports. In fact, carbon monoxide binds to hemoglobin more efficiently and tightly than oxygen does. Carbon monoxide tends to cause suffocation by occupying the high-speed transport system which in the human organism normally guarentees a steady renewal of the supply of oxygen necessary to maintain metabolism in the cells. When oxygen supply to the cells is reduced, the heart must work harder, as must the respiratory mechanism. These effects cause a strain in people with heart and lung diseases. Pollution may also give way to other respiratory diseases such as bronchitis and emphysema, contributing to the mainstay of viruses everywhere. I am firmly convinced that if we had cleaner air, we would not be sick as much.

Phintz can't really remember where in Ashley's essay, two weeks ago, he had suggested specific language and where he had drawn carets and written, "Find out the facts." He saw that Weatherby had incised a vertical line down one margin and written, "Yours?"

"I suppose in some disciplines the quotation mark has gone the way of the cedilla and the footnote," Weatherby says dryly, taking the paper and getting up in one motion. "I hope she passes next week, though I don't know what her chances are. You would know, I suppose."

Phintz sits in his office looking out at the trees, remembering with some irony the conversation he had had with the provost six years ago, bargaining for retreat rights back to his department should the WAC appointment not work out.

ACT IV

Whatever things are true . . . think on these things.

Ephesians 4:8

It is the Truman Reading Room, and the reading session for the junior writing exam is drawing to a close. There are only about thirty folders left in the "Unread" bin. One of them, Phintz happens to see, is Ashley Fairchild's. He picks it up, and looks around the room. Dorothy Craigmont and Jeff Salazar are still at it, though not reading at the same table. But there are plenty of other faculty readers he could give the folder to. Or he could simply put it on his own stack. He looks over at Sir Francis Bacon for an answer, but those meditative eyes are not looking in his direction, or in any direction, it would seem.

QUESTIONS FOR REFLECTION AND DISCUSSION

1. Do different academic departments hold different notions of truth? In writing done for their courses, do different teachers hold students to different standards of truth? If the answer is yes to either of these questions, how is it possible to construct campus-wide criteria for writing?

2. Or is truth not an important criterion in the evaluation of writing ability? Is passing on lies ever good writing? Should writers ever sell truth?

3. In Act II, Fairchild is caught between two incompatible responses to her writing. Her advanced-writing teacher, Professor Weatherby, has produced an edited version that satisfies him; the junior-examination readers have declared this version not qualified for upper-division work. Does she have a legitimate complaint? In the end, how many different verdicts are there on her writing competence? She is desperately trying to follow advice, but the advice conflicts. Generally, how does a university rationalize the fact of contradictory responses by faculty to student writing?

4. Phintz learns that Fairbanks is married, is pregnant, is trying to graduate within a semester, is submitting writing she did as a senior and not as a freshman, and other facts about her. Should these contingencies affect the evaluation of her portfolio?

5. Should Phintz have let Fairchild retake the junior examination? Should he have helped her rewrite her essay? At the end, should he rate her portfolio or let other examination readers do it? How much should a writing administrator stand free of the fray?

READINGS FOR FURTHER CONSIDERATION

Mallonee, Barbara C., and John R. Breihan. "Responding to Students' Drafts: Interdisciplinary Consensus." *College Composition and Communication* 36.2 (1985): 213–31.

Olson, Miriam M. "Writing for the Human Services." *Writing Talks: Views on Teaching Writing from Across the Disciplines*. Ed. Muffy E. A. Siegel. Upper Montclair: Boynton/Cook,1983. 112–24.

Rorty, Richard. "Science as Solidarity." *Dismantling Truth: Reality in the Post-Modern World* . Ed. Hilary Lawson and Lisa Appignanesi. New York: St. Martin's Press, 1989. 6–22.

31

Is This Writing?

Keith Hjortshoj

After the first hour of the Teaching Writing course, thirty-six graduate students filed out of the classroom and gathered around the refreshment table for a fifteen-minute break. Almost all of these graduate students were preparing to teach topical first-year writing seminars in their disciplines in the fall. Almost all of them were in fields of the humanities or social sciences, such as English, philosophy, political science, comparative literature, history, and archaeology. Most of them were also apprentice teachers in summer writing courses. And during the break, most of them clustered with people they knew in their own fields and departments. In this third week of the course, social barriers between fields of study had loosened slightly, but were still largely intact.

The exceptions in the class were three graduate students in the sciences who were involved in a new writing program in advanced courses for undergraduates. Holly was preparing to teach in a physical chemistry lab course for junior chemistry majors. Claudia, also a chemist, was collaborating with a professor to develop writing assignments that simulate the real challenges of experimental research, for another junior-level course in organic chemistry. Huan Ying was a PhD student in biology assigned to teach in a senior-level course on human genetics. All three of these courses included extensive writing but were core requirements for the major. Because this new upper-level program was still very small, its director, Clyde Olsen, decided to include these science graduate students in the course for teachers of first-year writing seminars, even though their courses, roles, and responsibilities were very different.

At the end of the break, the students divided into thirds and moved on to smaller seminar rooms for the second hour of the course, organized as workshops on course plans and teaching strategies. Clyde had made sure that all three of the science grads were in the same small group, which he led. For this session, he had asked the students to bring copies of writing assignments they had drafted, for distribution and discussion in the group at large. For most of the period, Clyde and the twelve graduate students sat in a loose circle, discussing the strengths and weaknesses of assignments that, in each case, asked first-year undergraduates to write three- to five-page essays based on assigned readings in the field.

"I think freshmen will head for the door when they see this," someone commented on a first assignment, for a philosophy course, that asked students to summarize an arcane passage from Derrida.

Others in the group observed that *they* would have trouble with this assignment, and recommended that Peter, the philosopher who wrote it, should either abandon it or save it for the end of the term. Discussion of the next three assignments focused on the clarity of specific words and phrases.

"What does *discuss* mean?" Claudia asked Aaron, the historian who had written an assignment based on *The Federalist Papers*.

After thinking about the question for a moment, Aaron said, "Well, I guess it means 'construct an argument,' and I suppose I can just use that wording instead." Two of the other participants urged Aaron to make this change, because "discuss" did not necessarily mean "argue" in their fields: political science and anthropology. College freshmen, they predicted, would simply summarize the reading.

Toward the end of the hour, Holly distributed material she was planning to use for work with abstracts of experimental reports in the physical chemistry laboratory. Aware that she was speaking to a group largely outside the sciences, she first explained what a scientific abstract was and why she wanted to emphasize this brief section of a report.

"Abstracts are really efficient ways to teach scientific writing," she explained, "because they encapsulate the most important information in the entire report—the purpose of the experiment, the method, the major results, and the conclusions—all in a paragraph or two. So we have to write them very carefully. Like poems, every word has to count."

Holly went on to explain the importance of abstracts in keyword literature searches and briefly referred to the assignment and classroom activities described in the material she had passed around. She planned to remove the abstract from a professional research article in physical chemistry and ask the students to produce the abstract from their reading of the article. In a workshop format, she would then pin all of the students' abstracts to the wall and have them pick out two or three that worked best. After discussion of the features that made these versions work, they would finally compare these versions with the original and consider similarities and differences. This exercise would give chemistry majors confidence that with some close attention to language they were capable of producing writing comparable to the work of professional chemists. With peer review she would extend this kind of attention to the abstracts, and then to other sections, of student lab reports.

To illustrate the kind of writing she was emphasizing in the course, Holly distributed copies of an abstract from a student report written for the course the previous year. For this group she chose an example that was not heavily interlarded with equations, from a report on the kinetic determination of activation energy:

In moving from reactants to products in any reaction, a high energy transition state must be attained before the products can be formed. The activation energy required to reach this state is related to the rate constant of the reaction by the Arrhenius equation:

$$k = Ae^{-Ea/RT}$$

By determining the rate constant of the iodination of cyclohexanone at different temperatures it is possible to experimentally determine the reaction's activation energy. A value of 53.62 kJ/mole was obtained for the activation energy of the acid catalyzed alpha mono-iodination of cyclohexanone. Examination of the proposed mechanism of the reaction in light of the activation energy suggests that the loss of a proton from the carbon alpha to the carbonyl may be involved in the rate-determining step.

Holly cheerfully began to explain what needed improvement in this example when she noticed that most members of the class were not reading it. They had looked at the abstract briefly and then stared at her or at one another with expressions of bewilderment and dismay.

"What's the matter?" Holly asked.

"This isn't writing," Aaron said in a tone of patient explanation. "You can't read it."

"What do you mean it isn't writing?" Holly asked with a look of disbelief. "It's what we write, and it's what we read."

"But it isn't clear," Aaron said.

"Well, it's clear to us!" Holly exclaimed with rising agitation.

"Just like scientists," someone muttered to another member of the group.

At this point Peter, the philosopher, tried to offer constructive advice. "What if you first asked them to pretend that they were explaining the experiment to their parents, in a letter, just in ordinary language anyone could understand. And then . . ."

"But they aren't writing to their parents," Holly protested, and she began once again to explain the function of an abstract in scientific research literature.

As this argument developed, Huan Ying, the biologist, listened silently from the other side of the room with a look of alarm, and Claudia, the other chemist, was becoming visibly angry. When Aaron looked away from Holly and began to shake his head, suggesting that his best efforts to help her had failed, Claudia turned on him.

"I can't believe how narrow you people are," Claudia said with controlled anger, looking first at Aaron and Peter, and then at other members of the group. "I thought people in chemistry were narrow-minded and isolated, but we would never try to tell you what writing is or what it isn't in your fields. I thought I had a lot to learn from this class, but this isn't what I expected to learn at all!"

No one replied to this outburst, and because the hour had passed, people began to gather their belongings and leave the room. Clyde, who had remained silent throughout the exchange, briefly reminded them of the next assignment, and the group dispersed without any effort to resolve or smooth over the disagreement.

INVERSION

The following summer, in the same course for graduate students, a senior chemistry major named Ahmad was a member of an undergraduate
panel that offered student perspectives on the topical writing seminars
the members of the audience were preparing to teach. Speaking to the
whole group in the first hour of the class, Ahmad described the challenges and benefits of writing courses taught by two of the most inspir-
ing teachers in the program—one a graduate student and the other a professor. One of these classes was taught in the English department and the
other in anthropology. Both, he said, engaged him in real critical reading, critical thinking, and reasoned argument, for the first time in his education. Close attention to language had raised his own standards and
performance far beyond the level that would have satisfied him and his
teachers in high school.

These experiences were so exciting that when he was a junior he had enrolled in an advanced expository writing class with another fine teacher,
who emphasized the development of voice and style, and greatly improved
his confidence that he could communicate what he believed in ways that
readers could understand, even if they didn't agree.

Unwilling to seem a poster child for the writing program, Ahmad also
spoke with candor about the kinds of writing instruction he did not like,
and mentioned complaints from friends about their teachers and writing
seminars. These included teachers who had specific, unstated expectations
for "good writing" that you had to guess at throughout the term, those
who simply corrected papers without acknowledging that students were
trying to communicate, and assignments that left no room for imagination.

The new teachers in the audience seemed impressed with these observations and hoped, perhaps, to have classes full of young Ahmads the following year. Administrators of the writing program were also pleased
with the way Ahmad's evaluations inspired good teaching and under-
mined stereotypes of science majors as students who avoided and disliked
writing.

During the question period, therefore, one of the program administrators
asked Ahmad to explain how all of his positive experiences in writing
courses affected his work in chemistry—especially in lab reports and other
kinds of scientific writing.

"Oh, not at all," Ahmad replied. "I didn't see any real connection
between what I was learning in my writing courses and my work in
chemistry, especially in the labs. Once you learn how to do a lab report
you just do it. There's a formula, and it doesn't require much thought.
A lab report isn't really writing," he concluded with a wry smile. "It's
just a matter of filling in the blanks, and that's also how teachers grade
it."

QUESTIONS FOR REFLECTION AND DISCUSSION

1. Aaron, Peter, and some other members of the group seemed to assume that real "writing"—or at least "good writing"—should be clear to any well-educated audience. Is there any basis for this assumption? Does it apply even to their own fields of study: history and philosophy?

2. We can possibly understand this disagreement as a conflict between the values attached to writing at the freshman level and those attached to writing at advanced levels of learning. Is it possible to teach values for writing at the freshman level that remain stable and true as students enter specialized fields and professions? Must an advanced writing program operate on assumptions different from those in a freshman program?

3. We can also understand this disagreement as evidence of prejudice against the sciences and scientific writing. To what extent do you think this is a valid understanding? If prejudice is based on fear or unfamiliarity, did you share any of the group's reactions when you read the abstract Holly provided? Did you actually try to read and understand it?

4. Claudia accused the group of being narrow-minded and arrogant, for assuming they could determine what real writing was in chemistry. Yet at least one member of the group reacted similarly to Holly's assertion, "Well, it's clear to us!" Is there any validity to this criticism that scientists just write for one another, in language that is unnecessarily obscure?

5. Clyde Olsen, the discussion leader, made no effort to moderate or resolve this disagreement. Was this a mistake? If so, what could he have done?

6. Can you think of any single way of understanding the two pieces of this scenario, where graduate students in chemistry argue that a lab report is writing, and a chemistry major argues that it is not? Note that both were speaking essentially to the same audience.

READINGS FOR FURTHER CONSIDERATION

Accreditation Board for Engineering and Technology (ABET). "ABET Evaluation Criteria." ⟨http://www.abet.org/criteria.htm⟩

Bazerman, Charles. *Shaping Written Knowledge: The Genre and Activity of the Experimental Article in Science.* Madison: U of Wisconsin P, 1988.

———. "Special Issue on Engineering Genre." *IEEE Transactions on Professional Communication* 42.1 (1999).

Bergmann, Linda S. "WAC Meets the Ethos of Engineering: Process, Collaboration, and Disciplinary Practices." *Language & Learning Across the Disciplines* 4:1 (May 2000): 4–15.

Herrington, Anne. "Writing in Academic Settings: A Study of the Contexts for Writing in Two College Chemical Engineering Courses." *Research in the Teaching of English* 19.4 (1985): 331–59.

Kalmbach, James R. "The Laboratory Reports of Engineering Students." *Writing Across the Disciplines Research into Practice.* Ed. Art Young and Toby Fulwiler. Upper Montclair: Boynton/Cook, 1986. 176–83.

Waitz, Ian A., and Edward C. Barrett. "Integrated Teaching of Experimental and

Communication Skills to Undergraduate Aerospace Engineering Students." *Journal of Engineering Education*, July 1997: 255–62.

Winsor, Dorothy A. *Writing Like an Engineer: A Rhetorical Education.* Mahwah: Erlbaum, 1996.

Youra, Steven, guest ed. *Communications Across the Engineering Curriculum,* Special issue of *Language & Learning Across the Disciplines* 3:2 (July 1999).

32

Showdown at Midwestern U
The First-Year Composition War Between English and Economics

Sharon Hamilton

Midwestern University (MU) is located in the heart of a thriving metropolis known primarily for its passion for college and professional sports. As the infamous coach on its sister campus in another part of the state purportedly said, "Most people learn to write by the time they finish second grade. Then they go on to bigger and better things."

Within this context, the English department at MU has supported the ongoing development of a writing program over the past two decades that is founded upon an ever-increasing understanding of rhetorical and pedagogical research, theory, and practice. More recently, an Office of Campus Writing was established to support faculty across the campus who wish to use writing more effectively to enhance as well as demonstrate learning in their disciplines.

Recently, the Faculty Council approved six principles of undergraduate learning, one of which explicitly addresses written composition, and all of which imply writing as a major vehicle for demonstrating and assessing student engagement with these principles. Now, the School of Liberal Arts and the School of Science are developing a common core curriculum based on these principles, with writing across the curriculum to be given a significant role in its implementation.

The prosaic serenity of this scene glosses over two years of turbulent discussions about the first-year writing sequence between Bob Aston, chair of the economics department and Sherry Hastings, the director of the Office of Campus Writing, both of whom hold influential positions on the Council of Liberal Arts and Sciences (CLAS) that is designing the new curriculum. While both agree on the importance of writing across the curriculum, they disagree vehemently on how the first-year writing sequence of two courses should prepare students to write in other courses.

The implication of their war of words is weighty: in the balance hangs the decision of whether the second course in the sequence will be mandated in the common core curriculum or will become one among many options. Because the course is highly subscribed in the English department, and already required by many professional schools, programs, and academic units across the campus as the second composition course, the economic fallout of its not being universally mandated will be substantial. At the same time, the course is acknowledged to have many problems, most particularly a very high "WDF" rate (withdrawal, non-completion, or failure).

Additionally, despite explicit advice to the contrary, many students elect not to take this requirement until their final semester before graduation, thereby strongly diminishing its intended value of preparing them to write in their chosen major or profession.

As Sherry prepares her presentation to CLAS to advocate mandating the second writing course in the sequence, she reviews portions of three sets of correspondence between her and Bob Aston, and what she sees as three distinct issues that she must address.

April 26

Dear Sherry,

The more we talk about the writing class, the more I realize we are worlds apart on what the class should be about and what are reasonable expectations.

The point of an essay is to write a closely reasoned argument about what an author says. This teaches the students to read carefully, take notes, back every assertion with evidence from the original sources, and synthesize the arguments in a text.

I looked through the two books for the first-year writing course in the bookstore, one on education and one on men versus women. The books are about two hundred pages long. The individual essays run one or two pages. I know we cannot duplicate the reading and writing requirements of the University of Chicago, but I cannot understand why we are asking our students to read less than one-tenth the material in terms of pages and an even smaller fraction in terms of difficulty.

I remain skeptical about the assertion that literature-based writing courses are less effective at teaching writing than composition courses that do not have a substantial reading component. Certainly the literature-based courses would be more effective at teaching students how to read, at expanding their vocabulary, and at making them think. I do not view the trend toward the composition course for teaching writing as any evidence of its efficacy. We are asking very little of our students in the first writing course in the sequence. As far as I can tell the faculty in Liberal Arts outside the English department and the faculty in the School of Science view the core writing sequence as an utter failure.

———

May 8

Dear Bob,

You open with the suggestion that "we are worlds apart" on what the W131 class should be about. That may or may not be the case, but we are not worlds apart on our desire to construct an excellent core general education program that offers learning experiences of verifiably high quality to our students.

You write that "the point of an essay is to write a closely reasoned argument about what an author says." You are quite right in asserting that this is one very important kind of writing in the university setting. And it is one of the kinds of writing that students do in both first-year writing courses. But it is only one kind. You are not correct in the first part of your assertion: "The point of an essay is . . . ." There may be many reasons for writing an essay, a "closely reasoned argument about what an author says" being only one. Montaigne, the purported originator of the "essai," wrote of it as being an attempt to discover meaning by exploring concepts. Over time, the essay in its most transactional form has been subverted to the needs of the academy to demonstrate learning rather than to discover meaning. Outside the wall of the university, the essay exists in many forms and for many purposes, and this wider range of forms and purposes, reflected in "real-world" publications, now influences the foundation of many current writing programs.

You also mention that there should be a substantial reading component in the first-year writing sequence. With respect to the amount of reading material, there is evidence to suggest that, over time, the more students read, the better their writing is likely to be, especially if what they are reading has vocabulary and structure similar to what is expected in the university. However, there is no direct correlation between length of assigned reading and quality of writing in response to that reading. Our expectations are less related to number of pages read than to the appropriate nature of the writing in relation to audience and function.

Furthermore, your letter suggests that the more traditional literature-based writing course is more effective than the "trendier" composition-focused writing course. I agree totally that the trendiness of something is no good reason for doing it. The way we teach composition is grounded in theories of language learning articulated in the '70's. But these theories of writing instruction are themselves grounded in psychological theories of thought and language from the late '30's. I write that only to indicate that our theoretical base is no passing fancy. Now to your point. Is a composition-based course better than a literature-based composition course? I offer no definitive answer. A literature-based composition course would probably prepare students to write better in literature courses, if they were learning to write literary analyses and critiques. However, I cannot find any research to prove that either way prepares students better to write economics or history papers. The features you emphasize—supporting every point with evidence and synthesizing arguments—are characteristics currently emphasized, among others, in the first-year core writing sequence. They are important in all academic writing.

June 17

Dear Sherry,

Thank you for your considered response to my letter. We may disagree on the means, but we both endorse the same end—a first rate education for arts and science majors. Your letter addressed all but one of the questions I raised. The missing question was about the minimum number of pages of their 200-page text.

Our students need to demonstrate learning before they can use essays to discover meaning. The kind of essay I am advocating is one that is based on the careful analysis of a text—the "analytical essay." The skills of synthesizing a large body of material, defending assertions by finding references in the text, and putting together a closely reasoned argument have an immediate payback in upper level courses. You have told me several times that a writing course requiring extensive reading and analysis of literature would give the students no skills that they could carry over to other courses. In your view it would merely train them to analyze literature. I think careful reading, reasoning, and documentation have universal application.

Because I was not familiar with Montaigne, I bought a copy of his essays to see what the originator of the essay had done. I agree with your description that he used the essay to "discover meaning" and "make sense of the universe to himself." However, I found it ironic that Montaigne would be held up as an example of what the essay is about by anyone advocating a writing course with minimal reading. Montaigne quoted classical authors such as Plutarch and Seneca on every page. He began his exploration of each subject with an examination of what the ancients had written. Even if the intention of the essays in the composition course was to discover meaning instead of demonstrating knowledge, I find it hard to imagine that Montaigne would advocate writing without reading.

I searched through the MLA and ERIC databases and found articles spanning 30 years that advocated the inclusion of literature in introductory writing courses. Unfortunately, the advocates argued the issue on its political merits, its social ramifications, or their experiences with a few students. Here are some of the articles I read: John J. Fenstermaker's "Literature in the Composition Class," *CCC*, Vol. 28, 1977: 34–37; Karen Scriven's "Composition as Content: Clarify the Limits of Literature in the Writing Classroom, *The Writing Instructor*, Spring/Summer 1988; and Mary C. Daane's "Good Readers Make Good Writers: A Description of Four College Students, *Journal of Reading,* Vol. 35, Nov. 1991: 181–88. That there has been sixty years of theorizing on the subject without a single empirical test disturbs me. What would be necessary to test my hypothesis that reading during the freshman year can improve students' writing would be a random assignment of students to W131 and a literature-based writing class with a blind evaluation of their writing at the end of the semester. There would have to be enough instructors of both treatments to control for any individual instructor effects. I imagine that such a study would be of wide interest to anyone who teaches writing. I would be willing to help with the statistical design.

I have one last reason for pushing for a literature-based composition sequence. The present sequence sends the wrong signal to our students. If we expect them to be able to write analytical essays based on careful reading, this should start at the beginning of the curriculum. The present sequence with its minimal reading belies what we expect and starts the students in a hole they may never climb out of.

June 19

Dear Bob:

You write that students should use writing to demonstrate meaning prior to using writing to discover meaning. How can students demonstrate learning before they have discovered meaning? Any "learning" in that situation would be primarily regurgitation of someone else's learning and meaning. We both agree that the analytical essay is fundamental to university writing. However, "the careful analysis of text" is only one form of the analytical essay. There are many phenomena and concepts and events to analyze, someone else's text being only one.

Length was never the basis for selection of texts. The set of shorter readings was considered to offer excellent examples of awareness of rhetorical context, which is the focus of the first course in the sequence. Your discussion of Montaigne makes an excellent point of the interrelationship between writing and reading, a relationship that I have never disclaimed. I do need to take issue with one phrase where you refer to me as "advocating a writing course with minimal reading." That label of "minimal" is yours, not mine. I advocate writing courses that have reading appropriate to the focus and function of the course. Length is secondary to those two considerations.

I have never said that "extensive reading and the analysis of literature would give students no skills that they could carry to other courses." I have said that it would develop their ability primarily to analyze literature. And I did not say merely to analyze literature, since I consider literary analysis an intellectually rich and challenging writing experience. What I did say was that the ability to analyze a literary text would not necessarily enhance students' ability to analyze an economics text. Certain principles hold true across the range of disciplines, such as supporting all general or abstract statements with concrete evidence, but many principles of reading and writing are very much discipline-specific. I agree with your last statement that "careful reading, reasoning, and documentation have universal application."

August 14
Dear Sherry,

If writing is idiosyncratic to the various disciplines, as you suggest, what is the point of English composition? Should we be granting six hours of college credit for a composition sequence that has the sole aim of promoting fluency and competency in writing? Competent writers should have an eye for vivid images, an ear sensitive to discordant language, and an intolerance for clichés. They should have the discipline to work through an extended argument and the fidelity to support every assertion about a text with examples or references. I cannot see any way of accomplishing these ends other than asking students to write substantial essays about serious books. If these goals are beyond some of our students, those students do not belong in college. We should not be giving a bachelor's degree to anyone who cannot write. I have been working doggedly to bring the rest of the liberal arts and science faculty around to my point of view. When CLAS meets today to decide upon the writing sequence, I plan to argue vehemently against mandating the second course in the common core curriculum.

QUESTIONS FOR REFLECTION AND DISCUSSION

1. How would you advise Sherry to prepare for the upcoming meeting?
2. How would you address each of the three main issues discussed in Sherry's correspondence with Bob?

READINGS FOR FURTHER CONSIDERATION

Daane, Mary C. "Good Readers Make Good Writers: A Description of Four College Students." *Journal of Reading* 35 (1991): 181–88.
Fenstermaker, John J. "Literature in the Composition Classroom." *College Composition and Communication* 28 (1977): 34–37.
Michel de Montaigne. *Essays.* Trans. J. M. Cohen. New York: Penguin, 1958.
Scriven, Karen. "Composition as Content: Clarifying the Limits of Literature in the Writing Classroom." *The Writing Instructor,* 7.3/4 (1988): 115–21.

33

Raising the Gates of Chem. 110

Jeffrey Jablonski and Irwin Weiser

In what's become a regular feature of Glenridge University's dual writing-across-the-curriculum/faculty development program, several faculty meet for lunch once a week to share stories about their teaching and their students' writing. While there's typically a core of regulars—the WAC director, her assistant, and those teachers who've most recently "graduated" from the summer workshop—veteran writing-emphasis (WE) course teachers often drop by on their own or visit at the WAC director's invitation. Sometimes, the WAC director invites various members of the campus community who might discover some relationship between their interests (or their program or department's interests) and the interests of the WE faculty.

Today is a case of the latter. Sharon, the WAC director, has asked that Barbara Woodford join them for lunch. As the head of Science Counseling in the School of Science at Glenridge, Barbara has a problem and has come looking for answers, if not moral support.

After an exchange of introductions—and a group trip to the buffet—Barbara begins to tell her story by first distributing photocopies of a memorandum. "I've been dealing with a student who's terribly upset, and I remember reading in the WAC newsletter about the workshop's focus on teaching. Well, do I have a dilemma about teaching!"

"A few days ago," continues Barbara, "a student brought this memo to me. She was in tears." Barbara quickly reads the memo aloud while the others follow along:

Interoffice Memorandum
Glenridge University
General Chemistry Office
To: Yichun Wang
From: Dr. Cheryl Stein, CHM 110 Course Supervisor
CC: Dr. William Rogers, CHM 110 Professor
           Office of the Dean of Students
RE: Lab Reports for *Commercial Sodas: Analyzing for Acid Content*

Your lab report for *Commercial Sodas: Analyzing for Acid Content* was brought to my attention by your TA. In the routine check of data included in the report with the data recorded in the lab, the TA discovered that you reported different data in the report than you had recorded during lab. This was the case for the density data collected for both sodas that were analyzed. I do not know where these numbers came from but in any case we do not alter lab data in order to get information that we think might be "more correct."

This is considered to be academic dishonesty and is not tolerated in CHM 110 nor at Glenridge University. As a consequence of your decision to alter lab data and turn in altered data as though it were data collected, you will receive a grade of "zero" for this report. In addition, I will override the computer at the end of the semester so that this will not be the lowest grade dropped before final grades are assigned.

I am returning a copy of your lab report to you. I will keep the original for the CHM 110 files. As stated in the CHM 110 course packet on page 8, this incident is being reported to the Office of the Dean of Students. If you have any further questions, you may direct them to the Office of the Dean of Students.

Enclosure: *Academic Integrity: A Guide for Students*

"Wow," gasps Doug from Education. "This memo sounds serious. I would say, judging from its tone, this student did something pretty inappropriate."

Others nod in agreement.

Sensing the call for more context, Barbara elaborates: "Let me first say I've changed the names of everyone involved for the sake of privacy, but I felt it important to preserve the student's background. We'll call her Yichun Wang, and the actual student is from an eastern province of China. As an eighteen-year-old international student, her second-language skills aren't great, but her TOEFL score is higher than our average, and she has previously spent some time in the U.S. as an exchange student."

"I'm not convinced," she adds, "that what Yichun did is inappropriate. She's a wonderful student, and I was floored when she came to me with the memo. She explained to me that she was called into Dr. Stein's office and summarily presented with this memo—without any opportunity to explain her position. Dr. Stein is the course supervisor for Introductory Chemistry, or Chem. 110."

Several of the faculty members' expressions evince the question, "course supervisor?"

"As I'm sure many of you know, Chem. 110 is a large lecture course with close to four hundred students. As part of the course, each student also participates in lab and recitation components. Graduate student teaching assistants teach the labs and recitations, and a faculty member teaches the lecture. But since faculty rotate teaching the large introductory lectures each semester, nonfaculty 'course supervisors' are hired to administer each section. These course supervisors handle everything from scheduling TA meetings to getting equipment to dealing with students. I guess you could liken the model to congressional staff who accrue knowledge and responsibility as the representatives come and go. But, for better or worse, these course supervisors aren't put in teaching roles."

"But what did the student do that was so terrible?"

"Well, I asked Yichun, 'Are these accusations true? Did you falsify your lab data or submit a falsified lab report?' She welled up with tears again. 'No, not true,' Yichun replied. She went on to explain what happened. She had conducted her latest lab experiment, recorded the results in her notes, and submitted the final report and her lab notebook to her TA. A week later she was confronted by Dr. Stein and told she would receive no credit for that particular assignment. But, more gravely according to Yichun, she was being accused of academic dishonesty, something she could not bear accepting or, worse, sharing with her family back in China. She did not know what the Dean of Students would do and feared expulsion, what she called the 'ultimate dishonor.'"

Barbara looks around the table to see if everyone follows. They are intensely interested but seem a little lost. "The test was a fairly commonplace experiment called a titration. Students created a reaction between chemicals—in this case, soda pop and sodium hydroxide—and weighed the results, or products, to measure some variable. The aim was to determine the concentration of acid in the two different brands of soda. Well, Yichun apparently went through the steps and recorded the data from the experiment in her lab notebook. Afterward, she returned to her dorm and naturally discussed the lab with her roommate who was in a different lab section of Chem. 110 but doing the same experiment. When they compared results, Yichun discovered she had forgotten to subtract the weight of the dish containing the product. Her calculations were off! Knowing the weight of the dish from previous experiments, she did some basic arithmetic in the margins of her lab notebook and submitted the revised weights as her final results."

"Yichun didn't see this as problematic. In fact, she was trying to follow what she had been told about not altering experiment results in her lab notebook. Of course, the goal is to help students understand the importance of rigorous research for making scientific claims. And it's safe to say that Yichun certainly learned never to forget the basic step of subtracting the product's container. But, in a routine review, the TA noticed the data discrepancy between Yichun's lab notebook and her lab report. He gave the documents to the course supervisor, who initiated disciplinary action following standard course policy regarding data inconsistencies. Dr. Stein met with Yichun briefly, explaining that Yichun was being informed of the disciplinary action. She was given the memo and a 'zero' for the assignment. According to Yichun, the course supervisor was unwilling to entertain explanations."

"So, what was the student's infraction again?" asks one of the faculty.

"Where the student made the mistake," answers Barbara, "was in not changing the lab notebook, particularly given the obvious mistake in her calculations. She went back and changed the final lab report but did not change the original calculation in her lab notebook. She believed changing 'original calculations' was inappropriate. What she did not understand—and where there's the possibility of a language misunderstanding—is the protocol for when and how one alters recorded results in lab notebooks."

"Well, but what about the course supervisor's point of view?" asks another.

Sighing, Barbara answers, "I pleaded the student's case to the course supervisor to no avail. The supervisor's attitude was, 'If she gets the total points allowable on the rest of her assignments, the 'zero' won't matter anyway.' She also stated that especially for the first few lab assignments, it was all but routine to hand out such notices. 'Nearly one in ten students taking Chem. 110 receives such a notice,' she said. 'So, naturally, there is very little emphasis placed on investigating such discrepancies, just in ensuring they don't happen again. The Dean of Students keeps a file in case the student develops a pattern of academic dishonesty. Besides, if the student had not collaborated with her roommate, she would have merely lost points for improperly calculating the results. When students compare notes, problems inevitably arise.' "

With that, Barbara pauses to let the group gather its thoughts.

"I know that WAC is just about the only forum here at Glenridge for discussing issues related to teaching. So when I told Sharon about this, she invited me to talk it over with you. This problem is not by any means isolated, and if the science professors are aware of it at all, they seem to turn their heads. What can I do?"

QUESTIONS FOR REFLECTION AND DISCUSSION

1. Respond to the following parts of a dialogue about this case:

    DOUG: "How is this related to teaching writing? It's a case about that student not following directions and not learning how to do science."

    LAWRENCE: "I agree. Writing-emphasis seminar courses are one thing, but those giant gatekeeping courses are another. Students know it's basically sink-or-swim. With four hundred students—heck, even with fifty students—it really can't be any other way. I'm sure between the professor, her TA, the course supervisor, and other student support services, there were plenty of resources she could have sought out if she was confused or had any questions. After all, I thought she was a *good* student."

    NITIKA: "Oh, Lawrence, *'gatekeeping'*? Why does Yichun—an Asian woman—and, for that matter, the other ten percent of the students in Chem. 110, have to be treated so insensitively? Haven't we been talking in the WAC workshops about how our individualized, competitive system of education oftentimes ignores the reasons underlying students' mistakes? About how if we give students more opportunities to use language and writing, they might not only come to better understand whatever it is they're supposed to be learning but also actually *discover* just what questions or confusions they have about the subject?"

SARAH: "The point is, and believe me I've been there, this is another example of the huge teaching bureaucracies that surround these introductory courses and their inability to recognize individual cases. This memo, unfortunately, is how students learn to do science."

LAWRENCE: "OK, I understand. But *my point* is that WAC is just not practicable in the large lecture model, particularly in the sciences, in math, and now even introductory computer programming classes. As Doug implied, there's the lab, the algorithm, the program code—each has either the right answer or the wrong answer; there's no in-between. And each of those four hundred students has to learn the right answer. In fact, I think this memo is very instructive insofar as modeling how the scientific community regulates methodological rigor. The course supervisor admitted the efficacy of this system for cutting down the cases of cheating each semester. It will be just like that out in the real world of science."

NITIKA: "Should first- or second-year students be expected to think and act like scientists? Or mathematicians? Or computer scientists? I'm really not comfortable with the sink-or-swim model of education.

LAWRENCE: Can't we get at the teaching practices—and the concomitant epistemological beliefs—underlying the high incidence of alleged 'academic dishonesty' in this case? A university can have all the student support systems in the world, but you know, for at least this one course they don't seem to be working—responsibly, proactively, humanely."

DOUG: "And WAC can do all that, huh? Tell me how, please; I'm all ears."

2. In the case and dialogue, there seems to be some ambiguity about the nature of the collaboration between Yichun and her roommate. Is it an incident of academic dishonesty? How is this issue related to Nitika's question about underlying epistemological beliefs?

3. Should the course supervisor, Dr. Stein, follow institutional procedures for reporting "academic dishonesty" in this case? What alternative courses of action might she have pursued?

4. Is Barbara's congressional metaphor fair? Does it inappropriately leave the course supervisor in a position of less authority than the course's professor? Who has power in this situation? Who can teach? If you were to diagram the "teaching bureaucracy" described in the case, how might WAC be incorporated into each level?

5. In the dialogue, Lawrence is skeptical about the possibilities of integrating WAC into large introductory and general education courses. Do you agree with him? Why or why not? What might be some ways to overcome roadblocks to integrating WAC into courses with more than thirty students, courses that often, but not always, have attached lab and/or recitation sections as well? What should be the relationship of any curricular or pedagogical changes in such courses to other existing WAC requirements?

READINGS FOR FURTHER CONSIDERATION

Bruffee, Kenneth. *Collaborative Learning: Higher Education, Interdependence, and the Authority of Knowledge.* Baltimore: Johns Hopkins UP, 1993.

Connolly, P., and T. Vilardi, eds. *Writing to Learn Mathematics and Science*. New York: Teachers College Press, 1989.

Howard, Rebecca Moore. *Standing in the Shadow of Giants: Plagiarists, Authors, Collaborators*. Stamford: Ablex, 1999.

Thaiss, Chris. "WAC and General Education Courses." *Writing Across the Curriculum: A Guide to Developing Programs*. Ed. Susan H. McLeod and Margot Soven. Newbury Park: Sage, 1992. 87–109.

34

The Strange Case of the Vanishing Very Bad Writing

Tom Fox

As chair of his campus's University Writing Committee (UWC), Dale Thibodeaux hosts an annual gathering of faculty to clarify the purpose and practices of the upper-division writing requirement. Canyon Verde University has an older, well-established series of writing requirements, most of which were created in 1975. Central to Dale's program are upper-division writing courses taught by faculty in the disciplines, called writing proficiency (WP) courses. Most (but not all) departments have come to accept this requirement. Many do a splendid job; others simply staff the course with whoever is willing. With the enormous number of retirements, however, and the tendency of departments to put newer faculty in charge of their writing courses, there are many faculty who do not understand the reasoning behind the requirement, or the importance of its being taught as a real course in the majors.

To lessen this problem, each year the UWC hosts an informal gathering of teachers of writing proficiency courses. It's held in the Creekside Café, where food is served. Dale takes the opportunity to highlight excellent assignments from exemplary WP courses in social work, industrial safety, marketing, or other majors. The previous year, two such meetings were held. The first was a happy gathering of friends that led to a great conversation about teaching. The second one, the following day, started the same way until a faculty member unknown to Dale walked in and took a seat in the back of the room. As Dale talked along in his friendly, workshop voice, he noticed that the stranger was grumbling and shaking his head. In the middle of Dale's presentation on the value of the exemplary social work assignments, he interrupted:

"If you guys would just teach them something in English 1 [first-year composition], we wouldn't have to do this! I have students who can't write a simple sentence. Why would I bother teaching them about my discipline when I'm so busy teaching them the basics that you [here he pointed his finger] were already supposed to have taught them!"

Blindsided, Dale at first thought that perhaps this latecomer was joking—his comments were so stereotypical that they were almost burlesque. But judging from his expression, Dale assumed the worst: a rude and disrespectful colleague. Recovering his composure, Dale took the opportunity to explain the work of the first-year composition program, concentrating on how the curriculum taught editing and how it made use of a developmental portfolio requirement. The unknown professor continued his tirade, and Dale took the opportunity to explain the research on error. For a moment he felt like he was in Monty Python's argument sketch (Yes, it is. No, it isn't. Yes it is. No it isn't). Thinly disguising his sarcasm, Dale invited the professor to look through the English portfolios and see all the simple sentences that students could write. Not to be squelched, the resistant professor kept going. Then, finally, Dale lost his temper. "You don't know what you're talking about; you're taking up all of the time of this meeting, and you need to be quiet." At which the professor stormed out of the meeting.

After a short bit of sleuthing ("who *was* that guy?"), Dale found out that the Unknown Professor was Walt Leiter, chair of the engineering department, a department that the writing-across-the-disciplines program was particularly interested in making connections to. Dale made an appointment with Leiter the very next morning, to mend fences and figure out what was really wrong. He had two discrete goals: (1) to explain the practices in English 1 so that the program could not be caricatured and (2) to find out what was causing this very bad writing that Leiter referred to in the meeting.

Dale was on time for his appointment and Leiter was waiting. Dale was impressed with his office, much nicer than in English. The bookshelves, to his surprise, contained both engineering manuals and literature. Toni Morrison, Alice Walker, Joseph Heller. Dale checked his stereotype of engineers, hoping that Leiter might do the same with English professors. Surprisingly, the conversation went very well. They were both out to mend fences. Leiter talked about the pressures on his faculty to teach writing, their sequence of courses (which were thoughtful and well informed), and their high standards for their students. Dale was impressed. He explained the English 1 program, showed Leiter the portfolio requirements, and gave him an article on error. Then he asked for examples of very bad student writing so he could understand what was going on. Leiter was eager to tag the problem on English 1, so Dale agreed that he would find out if these very bad student writers got good grades in the English 1 program.

Leiter looked around his office and gave Dale five portfolios from one of his courses. Back in his office, Dale skimmed through the portfolios. They weren't very bad. In fact, even the C students were quite competent. He did a quick error analysis on the portfolios, and typed up a list of errors for each student. One student made only three errors (misplaced or absent possessive markers, comma splices, and subject-verb disagreement), although in his ten-page paper, he made them several times. Dale made another appointment with Leiter.

As he headed to their meeting, Dale was a little worried that when he told Leiter that the very bad student writers were better than most in the university, Leiter's suspicions about Dale's lack of standards would be confirmed. But when they had sat down and Dale had shared his opinion, Leiter agreed. "I see what you mean," he said. "These aren't really bad. There are worse. Let me get back to you."

Dale waited patiently over the next few weeks, even emailing Leiter a couple of times. Leiter *was* really busy. The semester passed and then Dale got a phone call at the beginning of the semester in January. He had found the very bad student writing. Dale went over to pick it up. Leiter had collected five timed pieces of writing, all written by nonnative speakers of English, about their goals in life, written on the first day of class. Students were not allowed to revise. The students used UNIX, which didn't have a spellchecker on it.

Dale dutifully took the papers back to his office and prepared a small speech on reasonable expectations for nonnative speakers of English. He returned to Leiter's office the next day, delivered the speech, and offered writing-across-the-curriculum assistance focusing on teaching ESL literacy. Leiter listened, but became increasingly agitated.

"Look, Dale," Leiter said, his cheeks flushed. "I agree with you that some students in this department can write. We've seen that, you and I, in a few papers. But these students are clearly at the other end of the spectrum. I understand that one semester with these students isn't going to fix the problem. But that doesn't mean it's our problem. You can't expect engineers and nursing faculty and economists to teach writing. *You* create the foundation. *We* build on it. But there isn't a foolish faculty member among us who will work on the quicksand of your foundation. First you expect us to teach poorly prepared American writers. Now you're telling us we have to teach English as a foreign language as well. Who do you think you're kidding?"

Halfway back to his office, Dale thought about his options. It was no use, he concluded. This one was beyond him. He'd let Engineering go. Besides, ABET, their main accrediting agency, was breathing down their necks every few years. And writing was becoming a big thing for ABET. Let them account to ABET, he thought, tossing the photocopies of the timed writing samples into the wire waste bin in the middle of the quad. He was done with it.

QUESTIONS FOR REFLECTION AND DISCUSSION

1. Should Dale give up on Leiter? On Engineering? Why or why not?
2. If Dale decides to press ahead with his plans to draw Engineering into the WAC community, what else might he do to succeed?
3. What ideological issues does this scene raise about ways that faculty perceive student writing? Is there a point at which it is no longer worth the time and effort it takes to reconcile differences in such perceptions?

READINGS FOR FURTHER CONSIDERATION

Anderson, Worth, Cynthia Best, Alycia Black, John Hurst, Brandt Miller, and Susan Miller. "Cross-Curricular Underlife: A Collaborative Report on Academic Ways with Words." *College Composition and Communication* 41 (1900): 11–36.

Bartholomae, David. "The Study of Error." *College Composition and Communication* 31 (1980): 253–69.

Part 7

Seeds of Change
Scenes of Apprenticeship and the Role of Graduate Students

35

The Blind Man and the Elephant Called Writing

Patricia C. Harms and David R. Russell

Kenwood State University has recently begun a program called "Learning Communities." Each learning community sponsored by KSU is unique; however, many of them share similar basic components: often the students live on the same dorm floor, take some of the same classes, and participate in community-building activities. Some of the learning communities include "linked courses," courses that are in some way related, and for which students co-register. The goals of linking courses are multifaceted and include helping students to see courses as integrated units, to see similar material from different perspectives, and to apply material learned in one course to another course.

The degree of linkage and related material varies greatly from course link to course link and from instructor to instructor. In addition, the degree of collaboration by the teaching faculty varies a great deal. First-year composition is often included as a linked course, because it is a class required by all majors at KSU. Like a number of WAC programs across the country, Kenwood hires graduate students or temporary instructors from English to work with faculty—even senior faculty—from non-English departments. Commonly, the instructors in the non-English course are senior professors, teaching large-lecture or multisection introductory courses, while the instructors of the first-year composition course are generally teaching assistants or adjunct, temporary faculty.

One such first-year writing instructor is Judith Hansen, a doctoral student and graduate teaching assistant for the Department of English. Judith has agreed to meet with Pete Winters, an associate professor in the engineering department. Judith makes the trek across her large campus to one of the engineering buildings and climbs the old, wide staircase to Pete's office. Armed with some materials she has gathered from various sources, she hopes to have a productive meeting with Pete about a new learning-community link between first-year composition and first-year engineering.

JUDITH: (Enters Pete's office, where Pete is flipping through the pages of an engineering journal.) "Hi. I'm Judith Hansen from the English department." *[She thinks: Gosh, he's old!]*

PETE: (Glancing up) "Come on in and take a seat. Would you like a cup of coffee?" *[He thinks: Gosh, she's young!]*

JUDITH: "Thanks, no. I just had one. I understand we'll be working together next semester." *[I hope he knows what we're supposed to be doing.]*

PETE: "That's what I heard. I was recruited by my department chair to try out this new linked course idea. I'm not too sure what you're expecting me to do." *[I hope she knows what we're supposed to be doing.]*

JUDITH: *[Uh-oh. He's clueless too.]* "Well, quite honestly, I'm not sure. I haven't taught a linked course before either." *[I thought it would be good for the students, to motivate them—better than first-year comp.]* "I was told that your department was interested in having what they called a 'value added' first-year composition course. And that the plan was to link a section of first-year composition with a section of first-year engineering. Can you tell me a little bit about the course you teach?"

PETE: (Closes his journal and tosses it on the desk) *[God, where to start?]* "Sure. It's sort of a basic introduction to engineering. We teach students about many engineering principles by having them do 'reverse engineering.'" (Pete reaches over and finds a text on his shelf.) "That's where they take a model or a robot and take it apart in order to learn how it works and how it was put together. They then have to make a parts list and put the model or robot back together. They also learn how to draft using an advanced computer program."

JUDITH: *[Well, at least he knows about drafting—writing process.]* "My students do a lot of drafting with computers, too. What other kinds of writing do they do in the class?"

PETE: *[English students do computer drafting? Things have sure changed since I was a freshman.]* "They don't really do any writing, actually. They just write up their data. They solve a problem in teams. They do a literature search, create different versions of the robot, then compete to see which performs best. So they've got the specs. And an oral presentation using PowerPoint."

JUDITH: "So what do they write?" *[I'm missing something.]*

PETE: "Not too much." *[I'm missing something.]* "I give a few quizzes just to make sure they've done their reading. I don't use quizzes every day. Oh, and of course most of them take notes during lecture. You've been asking me about my class. How are you going to incorporate engineering into a freshman composition class?"

JUDITH: *[Does he expect me to teach engineering?]* "Well, that's a good question. I obviously can't teach engineering per se. What I'm imagining is pulling in readings related to engineering and technology, to give them a critical perspective on science and build their agency as writers."

PETE: "Hmm." [*What could she mean by "critical perspective?" Science bashing?*] (Pete gets up, opens a file drawer, and flips through files.) "You know, I have a bunch of magazine and newspaper articles about engineering-related topics that have been in the media. Here's a couple on water quality and field drainage. Are you interested in these?"

JUDITH: "Hmm." [*I don't think he gets it. God, where to start?*] "I'd be happy to look at whatever articles you're willing to share. I think I'll ask the students to watch for articles, too. There has been a lot in the media lately. Any other ideas?"

PETE: [*Well, let's talk about something we can agree on—bad grammar!*] "Would you be able to correct their reports in your class? Just the English. Their grammar is unbelievable. That would save a lot of time and really improve their writing."

JUDITH: [*Oh . . . my . . . God!*] "That's not really . . . well . . . I'll have to check with the director of the composition program. But we do work on revision techniques and principles in my course, global as well as local."

PETE: "That sounds great. Let me know how I can help." [*That went over like a lead balloon.*]

JUDITH: [*Change the subject, quick.*] "Ok; thanks. Well, I've got some great ideas for first-year comp. Let's talk about first-year engineering now."

PETE: [*She's got ideas for Freshman Engineering?*] "What do you mean?"

JUDITH: [*Let's talk about something we can agree on—more writing!*] "Well, do you have any ideas how we can incorporate more writing into your curriculum?"

PETE: "I don't think there's anything we can do there. I only teach one section out of a total of six sections. We have a standard syllabus that we all follow." (Pete takes papers from file drawer.) "Wait . . . here it is. You can keep this copy. Sorry I can't help you more." [*If I start messing with the standard syllabus my colleagues will kill me. I can just see the curriculum committee now.*]

JUDITH: [*We've got a lot of talking to do to work this out. What have I gotten into?*] (Judith takes the syllabus from Pete.) "Thanks. I'll give you a copy of my syllabus at our next meeting—when I've had time to develop it on the basis of our discussion here."

PETE: [*Next meeting?*] "Next meeting? What will we talk about? You mean there's no standard syllabus for freshman comp?" [*Let's just trade syllabi and get on with it!*]

JUDITH: (Looks down at the syllabus on her lap and tries to gather her thoughts. All she can think of is the John Jeffrey Saxe poem, "The Blind Men and the Elephant," in which six blind men encountering an elephant for the first time give very different descriptions of it on the basis of the very different parts each latches onto first.) "Well . . ."

QUESTIONS FOR REFLECTION AND DISCUSSION

1. What is necessary for instructors with different rank and teaching experiences to work together to improve students' writing and learning?
2. What is necessary for instructors with different disciplinary backgrounds to work together to improve students' writing and learning?
3. Can you imagine situations when it would be helpful to bring Judith into the engineering classroom or Pete into the composition classroom?
4. Judith skirted the request for editing service. Could she have handled that situation more effectively?
5. Considering Pete has to work within the structure of the standard syllabus, how could he incorporate WAC into his course?

READINGS FOR FURTHER CONSIDERATION

Burnett, Rebecca E. "Some People Weren't Able to Contribute Anything ut Their Technical Knowledge": The Anatomy of a Dysfunctional Team. *Nonacademic Writing: Social Theory and Technology*. Ed. Ann H. Duin and Craig J. Hansen. Mahwah: Erlbaum, 1996. 17—33.

Lenning, O.T., and L. H. Ebbers. *The Powerful Potential of Learning Communities: Improving Education for the Future*. ASHE-ERIC Higher Education Report, Vol. 26, No. 6. Washington: The George Washington University Graduate School of Education and Human Development, 1999.

Russell, David R. "Activity Theory and Its Implications for Writing Instruction." *Reconceiving Writing, Rethinking Writing Instruction*. Ed. Joseph Petraglia. Hillsdale: Erlbaum, 1995. 51—78.

Walvoord, Barbara E. *In the Long Run: A Study of Faculty in Three Writing-Across-the-Curriculum Programs*. Urbana: National Council of Teachers of English, 1997.

Winsor, Dorothy A. *Writing Like an Engineer: A Rhetorical Education*. Mahwah: Erlbaum, 1996.

36

Greta's Cacophony

Michael C. Flanigan

Greta Holmburg poured over the papers from her Introduction to Music class. She was appalled by the spelling mistakes, grammar errors, and lousy punctuation. She had no idea that grading student papers would be so hard. She felt at a loss, but she knew she had to plug on. The students expected the papers at the next class meeting, and departmental policy recommended papers be returned right away, no later than five days after being turned in.

Greta had joined the music department training to be an opera singer, not an English teacher. She needed the TAship to support herself and her daughter, and she loved the teaching of music, even if most of the syllabus requirements were determined for her by the curriculum committee of her department. She had met the faculty liaison, Candace Lowell, three days before the semester had begun. In what was called the "Familiarization Seminar," Greta and three other new TAs were given a syllabus, which Ms. Lowell went over for about an hour. She explained to the new TAs that they needed to go over the syllabus in class in the same way that she did, pointing out how the course focused on the breadth of music from before 1600, through the Baroque, the Classical, Romantic, Impressionistic, Neoclassical periods and into experimental and technological music. Just getting a grip on all these periods of music was going to be challenging, Greta thought, though she was familiar with most of them, and she could see the other new TAs looked as worried as she felt.

Ms. Lowell then discussed the goals, objectives, and requirements and the grading system of the course. Greta considered the four goals that were listed on the sample syllabus:

1. To develop a perception for aesthetic elements present in all kinds of music.
2. To describe music in terms of its aesthetic elements in both written and oral assignments.
3. To attend live performances of a variety of styles of music.
4. To gain understanding of the progression of music from the Western European notated tradition as it evolved and is evolving.

Judging from the eager nodding of their heads, the other new TAs seemed to understand these goals, and they made good sense to Greta as well. The objectives seemed clear enough, too:

1. Students will read assigned portions of the text.
2. Students will be able to identify definitions of musical terms, major composers, and representative genres with 60% or better accuracy on multiple choice tests.
3. Each unit test will include a listening portion requiring the same recognition of musical elements, forms, and styles.
4. Students will attend four live concerts and write essays summarizing the musical elements, structural designs, and historical styles of the music heard.

Under the "Requirements and Grading" section on the syllabus, all components totaled 1,000 points: 100 points each for the four unit exams; 100 points each for the four essays; and 200 points for the final exam.

By the time Ms. Lowell reached the requirements for the four essays, Greta felt as if her mind were swimming with information. On hindsight she wished she had asked more questions, but the syllabus seemed clear enough at the time. Under "Concert Essays" were listed the following rules and directions:

A. No essay will be accepted before or after the due date—no exceptions!
B. All essays must be typewritten and double-spaced.
C. All essays must be at least two pages long.
D. Notes from concert and printed program must be attached.
E. Complete sentences, correct punctuation, and proper grammar are expected.
F. Grading of essays: Essays will be graded on content and form (writing style, grammar, and spelling). Your paper must also contain comments in reference to specific musical features of the works heard, at first in your own words and later in the vocabulary you are learning in class. You may give your personal reactions to the compositions and the performances. Generally, you will need to write one paragraph for each work. Avoid "rewriting" what is in the printed program, and give only a brief description of the "environment" (clothing, hall, audience, appearance of the performers, etc.). This writing should represent your best scholarly effort, and should be well thought out and creative. Do not write jargon or fad language; be creative but fairly formal with your vocabulary. Read your essay out loud to find errors in construction and left-out words. Be sure to use the same tense in your descriptive remarks. Proof for grammar, style, and spelling!
G. Essays will be collected at the beginning of class on the date due. Any papers turned in after that will receive a zero.

Like the other new TAs, Greta was filled with apprehension about how often students would not do the assignments on time, whether they should be penalized for missing classes, how they would behave in class—and the last two hours of the seminar didn't even scratch the surface of her concerns. She remembered leaving the meeting clutching the five-hundred-page course text and her well marked-up sample syllabus feeling a little overwhelmed by her new venture into teaching. But she was also excited by the prospect of teaching, though she wasn't sure what it all entailed yet.

She knew, though, that she could prepare well, and that evening and the next day she read through the text. Then she made up her first syllabus following the guidelines in the sample syllabus almost verbatim. She gave her name, office hours, class meeting times, and phone number—all things that Ms. Lowell had pointed out in the seminar meeting. Under the title of the course she typed a favorite quote from William Congreve's "The Mourning Bride": "Music hath charms to soothe the savage breast,/To soften rocks, or bend the knotted oak."

Satisfied with the look of the syllabus, she prepared her first two lectures. She knew that the first would be about the course and its requirements; the next would cover the first chapter, on how to become an aware and etiquette-minded concertgoer, how to take notes quietly, and how to get into the spirit of the music. She celebrated the finished syllabus and lectures by taking her daughter to their favorite Japanese restaurant. One day later she taught her first class.

The first two weeks of class went well enough. Students seemed bored by the first "syllabus" lecture, though she saw them taking notes. After that things seemed to pick up, especially when she played excerpts to illustrate points in her lectures. Luckily Martha Pannini, who shared the same office with her, had been teaching Introduction to Music for almost three years. Martha showed her how the departmental recordings underlined in the syllabus went with the terminology, historical elements, and other musical nomenclature she was to cover. Greta wished she had had more time earlier to arrange the tapes and listen to them.

At the end of the third week Greta reminded the students that their first concert paper was due in one week. She also reminded them that they could get a copy of the music offerings for the month from the music office. One student in her class of forty-five students asked what should be in the essay. She pointed him to the syllabus and the guidelines laid out there.

"So grammar and spelling are really important?" he asked.

Awkwardly, Greta answered, "Well, yes, those things are central to good writing." No one else had any questions, so she dismissed the class.

On Friday of the following week she collected the papers, and noted that all but three students handed them in. She would have to give them a zero, she thought. That evening, after her daughter Hazel had gone to bed, she read over half the papers. She couldn't believe they were so poor. Most students seemed to have no idea how to organize a paper. Many essays were replete with careless spelling and punctuation errors. Those without errors seemed dull, unimaginatively following a pattern that went something like, "In the first performance . . . ," "In the second piece . . . ," "In the third . . . ," and on and on until all the pieces performed were sort of catalogued.

She suddenly had the feeling that she didn't know what to do. How was she going to put grades on these papers? She decided that those with careless mistakes would get C's and D's—five spelling or punctuation errors or flawed wording would get a C, and more than that a D. The half dozen papers that plowed paragraph by paragraph through the concert event would get a B or B+; it all depended on how she felt at the moment. Three papers were very well written, even though the students didn't have much command of the technical language of music, but two of these had two spelling or punctuation errors each. These she gave B−. The other she gave an A.

As she tried to make distinctions among the pile of papers, she found more and more that she wasn't sure what she was doing, how she would defend the grades, if students asked. She spent a good part of Saturday and Sunday grading the rest of the papers, and found herself often returning to earlier papers only to discover that at times she seemed to be contradicting herself. Exasperated, she finally finished late Sunday, well after her daughter had gone to sleep.

On Monday, still feeling uneasy about the grades she had given, she returned the papers just before the end of class. She watched as most students flipped to the back page to check out the grade; she heard several moans; one student swore at no one in particular as he left the room.

A short while later after Greta had returned to her office, Rhonda, a student who usually sat in the first row, came to see her.

"I wanted to talk about my grade," Rhonda ventured.

"Sure," said Greta, offering Rhonda a chair next to her desk. "What seems to be the problem?"

"Well," said Rhonda, her voice a little shaky, "you gave me a D, and I just can't believe it. I went to the concert and took notes, and I enjoyed it. I guess I don't know what you want."

"Here," Greta said, reaching toward Rhonda. "Let me see the paper and perhaps I can show you."

As Rhonda handed her the paper, Greta got a sudden sinking feeling. As she skimmed through what Rhonda had written, she realized that it had been one she had graded on Sunday after she had a fair sense of her grading standards. Rhonda's paper had four spelling errors, two punctuation errors, and a word at the beginning of a sentence that was not capitalized.

"Well," said Greta, leaning over the desk so she could show the errors to Rhonda, "you have too many errors. See, you misspelled four words, and you need commas here and here," she went on pointing to the marks on the page. "Oh, and you didn't capitalize here, see!"

Rhonda looked at the paper, and then said, "Well, I'm sorry about those, but what did you think of my review of the concert itself? Was that D writing?"

"You made a lot of errors; that's D writing."

"But," Rhonda replied, her voice starting to shake even more, "but didn't you think my attempts to use the new vocabulary and the details about the flutist, who was just wonderful, were right and decently written? I thought you would be more interested in my ideas and reactions to the music than in my grammar."

Feeling increasingly uncomfortable, Greta pulled the paper toward her. "Let me read it again."

As Greta read, with Rhonda looking down and then out the window, she did notice that Rhonda had used a lot of the vocabulary from the first three weeks of class, and that it was generally accurate, though she had misspelled *dissonance* and *polyphonic*. She also noticed that Rhonda's description of each performance was detailed, and—she had to admit to herself—at times even insightful. She also noticed that Rhonda's excitement about the concert came through in this reading. "Gads," she thought to herself, "What to do?" When she finished reading, she cleared her throat, searching her mind for a solution.

"Well?" said Rhonda expectantly.

Greta hesitated. "Well, you did seem to enjoy the concert."

"Oh, I loved it! Miss Watts was wonderful."

"Yes," Greta replied, "I think she's one of the best people we have. But back to your paper. On rereading it I think it has some real merit, but the careless mistakes just are not acceptable. They just distract me as I read." She hesitated again. "However, in that this is the first paper of the semester I'll raise the grade to a C, but you need to promise me to check for errors better next time."

Rhonda seemed a little disappointed with Greta's response, but quickly agreed and left the office.

About an hour later another student, Thomas, showed up to discuss his paper, but this student had not made any errors in his paper. Greta had given him a B, because the paper was rather dull, did not use new vocabulary as Rhonda had done (something that Greta had not realized in the first reading), and seemed more focused on giving general opinions than on discussing the performances in detail. On rereading Thomas's paper, Greta realized that Rhonda had done a much better job but she had given her a lower grade. She tried to explain to Thomas the problems she saw, but, as if armed for a debate, he then took out the syllabus and pointed to the section that said personal opinions were fine. "Plus," he went on, "you have this section here that says 'Generally, you will need to write one paragraph for each work."

Confronted with Thomas's assertiveness and the words in the syllabus that seemed to be working against her, Greta felt herself becoming irritated and defensive. She explained to Thomas that the directions for writing the paper were guidelines that did not include all possible problems. Standing his ground, Thomas snapped back, "How are we supposed to write something correctly if you don't tell us what you want?"

Greta tried to calm herself, and told Thomas she would try to make things clearer next time, but that his paper just wasn't developed enough, and that he needed to try to use the vocabulary from the course. Again pointing to his copy of the course syllabus, he countered: "The syllabus says explicitly that the paper can be written 'at first in your own words.' Well, I wrote it in my own words as you said I could in the syllabus."

Her patience growing thin, Greta pointed toward the syllabus. "But if you read it carefully, Thomas, you'll see that it also says, 'and in the vocabulary you are learning in class.' I introduced you to a lot of vocabulary, and I don't see any of it in your paper. I had hoped you would use some, make some attempt."

"Then why did you say, 'later?' Doesn't that mean it isn't necessary in the first paper?"

Greta struggled to retain her composure. "If you look just before that, it says you must refer to 'specific musical features,' and that means you need some of the vocabulary."

As if softened by her own growing dominance in this difficult conversation, Greta conceded that she would consider changing Thomas's grade, but that she needed time to think about it. As she gathered her things to go to a meeting and they ended the exchange, Thomas left still muttering about how unclear she was. Greta realized that her discussions with these two students exposed her uncertainty, and made her feel uncomfortable with the way she shifted her standards from one context to the next.

When Greta returned to her office later that day, at least a dozen students, mostly alone but some in pairs, came to see her to complain about their grades. Like the Thomas and Rhonda cases, she found herself flailing around trying to justify her grades, which made less and less sense to her, and made her feel like a phony, maybe even an opportunist. She wished she had thought more about this whole grading business. As she dealt with their complaints and concerns, she realized that the students were right: she didn't know what she was doing. Toward the end of the day, she shut her door and sank back in her chair, a lump rising in her throat. "Is it really worth it?" she thought aloud, staring at her course folder. "Is this what my love of music has come to?"

QUESTIONS FOR REFLECTION AND DISCUSSION

1. Think about what Greta has just experienced as a fledgling TA, and look over her brief history as a teacher. At what point do you think things started going wrong for Greta? What might have been done to prevent her first teaching/grading experience from going sour on her?

2. If you were to advise Greta, what would you tell her to do?

3. What larger problems do you think need to be addressed to help future Gretas in similar situations? How would you address them?

4. What basic problems underlie Greta's dilemma about grading? What do you think she needs to do to avoid these problems in the future?

5. What do you think Greta should do about the departmental guidelines for student essays?

6. Should Greta devote more time in class to writing issues, or developing the written work in class?

7. Would Greta be wise or unwise to change the assignments and syllabus without consulting the faculty liaison of the course? How much freedom does she

have to make changes? How much can she do on her own? What guidelines would you suggest?

8. If you were in charge of training new teaching assistants from across campus, what would you do to ensure that problems such as Greta's would be eliminated or reduced? What issues for Greta's school and campus are implicit in Greta's experience? How would you deal with these?

READINGS FOR FURTHER CONSIDERATION

Haskins, Ekaterina V. "Mimesis Between Poetics and Rhetoric: Performance Culture and Civic Education in Plato, Isocrates, and Aristotle." *Rhetoric Society Quarterly,* Summer 2000: 7–33.

Walvoord, Barbara, and Lucille McCarthy. *Thinking and Writing in College.* Urbana: National Council of Teachers of English, 1990.

Winterowd, W. Ross. "Where the Action Is: Doing Versus Being in the Academy." *Journal of Advanced Composition*, Spring 2000: 299–309.

37

Mistakes in Social Psychology

Chris M. Anson

PART ONE

Brandon Pulasky had always been a little ambivalent about the role of error in social psychology papers. But when he'd been hired as a teaching assistant in Rowayton University's psychology department, he'd heard the leaders of his teacher-training group loud and clear: this wasn't a course in writing, it was a course in social psychology . . . with lots of writing. Brandon's general agreement with the director's philosophy wasn't all that unusual in the program at Rowayton. Several other instructors said they had no problem ridding their courses of a preoccupation with error. In the context of a progressive program that focused on the uses of writing as a tool for learning psychology, error played second fiddle to what the administrators called "broader concerns."

But now, as he stared at his copy of the previous year's syllabus for Introduction to Social Psychology, Brandon was trying hard to adopt the approach of the new TA coordinator, Professor Carter Paxton. Elected by the department after the regular coordinator had accepted a position elsewhere, Paxton was making changes in the teaching program with what several instructors had called "a vengeance." One TA, Karl Spaulding, even recounted a conversation in which Paxton had said he thought the program was "bloated with complacency." True, Karl was prone to a bit of hyperbole. But Brandon knew this hearsay was probably not far from the truth. For one thing, Paxton had little background in teaching as a subject, and no experience in faculty development. In fact, he was known to talk disparagingly about the "so-called research" on teaching, the "dummies" who were accepted into the College of Education, and the "generally lousy writing" that its faculty produced in their journals. He was also a regular critic of the university's composition program which, he often claimed, preferred to have students chat in small groups than learn how to improve their prose.

In spite of all this, when Paxton appeared before the group of twenty teaching assistants at the opening meeting of the orientation and training seminar that fall, Brandon tried to keep an open mind. Addressing the group from a podium at the front of the room, Paxton spent the better part of an hour explaining policies and procedures and working through a list of suggestions for teaching the standardized syllabi for the four different courses assigned to TAs. He sure commanded attention, Brandon thought: you could hear a pin drop. Quite a change from last year's meeting, when the previous coordinator had joked with the group and given a pep talk about respecting students as learners. But Paxton spoke with plenty of conviction, Brandon thought, as if he really did care about the quality of things.

When Paxton turned to the matter of writing assignments, Brandon had the sense that his voice became louder and more tense. "Your students," Paxton said, "are immersed in a hostile campus environment where teachers have little patience for dangling modifiers, sentence fragments, and misused apostrophes." Paxton ran his thumbs behind his suspenders and continued. "Your role—no, your *duty*—is to bring the sounds of the real world into your assignments. Let's think a moment about those sounds." He paused, flipping a page of his notes. "They're the groans of disgust from a reader hitting the third misused comma in one page. They're the sounds of paper crumpling as a potential employer disposes of a job application in which he has found poorly constructed syntax and numerous spelling errors. They're the sounds . . . ," he looked out, eyes narrowed, over the group of instructors, "they're the sounds of laughter as a supervisor ridicules a recent graduate for punctuating like a third-grader."

As Paxton continued, a handout reached Brandon's row—one page titled "New Grading Policy for Writing Assignments." Strategically, Paxton paused in his oration until the handout had reached the back of the room. "Of my many goals for the introductory courses," he went on, "I'm starting with one so basic it virtually defines how you'll operate this year with respect to writing assignments." He held up a copy of the handout. "The policy before you is designed to address this ever-worsening problem of students' language habits. As of this semester, I'm requiring that you incorporate the policy into your syllabus and reinforce it when grading papers. For the time being, the rest of the courses haven't been altered one whit." Brandon mused over Paxton's use of "haven't"—did he mean other courses weren't altered, or the rest of each of the four courses the TAs were teaching? "If students are unable," Paxton continued, "to write clear, grammatically correct prose by the end of a course devoted to clear thinking, housed in a department with high academic standards, then we've failed at our mission. Put plainly, your very livelihoods—all our livelihoods—depend on it."

Paxton ended the meeting by encouraging instructors to meet with him if they needed suggestions about how to implement the policy. In spite of his rather formal demeanor, Brandon thought, Paxton seemed genuinely . . . well, maybe not passionate, but at least concerned about the progress of students and the success of the instructors. The tricky part, Brandon agreed later with some of his peers, was incorporating Paxton's new policy into a course designed to speak directly to students and inspire them to be interested in psychology. The language seemed rather direct and authoritative next to Brandon's more relaxed course overview.

Department of Psychology Policy on Correctness: Every student is expected to turn in final papers that are in every respect correct in grammar, punctuation, spelling, and other formal characteristics. An error or two will be tolerated for obvious pedagogical reasons. However, papers that have several errors will be docked one letter grade. Papers in which several errors appear on each page will be docked two letter grades. Papers in which there is a preponderance of errors throughout will automatically fail.

Clearly, Brandon admitted, he wasn't used to this sort of approach. But maybe Paxton's general direction wasn't all that bad. It wasn't right to let class after class of freshmen move beyond the introductory psychology courses still committing errors serious enough to compromise their success elsewhere. Still, it wasn't quite his style . . .

———————

In fulfilling the goals of Rowayton's writing-intensive curriculum, Brandon's Introduction to Social Psychology led the students through three writing assignments. The first, a personal narrative, allowed Brandon to help students connect some of the course concepts to their own lives and gave them a chance to practice writing in a form familiar to many of them. Following a kind of developmental trajectory that kept moving away from the self as the source of information and adding multiple perspectives, the second assignment was a summary and synthesis of two social psychological research experiments that studied the same phenomenon but reached different conclusions. The final assignment was a "short documented paper" in which students investigated a particular question raised in the course and synthesized several outside sources on the question.

Because Paxton hadn't made any major changes in the existing curriculum—at least for now—Brandon figured he could stick with the "old" program's writing assignments, which had also allowed the TAs some flexibility to teach these assignments as they wished. Maybe all that was needed was a change in the standards for final assessment. He could simply increase the weight of error in his grading policy.

After working for an hour on his computer, he looked at the new section of his syllabus that described grading policies in his course:

How You'll Be Graded on Writing Assignments: The grading emphasis will be on the final drafts you turn in at the end of each unit. Our class discussions of the writing assignments will focus on broad concerns such as the development of ideas, the structure and coherence of your essay, and the quality of your ideas or research. These and related issues will be the *primary* basis for your grade. Please see the handout on each assignment for more specific criteria. Note: The Rowayton Composition Program also has a special policy on correctness, which I am obliged to include below. Please be advised that even if your paper has strengths in the broad areas listed above, *you can fail* just because you make a lot of errors. Make sure you proofread your papers carefully before turning in the final version. Here's the policy. Please read it!

Just below this revised statement, Brandon inserted the new policy inside a box, in a different font, and labeled it "Official Policy on Error, Dept. of Psychology." There, he thought. Not much work after all.

QUESTIONS FOR REFLECTION AND DISCUSSION

1. How do you assess the way Brandon has incorporated the grading policy into his existing course design? Would you have suggested a different course of action?

2. Should Brandon subvert Paxton's authority? If a TA or teacher in a subordinate position has a strong and well-supported intuition about an instructional issue, should she or he have the right to follow it?

3. What issues does this first part of the case raise about instructional supervision and control of the curriculum? Is Paxton's approach an adequate way to create consistency of standards for writing across his introductory psychology curriculum?

PART TWO

The class was going well, Brandon felt. Since the previous year, he'd put a lot of thought into orchestrating his classroom activities so that the students spent their time productively. And the class, for its part, seemed attentive and energetic: twenty-one young men and women whose names he learned quickly and who seemed to warm to his personable style.

As he sat in his living room skimming through the final drafts of the first assignment, Brandon felt pleased with the class's progress after just three weeks. The students had done a good job applying some of the social psychological concepts to their narratives, and the writing (well, some of it, anyway) even appeared lively and interesting. The usual problems surfaced here and there—uneven style, topics that had not been very carefully developed—but on the whole the essays looked pretty decent.

After working his way through a dozen papers, most of which received B's or C's, he realized that he had yet to find a case in which the new error policy created a lower score. True, some of the papers were rather bland, but they were largely free of errors. Perhaps Paxton's approach really did work, Brandon mused. And to think that all it took was a simple, tough-minded statement. Maybe Paxton was right after all: you gotta be cruel to be kind.

To be sure he wasn't just overlooking any problems from the perspective of the error policy, he pulled out an essay he had already graded and glanced through the first few paragraphs. Carol Dernigan had written about "reverse culture shock," which she had experienced after she returned to the United States from an extended stay in Thailand with her family.

> As I walked off the plane, my eyes darted from side to side. People of all different shapes and sizes moved quickly in all directions. Conversations floated around me; whistling about my ears; rustling through my hair; flying angrily over my head. Nothing made sense. They were all speaking a language that I did not know or understand. I turned around and around and a sense of vertigo squeezed my brain until it hurt. I tried to walk straight, but I ended up bumping into a thin, black haired woman who gave me an evil stare. Where was I? How did I end up here? Why did nothing make sense? The signs said "Welcome to Los Angeles," but I didn't want to believe it.
>
> This was home. The home I had left only six months earlier. The home that I was born in, the home where I was raised, the home that I left unwillingly. My sophomore year of high school was ruined because I was forced to move to a foreign country with my family. Where in the world was Thailand anyway? Yet the faces, the movements, and the language became so normal, so safe, and so comforting. Home was in a jungle, in front of a lake, and next door to a zoo. The monkeys welcomed in the sun, not an alarm clock telling me that it was time for zero-period again. Sophomore year was no longer in shambles, it had become the most important year of my life.

As Brandon confirmed his positive impression of Carol's narrative, with its dramatic beginning and creative use of rhetorical questions, he also realized that, technically, Carol had employed several sentence fragments and had used some semicolons and commas somewhat dubiously. The overall sophistication of her writing had, he thought, pulled his attention away from these errors, but it wasn't entirely clear to him whether Carol was in control of her syntax and had erred deliberately and stylistically. The more he reread the paper, the more puzzled he became as to how the error policy might apply. Finally, frustrated that he was spending time rereading already graded essays, he decided that he might be able to justify ignoring these errors on rhetorical grounds. How would he explain it, he wondered. Well, Carol was in the know, obviously. Her errors were deliberate, and therefore exempt from the policy. And besides, the overall quality of her writing suggested that she knew what she was doing. It would be pretty rare to find a really effective writer who also suffered from major lapses in syntax, punctuation, or usage.

Not entirely consoled by this reasoning, Brandon nevertheless decided to push ahead, and returned to the stack of essays still to be read and graded.

Rebecca Eshelman was next. Becky had seemed a little quiet in class, but her contributions had been strong and she worked well in her small group. Brandon recalled joining her group briefly as the students discussed the concept of altruism. Becky had seemed animated, offering ideas and commenting on those of her other group members.

But as Brandon dug into Becky's opening paragraph and took a sip of his soda, he squinted, slowly put the can down, leaned forward, and started the paper over. This, he realized, was no ordinary freshman narrative.

WHEN YOUR HURT BY THE ONES YOU LOVE

Rebecca Eshelman

In the beginning their was the word. Or words. They soothed me as a infant, taught me as a toddler, reasoned with me as a child. My dad was a good man a honest man to most who knew him, he had a decent job and worked hard. To most who knew him he was a family man who cared for his wife and children and organized our house hold.

I loved my father like any kid would. But one day he turned from a caring individule, into a monster. I was only thirteen years old. My mom went out of town to funeral of an aunt who she didnt know real well, me and my dad and brother stayed at home for two days while she was gone. Over a Saturday and Sunday, when he was home with us. After my little brother was asleep and my dad thought I was there was a faint knock at the door, I heard the sound of a woman. I peered out my door and saw someone I had never seen before. They got drunk, I could hear them for most of the night. She was gone in the morning but you could smell the cigarette smoke and beer in the air.

After that weekend my father started to drink real bad. He always drank but now he was getting drunk constantly. My Mom and dad started fighting all the time he yelled at me and my brother and had no patience for us anymore. Finally he started to hit my mom in his rages and stay away for whole nights; and comeing home looking all worn out and smelling of alchohol. He hit my little brother a few times, which he had never done before and he kept acting like he was going to hit me until my mother pulled him away and then they fought instead.

Now only vaguely aware that he was evaluating papers, Brandon read the rest of Rebecca's essay. Vividly she recounted her father's decay over the next year—how he became more distant from Rebecca and her brother, how she cried herself to sleep at night, how conflicted she became in his presence, and how, finally, she began to panic every moment he was in her view or in her thoughts. She tried, not very successfully, to link these experiences to some material the class had read on the social bases of family behavior. The paper ended with only a hint of resolution, when Rebecca met someone whose mother was a family counselor specializing in cases of abuse. Her final, one-line paragraph read, "In the beginning their was the words. In the end, only silence."

As Brandon read and reread Rebecca's paper, wondering how on earth he would comment on and grade it, it dawned on him, through the intensity of his reaction and his sadness at the terrible experience she had disclosed, that her paper was riddled with errors. Maybe not a "preponderance," quite, but certainly enough to subject it to the two-letter downgrade. Comma splices. Misspelled words. Misused words. Verb problems. The grammar policy kept drifting into his mind, how effectively it had seemed to work on the papers up to now, how relieved he'd been to find such clean papers, how his view of Paxton had changed . . . Paxton, up there at the podium, waiving the policy around like a political decree.

The soda was gone. The rest of the papers sat, still ungraded, on the coffee table.

QUESTIONS FOR REFLECTION AND DISCUSSION

1. Should Brandon apply the new grading criteria to Rebecca's paper? Why or why not?

2. Who is Brandon more responsible to, Rebecca as a student or Paxton as a supervisor? What are the ethical implications of going with or against the grading policy in the case of Rebecca's paper?

3. What is the relationship between how Brandon might *grade* Rebecca's paper and how he might *respond* to it?

4. If Brandon can overlook possible errors in Carol's paper because they appear intentional, can he or should he find a different rationale for overlooking the errors in Rebecca's paper?

PART THREE

"But Dr. Paxton, this paper's just . . . just *different* from the rest," Brandon said, feeling about as authoritative as a freshman. "She's taken a huge risk. And it's so personal and, well, moving. I mean . . ."

Taking Paxton at his word, Brandon had come to get the coordinator's advice about how to implement the new grading policy. Paxton had greeted him warmly and they'd shared a few minutes of small talk about the department and Brandon's progress on a paper in a graduate seminar.

Paxton finished glancing through Rebecca's paper, which Brandon had photocopied for him, and leaned back in his chair, studying Brandon with a look of understanding that gave way to resolve. "You know, Brandon, I think there are some deeper problems with the writing in the introductory course, beyond the lack of concern for students' grammar and punctuation, and chief among them is this ubiquitous use of the personal narrative. Perhaps that should be the next thing to go. We simply can't encourage students to do all this . . . this highly personal drama in a course designed to acquaint them with the strictures of writing in the field."

As he went on, Brandon had the urge to tell him that he hadn't expected a lecture on the problems with the personal narrative—just some advice about how to apply the new error policy to a really tough case. As if sensing Brandon's growing impatience, Paxton shifted his focus. "Still, we have what we have: a personal drama shot through with error. What I think you should do—" He stopped himself, then looked up from the paper at Brandon. "Well, let me ask this. What grade would you give this paper, disregarding the new policy?"

Caught a bit off guard, Brandon flipped through his copy of Rebecca's paper. "Well, I think she's done a good job of making this an interesting, a moving paper. I mean, it's a little uneven, but . . . but then there are some nice little devices, the way she frames it with this thing about, this sort of theme of 'in the beginning, there was the word,' you know, it shows some creative flair, some sense of language, I think."

Paxton nodded. "So then, what grade?"

"Well, then the connections to the course are a bit weak. But I guess, I'd say at least a low B. B minus, maybe."

"Discounting all the errors?"

"Yes, right, without including the errors."

"And she did a draft, correct?"

"Yes," Brandon replied, "everyone takes their . . . his or her paper through at least one draft and a revision."

"OK," Paxton said, "so she's had a chance to work on this; she's been given time to look at her screen and edit and use the spellchecker and all the rest."

"Right, between a Thursday and a Tuesday, when the papers were due."

"So then," Paxton continued, "let's go with your B minus. Good, solid effort. Decent structure, even if just a chronology. Rather weak links to the material but at least adequate. Then we apply the error policy and I think your decision is quite clear."

"Clear?"

"Sure. She's read the policy, so there should be no surprise at the lower grade. Right?" He raised his eyebrows and looked at Brandon.

Brandon's uncertainty had increased in direct proportion to Paxton's sense of clarity. "But Dr. Paxton," he heard himself almost plead, "this student, this whole scene is so close to her. I mean, the literature . . ." He paused, realizing it was a risk. "The literature on teaching, there's a lot out there that talks about how it's really not good to switch goals midstream, I mean, to change from, say, encouraging a personal connection to the material and then suddenly looking at grammar.

"Sure," Paxton said, nodding, "you want to be consistent. But you don't have to respond personally to a student's work, no matter how personal it may be. As an assignment, the personal narrative is tricking too many instructors into that false assumption, seducing them into putting aside form in favor of a positive response to content." He signaled to a student in the hall outside his office that he would need a minute longer. "Some kinds of writing are less prone to this seduction, but the personal narrative isn't one of them."

Brandon glanced out Paxton's office window to formulate a response. "But even our other assignments sometimes allow students to respond to the material personally, and we do it in class all the time. I'm not so sure that it really is about the personal versus the objective." Brandon could feel himself becoming more confident. He cleared this throat. "I mean, that's a false dichotomy . . ."

Paxton was reaching across his desk to a pile of paper and books, and produced an issue of a journal that Brandon immediately recognized as *Teaching Psychology*. "That's not what, let's see—" Paxton flipped through the pages— "that's not what Bruce Peyton says here, exactly. These binaries do set up certain tensions. Here—page 513—he's commenting on the goals of writing assignments in psychology courses." Paxton pulled his glasses down on his nose and squinted at the page. "'Writing assignments in the psychology curriculum,' he says, 'should prepare students to be writers in the discipline. The problem with many writing-intensive systems is that they encourage weak, flabby, uncritical, or hastily formulated writing in the name of learning.'" He closed the journal and tossed it on his desk.

Picking up the journal, Brandon tried to collect his thoughts as Paxton continued. "So you see, Brandon, I don't think there's all that much consensus about the effectiveness of narrative as a form of writing in psychology. But let's deal with that problem next semester. In the meantime, I'm afraid that some of these narratives will simply have to go down hard."

"I'm just not sure that's entirely fair," Brandon replied, feeling almost desperate. "How can I send this student the message that her experiences and ideas are worth a D just because she didn't use her spellcheck?"

Before Paxton could respond, Brandon had a sudden idea. "Could I give her another chance, maybe? Let her fix these things?"

"I wish you could," Paxton replied. "But you should read the policy manual you got during orientation. The college policy states that you can't give to one student an opportunity that you don't also give to all the students." He folded his arms across this chest. "And I certainly couldn't recommend, in good conscience, that you offer that opportunity to the whole class."

Brandon glanced at the stack of student papers on his lap. "Well, then, I might be willing to—"

"Look, Brandon," Paxton interrupted. "Let's just say that you have my backing. She gives you trouble, you can send her to me. OK?"

Brandon wanted to say that Rebecca had been having trouble for years. He wanted to say that slapping Rebecca down for her errors was like her father slapping her down just for who she was in his life, for her annoyance, for being an error to him. He wanted to say that the academy was hurting the ones it loved. He wanted to say that what Rebecca needed was someone to listen without judgment, to pay attention to her thoughts and not her expression. For a second, he wanted to say that all those scholarly debates and articles had no relevance here, that it was about something interpersonal that he couldn't quite formulate, something important about language and self, stories and listeners. But the thought of the university enterprise that Paxton represented stopped him, and he felt utterly torn between wanting to agree with Paxton that probably the standards really did matter and he was there to uphold them, and wanting to believe that making Rebecca a successful student meant welcoming her into college instead of telling her, once again, from a new angle, that she was bad.

As Paxton glanced out toward the student waiting in the hall, Brandon realized that the conversation had ended. Thanking him for his advice, he left the office and wandered toward his favorite coffee house, Paxton's words still echoing in his head. Maybe the problem really was with the narrative, he thought. He'd have had no real dilemma downgrading, say, a short documented paper that had a lot of mistakes, even if there *was* a bit of personal anecdote mixed in. Or a resume, which is, well, *all* personal.

In a final moment of resolve, he decided that next time around he would toss out the narrative entirely. Paxton was right, it had just tricked him into too personal a response to the students' papers, and probably tricked them into too sentimental a mode of writing that did little to help them learn social psychology.

As he ordered a cappuccino and sat down at an empty table, he wondered what, in the meantime, he would write on Rebecca's paper.

QUESTIONS FOR REFLECTION AND DISCUSSION

1. What is the source of Brandon's feeling torn about Rebecca's paper? Why does the error policy appear to play such an important role?
2. What are the institutional consequences of teachers being "bound to" certain requirements and procedures but also free to develop their own courses and teach them as they wish? Is it unfair for senior-rank faculty to think their way through, and experiment with, various teaching methods but for TAs, adjuncts, part-timers, and other subordinate instructors to be denied that freedom?
3. Should writing assignments in the disciplines avoid personal responses or the use of the personal narrative?
4. If Rebecca's paper had been as personal but had described a very happy and nurturing family life, would it have been easier for Brandon to apply the error policy? If so, what are the implications of the difference?

NOTE

1. This case previously appeared under the title "Errors at Pound Ridge" on *Teaching Comp* (http://www.mhhe.com/socscience/english/tc/), a listserv sponsored by McGraw-Hill Publishers. All resemblance to actual people or events is entirely coincidental; excerpts from student papers are used with permission of the authors.

READINGS FOR FURTHER CONSIDERATION

Daiker, Donald A. "Learning to Praise." *Writing and Response: Theory, Practice, and Research.* Ed. C. M. Anson. Urbana: National Council of Teachers of English, 1989. 103–13.

Daniels, Harvey A. *Famous Last Words: The American Language Crisis Reconsidered.* Carbondale: Southern Illinois UP, 1983.

Elbow, Peter. "Ranking, Evaluating, and Liking." *College English* 55 (1993): 187–206.

Williams, Joseph M. "The Phenomenology of Error." *College Composition and Communication* 32 (1981): 152–68.

38

To Teach or Not to Teach

Martha A. Townsend

Dear University Writing Board Members,

Enclosed is my proposal for "Rural Sociology 241: The Contemporary Mennonite Community" to be offered as writing intensive next semester. There is an anomaly with regard to my proposal, however, that I should call to your attention: I am a doctoral student, about to complete my dissertation. I will go on the job market within a few months.

I am aware of the University Writing Program's longstanding regulation that prohibits graduate students teaching WI courses. But I am not deterred. I have discussed my teaching this course as WI with the department's director of Undergraduate Studies, Professor Joan Kincaid. She has fully apprised me of the pros and cons of teaching WI courses, and I am submitting this application with her knowledge and approval.

Moreover, I met at length last summer with UWP director Dr. Jonathon Neal and his colleague Ms. Carol Brown. They reviewed my course materials and we discussed the requirements of WI courses. Although they cautioned that my being approved to teach the course was unlikely, they encouraged me to apply anyway as a "test case," knowing that the Board periodically reviews its policies and thinking that my case might warrant consideration. At their invitation, I attended the three-day workshop for new WI faculty last week.

In support of my unusual petition, I'd like to point out that I have considerable college teaching experience, that I've taught this particular course three times already, and that even with a class as large as forty, I've stuck to my pedagogical principles, insisting that students write four papers that demand critical thinking. I have always received positive teaching evaluations. I was voted one of the three best GTAs at my previous institution (Stanford). And I've just received this university's Marion M. Martin Teaching Award for outstanding GTAs. My curriculum vitae is attached for your perusal.

Prof. Kincaid, Dr. Neal, and Ms. Brown all asked me the same pointed question: "Why are you so insistent upon changing your course to WI?" I have three primary answers: I feel a professional responsibility to offer courses that help students meet institutional requirements. I would enjoy having only twenty students in my class (which your guidelines require) instead of forty. And I believe that having formal WI teaching experience would strengthen my candidacy on the job market.

Even if my application fails to meet your requirements, I am pleased to know that the university places such a strong emphasis on writing and I am proud to be a member of such a community. Thank you for considering my proposal.

Sincerely,
Patricia O'Brien

"Oh, sheesh, " Craig Thurman muttered after reading the letter that fell out of the large campus envelope stuffed with WI proposals. "Here I am, brand new university Writing Board member, staring at a stack of proposals that have to be read by tomorrow. I thought this was going to be a breeze. There are more proposals than I expected, and this first one seems way out of line."

Craig's psychology colleague listened halfheartedly, then offered, "Well, at least you've got plenty to work with. When I did a stint on the board a while back, we had a hard time getting enough WI courses."

The next day, as the Writing Board's social science subcommittee began its monthly vetting of new proposals, the chair suggested they simply approve those on which everyone agreed, ensuring time for discussion of the more problematic ones. All six of the subcommittee members—Craig from psychology and one each from history, sociology, economics, political science, and communication—quickly agreed that Patricia O'Brien's proposal required further examination.

The more senior faculty in the group recalled that the sixteen-year-old WAC program had specifically disallowed WI teaching by graduate students when the first guidelines were developed. At a large public research university such as theirs, courses taught by graduate students were common. So, in the program's early days, the board had taken steps to ensure that WI courses, which could be seen as "less crucial" than faculty's "real work" (i.e., research), could not be handed off to subordinates—graduate students lacking the clout to refuse. Early program planners had also realized that if graduate students were permitted to teach WI courses, their time to degree completion could be lengthened. The university was already under pressure from the state's Board of Regents to ensure timely graduation rates. So, the stringent policy had been enacted early on. After a few challenges, which the board successfully withstood, the policy became the norm.

In recent years, though, as more and more institutions faced budget cuts, faculty retirements without replacements, and difficulty in finding enough faculty to cover all classes, Misty Mountain State University was no exception. From time to time departments would make urgent pleas for one of their "top" graduate students to teach a WI course, always a course that their undergraduates had to have in order to graduate. The university Writing Board was proud of its record in upholding its policy on these requests.

Never one to hold back, Craig started the exchange. "I found Patricia's course well put together and her cover letter well composed. She's obviously a good writer herself. What would be the harm?"

The subcommittee representative from economics, also new to the group, chimed in. "Seems to me Patricia's made a pretty good case for herself, covered all her bases. I'm not opposed to making an exception in her case."

A second-year member, from Patricia's home department of rural sociology, added, "She's a nontraditional student, very bright, and exceptionally well prepared to do this. I can vouch that she'd do a finer job than several of our senior faculty. She's certainly more committed to teaching and understands the principles of WI better than they do."

The longest-serving member of the group, from history, continued, "I've read a lot of WI proposals in my two-and-a-half years on the board, seen a lot of syllabi and writing assignments. Patricia knows what she's doing. The short dialectical papers require succinct but critical thinking. And this essay she calls a "black-white to gray shift" is innovative. The grading criteria for all assignments are clear. Best of all, the assignments directly reinforce the course goals."

"Well, yes, I'm with you on all this," averred the member from communication, "but she is a graduate student. While I don't espouse rules for rules' sake, I'm concerned that if we make an exception for Patricia, others will quickly follow. Even though she's applying for her own reasons, many departments are having trouble covering their courses. We could be headed down a slippery slope."

The political science professor was perhaps the most outspoken and blunt. "It doesn't matter how good the proposal is or how well qualified Patricia is, the board needs to stick to its guns. WAC and WI courses are just as much a faculty development issue as a student writing issue. We need to foreground WI teaching as faculty's responsibility, not GTAs, so that our own goals for this program continue to be addressed."

Quiet until all subcommittee members had spoken, as was his custom, UWP director Neal spoke up. "This is clearly one of those issues upon which reasonable people disagree, isn't it?" he said, referring to the main premise underlying one of the WI guidelines for developing writing assignments. "Let me muddy the water even more: we claim that the use of GTAs to assist WI faculty isn't just to keep the student-teacher ratio down and the workload manageable. We also claim the GTAs are receiving valuable professional development, that they're being acculturated to teach in their disciplines, with writing as a learning tool. If UWP is serious about preparing future faculty through WI teaching, doesn't Patricia's proposal take that mission one more valid step further? She's probably right that the experience will enhance her marketability."

Thoughtful, collegial discussion and disagreement continued for several minutes. Finally, convinced by the "other side," the rural sociology professor offered a way out of the dilemma: "I move that the subcommittee not put this proposal forward for approval by the board. But I also suggest that we describe the situation in detail—including our reservations—at our upcoming board meeting, so that we can revisit our policy. Perhaps others will have changed their minds. A lot has happened in higher education in the sixteen years we've been doing things this way."

Next week's meeting of the full board brought lively conversation on the topic. A representative from the humanities and fine arts subcommittee, an English professor, raised a new angle: "We encourage faculty-GTA teams to collaborate in teaching WI classes. We've even featured the most successful of these in our campus-wide newsletter, as models for accomplishing multiple goals in one class—students receive high-quality WI instruction, including the chance to observe two enthusiastic teachers debate one another in the classroom; faculty receive GTA help in grading the papers; and GTAs receive extraordinary mentoring. It wouldn't make much sense, though, to ask this GTA to 'go back' and collaborate with a faculty member—just for the sake of making it jibe with our policy—when she's already taught the class three times on her own. Maybe we should allow her to teach the class as WI, just this once. What do the rest of you think?"

QUESTIONS FOR REFLECTION AND DISCUSSION

1. What should the board do? Allow the GTA to teach the WI class? Reject the proposal and uphold the policy? What are the implications for either decision?
2. If Patricia's proposal is approved, should any limitations be placed on it? What? If Patricia's proposal is rejected, could any appeasement be offered? What?
3. Does gender factor into the discussion in any way? How?
4. What should the role of GTAs be in institutions that have WAC/WI requirements? Should this board rethink its policy?
5. How should institutions best use WAC/WI as training ground for GTAs?

READINGS FOR FURTHER CONSIDERATION

Lambert, Leo M., and Stacey Lane Tice, eds. *Preparing Graduate Students To Teach: A Guide to Programs That Improve Undergraduate Education and Develop Tomorrow's Faculty*. Washington, DC: American Association for Higher Education, 1993.

McLeod, Susan, Margot Soven, Chris Thaiss, and Eric Miraglia, eds. *WAC for the New Millennium*. Urbana: NCTE, in press.

Preparing Future Faculty Website. Washington, DC: Preparing Future Faculty National Office, 2000. ⟨http://www.preparing-faculty.org/⟩

Yancey, Kathleen Blake, and Brian Huot, eds. *Assessing Writing Across the Curriculum: Diverse Approaches and Practices*. Greenwich: Ablex, 1997.

39

Ranks, Roles, and Responsibilities
Crossing the Fine Lines in Cross-Disciplinary Mentorship

Julie M. Zeleznik, Rebecca E. Burnett, Thomas Polito, David Roberts, and John Schafer

O ur cross-disciplinary teaching/research team meets every Wednesday morning for an hour to strategize pedagogy and discuss research progress for our pair of upper-level, integrated courses—an agronomy course in soil, fertilizer, and water management and a writing course in report and proposal writing.

As a fourth-year PhD student with interests in writing across the curriculum and program assessment, Julie has been a member of the team since it was formed three years ago. Since then she has been assessing our integrated courses, and our research results are the focus of her dissertation. (A significant portion of our research efforts has been and continues to be funded by the Provost's Office at Iowa State University.)

On this particular Wednesday, Roger Kendall, an associate professor for the department of agronomy who is interested in our integrated courses approach, is sitting in on our weekly team meeting. Roger knows the members of our team and is familiar with our integrated approach to teaching these two courses. That is, he knows that our team has a mixed purpose—both pedagogy and research.

Roger has observed the agronomy course, so he understands that the instructors assign students to work in teams as certified crop advisors on their major project, a farm plan (a special kind of management recommendation report) to the owners of a large diversified farm. The students also work on individual assignments for both the agronomy course and the writing course; however, the farm plan is one of several projects that the students complete for both courses. The farm plans that students produce are complex, and the recommendations have to be agronomically sound, economically feasible, socially acceptable, and environmentally responsible.

Our discussion with Roger Kendall captures a number of critical features of our team's character and function. As we recreate the narrative of this meeting, Julie shares her thoughts about the questions and issues raised by Roger, who is, quite frankly, somewhat doubtful about the good press he's heard about our team. We have also incorporated comments from other team members as we considered Roger's questions about our individual roles and responsibilities, the flat rather than hierarchical structure of our team, and the usefulness of cross-disciplinary mentorship.

WHO'S ON OUR TEAM?

Along with Rebecca Burnett, Julie's dissertation director and a professor in the Department of English, our team also includes two colleagues from the Department of Agronomy who team teach the agronomy course—Tom Polito, an assistant professor who is also the director of the College of Agriculture's Student Services, and John Schafer, a University professor—and an associate professor from the Department of English, Dave Roberts, who teaches the writing course.

The rest of this case is presented in first person, in Julie's voice, but the case itself was collaboratively conceived and written by the entire team. Julie's observations respond to the team's conversation with Roger.

HOW ARE RESPONSIBILITIES ALLOCATED IN THE TEAM?

One way to ensure a team will break down is to have unfair allocation of responsibilities, a situation Roger pointedly asks about as our Wednesday meeting gets started.

ROGER: Since your team's purpose includes both pedagogical and research responsibilities, how are they shared by team members?

When our team started this integrated teaching approach, we knew that Tom, John, and Dave would teach the courses and that Rebecca would direct the research and well as facilitate selected discussions in the courses—e.g., group collaboration techniques, oral presentation strategies (in addition to coordinating the research). Everyone agreed that I would not have any teaching responsibilities.

TOM: In the fall semester when the classes are taught, Dave, John and I concentrate on the teaching and on coordinating our syllabi. Julie and Rebecca concentrate on gathering data. That doesn't mean we don't contribute to the research or they to our teaching approach. It's just that different people take the lead on different parts of the project. This approach works because of our mutual respect for each other's strengths and tendencies. For example, I'm an administrator and tend to focus on deadlines and organizing our weekly meetings. I always make sure I have the first agenda item for those meetings. I don't need a second one because after we get started Rebecca takes over. It's her tendency. [laughter]

ROGER: [smiling but certainly not convinced] Okay, it seems like you're all taking the lead on different aspects of the courses and the research. That makes me wonder what the students feel about this team. Julie seems to have a unique relationship with them . . . it's not teacher/student, but do students see her as a team member?

Defining my team role (as we believe the students interpret it) is complicated. From the beginning, I have felt strongly about distinguishing myself from the teaching of the courses—that is, I wanted to preserve my role as researcher-participant and to be a person in whom students could comfortably confide about the courses, teachers, and other students.

DAVE: Julie's role as not-a-teacher is critical to the success of our team. I doubt that students think of her as "on their side," necessarily, but they *do* tell her [evaluative] things they would never tell one of us, and they *do* use her as an additional resource.

REBECCA: I agree. While Julie sits in on many of the classes and all of the labs and goes on all of the on-site farm trips, students don't see her as one of the teachers. But they do see her as an expert in communication because they often ask for her opinion about how to approach their tasks.

The students, then, know me as a graduate student researcher who is interested in their perceptions about the courses. I can't be effective in collecting data about student perceptions if they don't trust me. Perhaps it is as much removing myself from the grading function as being removed from the teaching function that causes the students to be more open with me.

JOHN: From my perspective, Roger, Julie has always played a fundamental and unique role. She is our feedback mechanism. Most of us as teachers have goals and objectives and outcomes, and we develop some way of establishing a feeling as to whether or not we are accomplishing them. These mechanisms include student questions in and out of class, test results, quality of assignments, course evaluations, conversations with students outside of class, etc. But these are weak at best and subject to interpretations based on our own biases and egos.

ROGER: But how does Julie fit in all this?

JOHN: Julie's role is to get honest feedback—both positive and negative—and to help us to get a more accurate picture of whether or not we are accomplishing our goals. Since she has no teaching goals, her interpretations of student comments are more accurate and meaningful. Julie has a real talent for seeing patterns and trends in the thinking of individuals and the class over the semester.

Sometimes she can share these with us during the semester, and sometimes she must wait until the semester is over and the grades turned in before she shares. But never in my teaching career have I had such meaningful feedback. Her responses have caused several shifts in our teaching approaches and the methods we use in the course.

From a professional point-of-view, when she is able to quantify these observations and analyze them statistically, we have something that we can publish and share professionally both with our fellow teachers and our research colleagues.

My role, then, on the teaching/research team—like the roles of all of the other team members—is not straightforward. That is, our entire team takes responsibility for both pedagogy and research. For instance, while collecting data is my responsibility, analyzing and interpreting the data is our team's collective responsibility. While John and Tom take the most responsibility for teaching the agronomy course, our entire team feels responsible for the students' agronomic success and development. And similarly, while Dave takes the most responsibility for teaching the communication course, our entire team feels responsible for the students' communication success and development.

WHO'S IN CHARGE?

Clearly, hierarchy and leadership affect team function. Roger captures the point with a blunt question:

ROGER: I can see that your group members divide up the teaching/research responsibilities, but when it comes down to it—who's in charge?

TOM: Who's in charge? What day? What topic? What project? We each have unique talents, backgrounds and interests. We are fortunate that we all realize it and no one tries to dominate. Actually, each of us is in charge at some point.

As Tom notes, I don't ever get the sense that there is one person who's "in charge"; however, we all exert different levels of authority depending on the nature of the task. For instance, since I've written and updated the human subjects materials for this project and others, I feel like an authority on our team about these issues.

JOHN: Who's in charge has never been a real concern of mine. As Tom and I team-taught the agronomy course over several years we established a working relationship. We had a natural give and take, but we always reached consensus. Sometimes I bent a little more than Tom, and sometimes the opposite occurred. But I never considered "who was in charge." For me it was not a relevant question. The relevant question was, "What is best for the student?" Neither Tom nor I have such a big ego that it ever got in the way of answering that question. And neither of us was so inflexible that we were unable to come to some compromise. Whose idea ultimately prevailed was not important. In fact, by the time we were done, the final outcome was truly jointly developed. In retrospect, I was perhaps rather naive when I just assumed that when Dave joined the team he would share this view, and we would move forward as Tom and I had always done. I realize now that it could have been a disaster. But that thought never occurred to me early on, and from the very beginning it was very obvious that Dave, too, put the interest of the student and student learning above all else.

John brings up an interesting point about the nature of cross-disciplinary collaboration; that is, another benefit of being on this team has been my increased awareness of and respect for John and Tom's communication skills— the communication skills of scientists.

DAVE: From the very beginning of our project I realized that John and Tom were absolutely committed to the idea that agronomic knowledge and skills are virtually useless without strong communication skills. They do a fantastic job of weaving communication concerns into their agronomy lectures and labs. I've been delighted to see that one or both of them mark some of the same things on papers that I mark. And not just grammar and mechanics—I'm talking improper use of headings, insufficient claim support, lack of professionalism in document design.

The cross-disciplinary nature of our group also puts an interesting slant on the issue of disciplinarity and professionalism. Because of John and Tom's expertise in agronomy, I'm learning what their discipline values, and I'm afforded a view of the ways in which those outside professional communication value what we do in our field. The reality is that this is a team of professionals—all five of us—who value collaboration and respect the expertise that each of us shares with the group.

WHAT'S CROSS-DISCIPLINARY MENTORING?

One of the unexpected benefits of my participation in this teaching/research team is the cross-disciplinary mentoring. On our team, we've come to define cross-disciplinary mentoring this way (a definition, by the way, not limited to graduate students or junior colleagues):

Cross-disciplinary mentoring gives colleagues from various disciplines and professions a chance to learn from each other as we seek a common goal. Cross-disciplinary mentoring nurtures and encourages professional growth and development, while respecting the experience and background of each other. Such relationships have no place for misdirected personal egos or for professional snobbery toward other disciplines or colleagues. Cross-disciplinary mentoring is interaction that includes opportunities for engaging in professional activities, modeling of professional behavior, receiving support during new and/or difficult tasks, and learning about alternative approaches and perspectives.

During my three years on this team, I've had many opportunities to engage in professional activities not available to many graduate students, including collaborative presentations at a number of national conferences, not only in professional communication but also in agronomy and education. Additionally, I've seen professional behavior modeled in multiple settings, and I've seen members of our team reinforce the importance of establishing friendships and providing time for personal concerns. I've seen the team take time for self-reflection as a group. I've been encouraged and supported in new tasks—for example, developing skill in research methods such as conducting surveys, interviewing study participants, and utilizing statistical analyses.

I came to this project with experience in qualitative research, but due in large part to cross-disciplinary mentoring, I've learned to appreciate the value of using both quantitative and qualitative measures for answering research questions; I now believe that collecting both quantitative and qualitative data provides a stronger, richer base for analysis and interpretation. This idea of cross-disciplinary mentoring was completely new to Roger.

ROGER: I can understand that Rebecca and Dave feel responsible for your professional development, but it sounds as if Tom and John may play a role, too. What's that all about?

They all share in mentoring me in various ways. I feel free to seek advice from them, depending on their experiences and areas of expertise.

REBECCA: I am immensely grateful to Dave, John, and Tom for sharing in Julie's mentoring, which, in fact, benefits us all. Her career will be far better because of the experiences she has had as a team member. The other team members complement my dual responsibility: as a dissertation director and as the principal researcher for the project.

As Julie's dissertation director, I try to provide her with support and guidance to make the very challenging task of researching and writing a dissertation exciting rather than daunting, manageable rather than unwieldy, articulatable rather than mysterious.

As the principal researcher mentoring a junior colleague, I want to provide Julie with experiences that she'll need as a researcher: understanding the exigencies of research such as politics and funding; situating our work in relation to existing theory and research; designing a research plan; forming and revising critical research questions; collecting, cataloguing, and managing immense amounts of data; complying with human subjects requirements; understanding research budgets; analyzing data to respond to the research questions; and shaping results into formal presentations and publications.

But I don't do these things alone because the team is involved (though not necessarily at the same time; for example, the course instructors don't see student data during the semester they're teaching those students).

DAVE: I'm a member of Julie's PhD Program-of-Study committee, so some of the mentoring I do reinforces what Rebecca tells her, but because my own outlook is so driven by practice, I talk to her about hands-on teaching issues, concerns about the job market, and even give her advice about handling her comprehensive exams. And I've taught her to cuss like a muleskinner, too.

JOHN: Again I guess my naiveté is showing, but I never thought about myself as a mentor, and yet I can see from the conversation that surely I am. My concept has been that Julie could make unique and important contributions to this team. As a less experienced member, she sometimes needed a little more coaching. Perhaps at times we had to suggest things that with experience would become obvious to her.

Throughout my career, I have taught a large introductory class and of necessity worked with TAs and full-time instructors below the rank of professor. Yes, I played the role of mentor to them. That is, I provided training and direction for them until their experience and understanding allowed them to play a more independent role in the overall teaching effort. But at the same time, from day one, I considered each of them to be fellow teachers who had insights and experiences that would be beneficial to the students and to me.

In many ways in my mind I placed Rebecca, Dave, Tom, and Julie in that role. If I paid attention, I could learn something valuable. And while Julie had less experience and we needed to share more with her, she did have experiences to share and she has unique abilities. Therefore she had something of value to share with me and to teach me.

TOM: I agree with John. The strongest point I can make is that Julie is not the only one being mentored. We all are. Julie is also doing some mentoring. She has certainly mentored us agronomy types on visual communication when we developed our posters. In addition, I have tried to help her better understand the communication needs and quantitative research biases of science faculty. It is inconceivable to me that someone could be doing what we are and not believe in cross-disciplinary mentoring.

WHAT'S A TYPICAL OCCURRENCE?

This cross-disciplinary mentoring plays out every week in lots of different ways. One particular incident that occurred during the previous semester not only demonstrates some of the ways this cross-disciplinary mentoring works, but also demonstrates a way that authority is shared.

During one of last semester's team meetings, Tom reminded our team about the national Agronomy Society of America (ASA) conference:

TOM: The deadline to submit proposals for the next ASA conference is rapidly approaching. I'd like us to submit a poster presentation proposal that focuses on our research results. Last year we presented the nature of our integrated courses approach at the ASA, so I'd like to focus on what our courses have accomplished since then.

DAVE: Well, we certainly have research results! We should be able to submit a crackerjack poster proposal.

The year before, our team presented our integrated courses project in a poster session at the ASA conference. Since I had a class in visual rhetoric and had read about scientific poster design but had never designed one myself, Tom helped me to prepare the team's poster presentation. I enjoyed working on the poster design, and I was looking forward to designing another poster for this year's ASA conference.

TOM: I'm concerned, though, because the folks who attend ASA—professional agronomists, scientists, academics—expect statistical support, and up until this point our results has been largely qualitative.

REBECCA: I won't have the statistics you need calculated before the proposal is due, but I can certainly have them before the poster needs to be done. I'll call the Stat Lab right after our meeting and set up a meeting for Julie and me.

HOW DOES OUR TEAM COLLABORATE ON THE POSTER DESIGN?

Once our ASA proposal was accepted, Tom and I exchanged a sketch of the preliminary poster design. After that, I assumed the primary responsibility for creating and refining the poster, which would eventually be printed on a color laser printer on a single 40" × 60" piece of paper. Virtually every aspect of creating the poster, which took about six weeks, was in some way collaborative.

- *Design and visuals.* Was I the designer? While I was responsible for creating a professional poster for the ASA convention, I was not solely responsible. I came to the task with an academic background in visual rhetoric, with the experience of seeing dozens upon dozens of agronomy posters in Agronomy Hall where we meet every week, and the experience of assisting with last year's poster design. I took the photos used on the poster with a digital camera on one of several field trips to the client's farm.

- *Writing and editing.* Was I the writer and editor? I was responsible for writing and editing all the text on the poster, but I drew on existing text. For example, the research question was created by our team; I refined it. The source text came from various existing documents drafted by our entire team: funding proposals, annual reports, conference proposals. I selected appropriate sections from these texts and edited them. I sent drafts of the poster electronically to the team members for multiple rounds of comments. Naturally, everyone tweaked the design and the text. I synthesized and incorporated the suggestions that came from the team during each round of review (three rounds of full or partial review and revision).

- *Statistics.* Was I the statistician? The statistics came from a study Rebecca and I had designed and conducted. The study had been approved by the team (and approved by the university's human subjects committee). The actual calculations were done by Mack Shelley, director of RISE, one of the support units on campus. We all collaborated to ensure that the statistics made sense to the intended audience, complying with their expectations and conventions.
- *Ownership.* Was this *my* project? No, it was a team project. Everyone had a vested interest, but Tom and John had an especially strong interest because it was a poster for their professional conference and they knew the audience best.

WHAT'S THE FUTURE FOR OUR TEAM?

Our team continues to teach and research the integrated agronomy and English courses. Roger Kendall left our team meeting that morning with a better sense of the ways in which we balance pedagogy and research, maintain the team's collaborative nature, and promote cross-disciplinary mentorship. However, he still had important questions regarding our team's approach.

ROGER: Well, I'm impressed that your team is able to collaborate and provide mentorship in this way. However, I'm not convinced that some central political questions have been answered regarding the ASA poster. For instance, was Julie just serving as a technician creating this poster? Was she just a pair of hands completing mechanical tasks?

What about Roger's questions? Basically he doesn't understand the dynamics that take place within our team. His searching for some hidden "political question" comes from, perhaps, his own experience where he has observed that personal ambition, egos, or political agendas of others tended to get in the way.

Even though Roger's concluding questions show continuing doubt, he raises important issues about the fine line that must be considered in cross-disciplinary mentoring. How would you answer them?

QUESTIONS FOR REFLECTION AND DISCUSSION

1. *Defining and Sharing Authority.* One point made by the members of this cross-disciplinary team is that defining authority and discussing ways in which to share that authority continue to be critical tasks. In what ways can you share authority in your own group?

2. *Collaborating Across Ranks and Disciplines.* One of the tensions in cross-disciplinary collaboration may occur when members have unequal ranks. What seems to have contributed to the relatively flat team structure of this group? How can collaboration work—within disciplines as well as across disciplines—when ranks are unequal?

3. *Learning About Alternative Approaches/Perspectives.* One way to learn about alternative approaches to pedagogical or research issues is to collaborate with colleagues outside of your discipline or area of expertise. Once you become involved in a project with others, what are useful ways to encourage them to share their approaches/ perspectives with you? In what ways can you offer your expertise to others?

4. *Defining and Demonstrating Professionalism.* What defines professionalism? What's the fine line between providing opportunities for graduate students and making graduate students do all of the work? In what ways can we demonstrate professionalism to others? In terms of demonstrating professionalism, why is modeling of professional behavior important? How can such modeling be useful to junior colleagues?

5. *Balancing Pedagogy and Research.* In what ways can we define the fine line between pedagogy and research? How can colleges and universities better support this balance? An important way to balance pedagogy and research is to learn and receive support from others during new and/or difficult tasks. What are effective ways to encourage support from others and to provide support in your own cross-disciplinary teams?

6. *Mentoring Across Disciplines.* Why is cross-disciplinary mentorship beneficial for WAC/CAC? How can you define the line between cross-disciplinary support and disciplinary territoriality? How can cross-disciplinary mentoring be prompted or encouraged?

READINGS FOR FURTHER CONSIDERATION

Barton, Ellen. "Design in Observational Research on the Discourse of Medicine: Toward Disciplined Interdisciplinarity." *Journal of Business and Technical Communication* 15.3 (2001): 309–32.

Shapiro, Nancy S., and Jodi H. Levine. *Creating Learning Communities: A Practical Guide to Winning Support, Organizing for Change, and Implementing Programs.* San Francisco: Jossey-Bass, 1999.

Part 8

Tending the Garden
Scenes of Program Development

40

Been There, Done That
A Problem in WAC Funding

Chris Thaiss

rofessor Kerry Ross has been director of WAC at Northeast State for ten years. Ross, who has a talent for working with faculty from across disciplines as well as a solid reputation as a teacher, has built the program steadily, from early, unfunded "get acquainted" meetings for faculty through funded workshops and on to guiding the design and progress of an ambitious "writing-intensive" curriculum proposal. After unanimous passage of this proposal by the Faculty Senate three years ago, Ross has led a university-wide committee toward implementation, meanwhile continuing to lead workshops and edit a newsletter. Ross has tenure in the English department and teaches two courses a semester in addition to running the WAC program.

Funding of the program has steadily increased, but has always been precarious in terms of sources and reporting procedures. Every year, Ross has "cobbled together" support from offices on campus. There have been two outside grants over the years, from a state agency and a private source, and these provided most of the support for faculty development for four years early in the program. In recent years, the most consistent source of funding has been the Office of the Provost, which sponsored the course release for Ross; paid for workshops, the newsletter, and some travel; and provided secretarial assistance on an "as needed" basis. Ross had an excellent working relationship with the provost, who saw WAC as an important aspect of the teaching mission of the university, so gave money for the projects the director proposed. Ross sometimes supplemented the provost's support with contributions from specific departments for activities pertinent to their curriculum, such as department "brown bags."

Ross would have preferred a more stable, less varied funding situation, particularly an annual budget and the ability to hire staff support, but tolerated the unpredictability as long as the money and ad hoc staff assistance were forthcoming. Now, however, the provost has departed to become president at another school. During the interviews of candidates for the vacant position, Ross had been sure to meet the candidates and get their views on WAC, and the person selected for the job had had experience with WAC at her former school and had spoken to Ross positively about it as a model of cross-curricular cooperation.

Ross is now about to meet with the new provost, Eve Newman, to discuss funding of activities for the coming year. Now that the writing-intensive curriculum has been in place for a year, Ross wants to bring the provost up to date on its scope and successes, and then to outline a plan for assessment and continuing training of faculty to teach the WI courses. The plan calls for a slight increase in support over the previous year, but Ross is confident of a positive response, particularly because the implementation has gone smoothly and faculty have been so pleased by the workshops.

After a few pleasantries, Professor Ross gets down to business. "I hope you've had a chance to read the outline I sent. I'll be happy to fill in any items and answer any questions. I brought along an extra copy, if you'd like to have it." Ross is always nervous in these budget meetings, but tries, as usual, to project a sense of being at ease.

The provost waves away, not impatiently, the proffered document, and smiles. "Thanks, but I have my copy right here. I'm glad you sent it. I can see why you're proud of what's been accomplished. When Provost Oldham was briefing me, he mentioned WAC, especially the new requirement, as a model of what we might try to accomplish in some other areas, such as oral communication and, of course, technology. When I was meeting with the Board of Regents during my interview in the spring, there was considerable interest in our improving the curriculum in both those areas. Apparently, you've also done a good job of getting your message to the board, because one of the members—do you know Judge Stern?—mentioned the good job we were doing with writing. Believe me, it's rare when a board at any college approves of student writing. Hat's off to you."

Newman sits back in her chair, no doubt proud of being able to relay a compliment. Ross can see the executive psychology on display: by complimenting the program, even though she has had nothing to do with the achievement, Newman is already taking credit. "That's OK," thinks Ross. "But let's see if she'll earn the credit she's taking." Ross wants to feel at ease, but the voice of pessimism is saying, "I haven't heard anything about the request yet. Get to the point."

Ross approaches from a slight angle. "Wow! Thanks for sharing that. It's great to know that your new boss has confidence in what you're doing." Smile meets smile. Ross goes on: "Of course, the credit doesn't belong to me. The committee and I could never have gotten all the approvals and implemented the program at all, if we didn't have the cooperation and understanding of all the chairs—and if there hadn't been faculty in every department who could teach the courses in a really writing-intensive way. We have the faculty development workshops and the follow-up support to thank for that. You know, it's quite common at schools for a WI requirement to be approved and then for it to fall apart because the support mechanisms don't continue—faculty development workshops, a program director, rewards for good teaching."

Ross is looking for a nod, and receives several during the monologue. Newman leans forward, elbows on desk. She's warming to the subject. "I couldn't agree more. That's one of the most attractive things about your model. From the annual reports you sent—I really appreciate those evaluation statistics—you know how rare it is, I trust, for administrators to get data like that—anyway, from those reports it's pretty clear that you've created a strong foundation that'll make it much easier for the departments to keep up the momentum. How many faculty have been through those workshops over the past few years? A couple hundred? That's a really large nucleus to spread the word, almost a critical mass, I'd say."

Ross wants to agree, but doesn't like the sound of this enthusiasm. "Out of two thousand faculty, with all that turnover of adjuncts and TA's? I'd like to think we had a critical mass, but I'd have to say we're far from it. I guess I'll feel more comfortable when the program has been in place a few more years and we've had a chance not only to train more faculty but also to give some of the experienced faculty the chance to work with their colleagues in the development sessions."

The provost looks bemused, shaking her head slightly, and chuckles. "I can understand your concern—you wouldn't be a good director if you didn't feel that way—but I can assure you that in comparison with most other initiatives I've been around for the last twenty years, this one has a strong core that I don't see crumbling. One of the beauties of the WI concept, as I understand it, is that it decentralizes responsibility for writing; it respects differences among disciplines and authorizes them to teach writing according to their needs. I'm right about that, aren't I?"

Ross can't believe it. The provost is actually using the antifoundational rhetoric of WAC to argue against continuing the program administration. How can the WAC director get the provost to see that spending $13K on a one-course release and on nominal stipends and printing costs will ensure that decentering, not undermine it? Meanwhile, the optimist in Ross remembers that Newman has not yet categorically denied funding, so the director decides to play along. "Yes, you're right, but one of the tricky things to balance in WAC, as in any cross-curricular endeavor, is disciplinary autonomy with a sense of sound principles that cut across those boundaries. I don't know if you've ever had a chance to take part in a WAC workshop, but one of its most exciting aspects is how consensus is reached, as well as how the readings and the presenters can give faculty ways to work with student writing so that each person doesn't have to reinvent the wheel."

Newman nods reflectively, with wrinkled brow, at Ross's words. She pauses before responding, then speaks in a speculative tone. "That makes good sense." Another reflective pause. "Let me propose something. I do think that the foundation you and your associates have built is strong. I don't know Northeast as well as you do, of course, but I do trust the ability and good will of faculty to use good ideas in productive ways—and to share them with their colleagues. Now I'm not saying that WAC doesn't deserve continued funding, and what you're asking for isn't a lot in terms of our whole budget, but, to be honest, I'm under orders from the board and the president—this is part of why I was hired—to use my discretionary funding to support worthwhile new initiatives. This doesn't mean leaving the worthwhile continuing programs high and dry, but it does mean my looking for ways to have the colleges and the departments take more direct financial and monitoring responsibility for some programs the provost has funded in the past. That's also a way of giving them more freedom, and I believe that's the way academic administration should work."

Ross is getting that sinking feeling; the new provost has evidently read her Orwell—she uses "freedom" in an interesting way. The provost continues: "So what I'd like to do is this. I'm going to give the funding for your course release to Dean Klymer in Arts and Sciences, your home college, and let you and your chair work it out with the dean as to its best use. That way you won't be tied to doing WAC direction forever, which is what you'd do as long as the funding stayed with us, and the dean and your chair will have autonomy in this. What do you think?" Newman has leaned forward again. Her tone, which began as speculative, has ended in a good impression of the car salesman who has just tallied all the "free extras" and knocked off all the discounts and miraculously arrived at just about the sticker price. Ross visualizes the provost sliding a sheet of figures across the desk and asking, all smiles, "So, we have a deal?"

Ross momentarily imagines asking, "What if I wanted to direct WAC forever?", and inwardly laughs. Already knowing the answer, Ross asks anyway, "Will we keep the funding for the newsletter and the workshops?" The provost takes on a sympathetic look and shakes her head. "I'd love to keep that money, but it's already gone to the vice president for information technology, to use for Web workshops for faculty. Incidentally, he'll probably be in touch with you in the next week or so. Bill would like to pick your brain on the interface between the technology and teaching. I told him that you were the expert on faculty development at this campus. You won't have to do that for free, by the way. Bill said he could pay you as a consultant."

Now it is Ross's turn to nod without meaning. "So I'm assuming that you're saying that any workshop we do for the WI courses will have to be paid for out of college and department budgets." "Yes. At this point in the development of WAC, as strong as it is, we'll be depending on the judgment of the colleges and departments to determine what they need. Of course, if a dean comes to me to argue for help with a WAC-related initiative, I'll listen. Oh, yes, and I 'll be happy to write a memo to the deans praising the program and encouraging their support." Once again, the smiling provost leans back in her chair, the leather crackling for emphasis, her hands resting on the arms.

QUESTIONS FOR REFLECTION AND DISCUSSION

1. In the context of this dialogue, how is "WAC" being defined, both explicitly and implicitly? What seems to be Ross's definition? Newman's? Are there other ways of defining WAC that neither party seems aware of and that could have made this meeting less adversarial and more collaborative?

2. Analyze the provost's arguments to Ross. In what ways is Newman laying out a reasonable picture of university priorities, and in what ways may she be just exemplifying a "been there, done that" viewpoint that disregards the continuing needs of a strong program?

3. Note all the ways in which "funding" and "support" are defined and illustrated in this case. Compare them with all the ways that you and others are familiar with from your own academic or other professional experience. How can you benefit from what you learn here of Ross's success as a program director? What might Ross learn from you and from others considering this case?

4. Newman names oral communication and technology as programs in need of funding for faculty development and, as it turns out, in competition with WAC for funds. To what extent is it accurate to portray all these as separate programs in need of separate budgets? What more collaborative models might be useful here? Consider your own experience with the same or similar competitions/collaborations.

5. Rate Newman's techniques in orchestrating this meeting. Is she successful in making Ross feel like a valued member of the university and in showing that she values WAC? How and how not? How might she have reframed the dialogue—and perhaps have redistributed the funds—so that Ross would not have felt that WAC was being undercut, and so that the new ventures were funded also? (If helpful to you, consider these questions from your perspective as one who, like Eve Newman, has to consider requests for funding or approvals from people who look to you as authority or administrator.)

6. Looking into the crystal ball, what is your prognosis for WAC at Northeast State? With Ross's standard methods now unfunded by the customary source, and with authority and responsibility given to colleges and departments, what steps seem vital toward keeping the WI requirement meaningfully implemented? Should the effort be made?

7. If Kerry Ross were to seek your advice on a next step, what's the most important suggestion you would offer? Is this advice that you currently follow? How has it worked for you and others?

READINGS FOR FURTHER CONSIDERATION

McLeod, Susan, and Eric Miraglia. "WAC in the Next Millennium: The Challenges of a Changing Culture in Higher Education." *WAC for the New Millennium: Strategies for/of Continuing Writing Across the Curriculum Programs*. Ed. Susan McLeod et al. Urbana: National Council of Teachers of English, 2001.

Sandler, Karen Wiley. "Starting a WAC Program: Strategies for Administrators." *Writing Across the Curriculum: A Guide to Developing Programs*. Ed. Susan H. McLeod and Margot Soven. Thousand Oaks: Sage, 1992. ⟨http://aw.colostate.edu/books/mcleod_soven⟩

Thaiss, Christopher. "Launching a WAC Program." *The Harcourt Brace Guide to Writing Across the Curriculum*. Fort Worth: Harcourt Brace, 1998. 58–68.

Walvoord, Barbara. "The Future of WAC." *College English* 58.1 (1996): 58–79

41

A Chemistry Experiment in Writing

Carol Rutz

"Everyone's trying these interdisciplinary freshman seminars, so I thought I could put one together." Miriam Grant tilted her head and scanned the book spines on her office shelves as she talked. Miriam, an associate professor of chemistry, had just submitted a course proposal for a freshman seminar on energy production and consumption. Because her course lacked specifics on writing assignments, Larry West, the WAC coordinator at their small liberal arts college, was visiting during her office hours to offer any help she might need.

Running her finger along a shelf, Miriam continued, "I'm trying to scale down a course I did for our junior chemistry majors' colloquium last year. Those students had a good time with field trips to power plants and so on, but they also had the background to evaluate critically what they saw and heard. I'm worried about preparing freshmen well enough to take advantage of those opportunities. I don't know. Maybe it's too much to expect. And I'm really nervous about coming up with enough writing assignments to qualify for 'writing intensive' designation. Without that, no one will register for it. But if it really isn't a writing-intensive course, I'm wasting my time."

Larry closed his eyes and bit his lower lip. He didn't like the sound of that—wasting her time?

Miriam stepped back from the shelves and wearily looked at the papers and books heaped on her desk. She lifted her hair off her shoulders, shrugged, sat down, and started rummaging through a pile. Setting that pile on the floor, she started on another one.

"I'm not sure how to think about the assignments, but that's not because of a shortage of material. Where did I put the—? Here it is!" Miriam pulled a heavy paperbound book out of the middle of a tottering pile and flipped the pages for Larry to see. "This is magnificent data I got from the Department of Energy. This whole big book is full of information on every power-generating facility in the country, plus topographical, census, agricultural, and other stuff—all in one place. If students wanted to do projects that correlated population and energy distribution, for instance, they could start here. And I have lots of other stuff, too—not to mention all the usual library resources.

"In a way," she mused, "that's the problem—too many sources. Too much good information to be analyzed The projects I think about as a research chemist are more appropriate for a senior comprehensive project—or a PhD thesis—than a first-year course that has to get students into working in a college mode."

Larry listened to Miriam without comment, but he was getting impatient. She seemed to need to talk through the problem, and he wasn't sure whether to direct her with advice, or just let her explore by thinking aloud. But now she was out of steam, so he decided to nudge her.

Clearing his throat, Larry leaned toward her desk. "Miriam, it would help me to know what you think your course has to accomplish."

"You mean what I want the students to learn?"

"Well, that, and also what you think the college expects—you keep talking about the freshman seminar as if you had specific ideas about what it is and how it's supposed to function in the curriculum."

Miriam sat back in her chair. "Oh. OK. Well, like I said, we're supposed to, well—hmm. Maybe I'm making this harder than it has to be. My idea—and I'm realizing as I talk to you that maybe it's just my idea—is that a freshman seminar does a number of things, especially if it's writing intensive. It gives students their first college experience, a place where they are sort of socialized into college behavior. They have to learn how to get their homework done, discuss in class, meet deadlines, use office hours and help sessions, and that kind of general academic survival stuff. Are you with me so far?"

Larry forced himself to smile. "Completely. Go on, Professor!"

Miriam turned to look out the window. "But this isn't kindergarten. It's college. Students should expect to work hard and to perform at a level that exceeds the expectations in high school. They have to manage their reading, writing, labs, and other work without a lot of babysitting. OK, everyone knows that. The students know it too. But a freshman seminar carries some other baggage, or at least I think it does."

"Baggage?" asked Larry, lifting an eyebrow.

Miriam shifted in her chair and looked straight at Larry. "Yeah. Baggage. No one admits it openly, but even though these seminars are billed as 'interdisciplinary,' they are often recruiting vehicles for majors. Some departments are very adept at designing courses that draw students into the major, sometimes before they have a chance to experience introductory courses in other disciplines. I don't want to overstate this, but let me put it this way: I don't want to be accused of seducing people into a chemistry major by offering a course with lots of practical, exciting, politically relevant material and writing assignments that don't remotely resemble real writing in chemistry."

"Miriam, that's baloney. We're talking about a small freshman seminar here. How could it possibly make that kind of difference to anybody?" Larry uncrossed his legs and glanced at his watch.

Miriam eyed him warily. "I don't know. We've talked in the department about ways to attract more majors, and I get the impression that my colleagues would like to see people from my seminar choose chemistry as a major. If that happened, the department would have more numbers, but would the students really know what they're getting into?"

"Hold it, Miriam. You lost me. You say your department wants more majors, and they think your seminar will bring some in?"

"No one would put it quite that directly, but yes, that's exactly what I think is going on."

Larry snorted. "So what? Is there anything wrong with your first-year students, some of whom probably will have registered for the course specifically because it has to do with chemistry, something they're interested in—is there something wrong with their wanting to pursue chemistry after seeing some 'exciting, practical' (to use your words) applications?"

Miriam shook her head. "No, not 'wrong.' But I worry about misleading them. I worry that if they take a course that has a field trip once a week to a nuclear plant, a garbage burner and so on, that they will get the wrong idea about chemistry as a major. They may start thinking of chemistry as a field that doesn't require rigorous background knowledge, sophisticated analysis, and all the rest. If I had them writing up formal field notes and proposing research questions, that would be one thing. But that kind of writing goes against the goals—the institutional goals—of the freshman seminars."

Larry frowned and rubbed his chin. "Let's talk more about the writing you want to do in this class. You're trying to mix the whole liberal arts project with an invitation to major in chemistry?"

Miriam winced. "Oof. When you put it that way, the problem seems really daunting. I just don't know what to assign. I'm planning readings on energy from a range of perspectives: industry, regulatory agencies, politicians, journalists. We will be doing these field trips, which should give students a completely new perspective on energy production. Most of them come in with a conservation bias that assumes that a power company is an evil, capitalist entity. You can imagine."

Larry nodded. "Indeed I can." Privately, he thought, "Get to the point, please."

"It's not that I'm trying to win them for a particular political position, but I do want them to begin to appreciate the complexity of energy production and consumption. They need to know more about the science that goes into it, as well as the relevant regulations, applications, and the controversial stuff like waste management. As you can see, any of those issues would lead to marvelous research questions. But for freshmen, who are supposed to be writing in ways that will help them in their college careers—what kind of writing will work? How I can get them to use the material and the field experiences in their writing without making them do formal chemistry? And if they don't write the way chemists write, how do I make it clear that these problems are still very much the kind of thing that chemists do, even if the product the students produce is different? How do I reconcile the institution's need to have students write in many disciplines for many purposes with my department's need for more good majors?"

Larry stood up and reached for his baseball cap. "Look, Miriam, you said it yourself. You're making this a whole lot harder than it has to be. If you can't pull a freshman seminar together using topics that chemists find interesting, there's something wrong with you. Honestly, I get so tired of experts who can't tolerate the dilution of their holy disciplines. I'm surprised you guys over here deal with freshmen at all. And I'm surprised that you get any majors with the attitude you have!"

Miriam stared at him and gripped the arms of her chair. "Now just a minute, Larry. You came over here to help me with writing assignments. I don't need a lecture on chemistry as some sort of elite calling. That's not the point!"

"Oh?" sneered Larry. "Isn't it? Listen to yourself—and your colleagues in this department before you dismiss the charge of elitism. You people aren't interested in writing, you're interested in recruiting majors, pre-meds, whatever. And you want to brainwash them into your exclusive, disciplinary notions of 'rigor' and 'sophisticated analysis.' Give me a break."

Miriam leapt to her feet. "Larry, you're being unfair and obnoxious!"

"I suppose I am," Larry replied with a grim smile. "But imagine what it feels like to have people approach you with WI course designs as self-serving as yours. All you want is enrollment—and chemistry majors. Your high and mighty talk about socialization and the other functions of freshman seminars—it's all smoke. Well, lady, I see through it, and on behalf of our incoming students, I'm aiming the fire extinguisher right at you. Forget about your WI designation—I'm not approving it. Go ahead and design a course to lure in majors. I wish you the best of luck."

With a tug on his cap, Larry made for the door. Miriam glared in his wake.

QUESTIONS FOR REFLECTION AND DISCUSSION

1. Do you see problems with Miriam's plan for her first-year seminar? What suggestions could you offer her?

2. As you think about WAC models, how does Miriam's course compare with courses you are familiar with, especially in the sciences?

3. In your experience, do first-year seminars affect students' choice of major? How often? In what ways?

4. Larry's response to Miriam suggests some personal and institutional history that emerges only obliquely in this case. If you were to fill in the blanks, what would you imagine Larry has encountered at his school that might account for his outburst?

READINGS FOR FURTHER CONSIDERATION

Day, Robert A. *How to Write and Publish a Scientific Paper*. 4th ed. Phoenix: Oryx, 1994.

Fulwiler, Toby, and Art Young. *Programs That Work: Models and Methods for Writing Across the Curriculum*. Portsmouth: Boynton/Cook, 1990.

Walvoord, Barbara E., Linda Lawrence Hunt, H. Fil Dowling, Jr., and Joan D. McMahon. *In the Long Run: A Study of Faculty in Three Writing-Across-the-Curriculum Programs*. Urbana: National Council of Teachers of English, 1997.

42

Thoughts from the Rank and File

Chris M. Anson

Whoah, Chikilah Johnson thought as she slipped another memo into the thickening file folder on her desk. At first the Writing Task Force had *wanted* to be inundated with responses to their call for reactions to the new university-wide WAC proposal. It would be a sign of engagement. But after glancing through some of the notes and email messages she'd received over the past week, she realized that she and her colleagues had one heck of a task ahead.

Two Rivers State University wasn't known for its great curricular innovations, Chikilah had to admit; but it was a solid campus with an assortment of decent majors and some pretty good leadership higher up—well, at least after the campus had been blessed with the retirement of Sanford Brown, their last provost. She recalled the joke about Sanford that her colleague Thomas Averton had shared: Question: How many Sanford Browns does it take to change a lightbulb? Answer: What, *change*???

Over the past year, TRU State, as it was affectionately known, had listened to its faculty all too well, about the questionable retention rate of freshmen, about the cruddy condition of the labs in Peale Hall, about the lack of adequate lighting along the woodland walk between the union and one of the dorm complexes . . . and about the generally pathetic state of student writing. These were the kinds of gripes that any campus hears from its members, of course, and although most of the complaints didn't reflect any serious deficiencies in the curriculum, the frequent refrain about writing skills had the administration disconcerted. Lighting could be fixed with some reallocated funds. The Peale Hall labs could get a makeover with some of the money raised by the capital campaign. The new freshman orientation and mentoring program, and a suite of exciting, limited-enrollment first-year seminars, would almost certainly increase retention—or provide some good data about what to do next. But writing ability . . . this was uncharted territory at TRU. Worse, it wasn't just the faculty who were griping. The chancellor had experienced it first-hand during a leadership forum involving local businesses and nonprofits: graduates made adequate new employees, but their writing? Frowns, winks, whispers.

In creating the TRU State Writing Task Force, newly arrived provost Derek Hadley had chosen wisely. Its eight members were some of the most persistently outspoken critics of students' writing abilities. "Hadley's Eight," they were soon dubbed. Well, seven, Chikilah mused: even though she'd been named chair, she didn't quite fit the mold of her other task force members, most of whom had at least ten years on her and five of whom were men. But those seven were quite a bunch, she had to admit. You'd have thought that students in the 1960s all must have been Pulitzer-prize candidates, the way the task force members invoked the years when TRU State students could *really* think and had a gift for putting it all down on paper. By God, those were writers, they intoned, almost dreamy-eyed.

But Hadley had indeed chosen well. In selecting faculty vocal about writing, he also avoided the fingerpointers. Instead of blaming the English department, the high schools, the elementary schools, day care, TV, video games, and parents who didn't read to their kids, the task force members were often heard to place the blame on a lack of student experience with writing in all disciplines—*at TRU*. Stu Leppert, from history, repeated a sort of writing mantra at committee meetings and luncheons: "*I*, Stu Leppert, teach writing in my history courses. What do *you* do?" And so it was with the others, from Martha Paltrow's insistence that every one of her students write a major research paper in biology to Kent Saggett's "daily themes" in international relations.

Provost Hadley had given the Writing Task Force a simple charge: in six weeks, get a bead on the prospects of saturating this curriculum with writing, he said. Chikilah remembered thinking about that word, "saturation." It was like what she told her nine-year-old about the word "hate." "Hate's a very strong word, Paris," she'd tell him. "Use it carefully." Saturation. Strong word. She hoped it wouldn't set up a mass drowning.

Still, the task force didn't have to be all that radical. Get a bead on it. Ask the faculty about writing. Ask them, the task force finally decided, to react to a simple prospect, stated in plain language: How do you respond to the idea of increasing attention to writing in your department?

The first meeting was pleasant and relaxed. And unlike so many of Chikilah's experiences in "writing something by committee," this one took less than an hour. By the end of the meeting, Chikilah was feeling pretty good about her role as chair: she'd taken care of business, collaboratively drafted a call for responses, and done it all without a word of contention among her colleagues.

By the end of the next hour, she had sent off the email version of the task force's note to Shi-Pau Yang, the administrator of the "magic list," which got an email posting into the mailbox of every faculty member on campus, on sabbatical, on medical leave, heck, on retirement: even the emeriti got it. And now it had just appeared on her own computer. She smiled and leaned back in her chair. Good; the deed was done.

Subject: Responses to Task Force Charge
Date: Thurs, 08 April 14:59:42
From: WAC-COMM
To: FACLIST@TRU.edu

Colleagues:

As you may know, a faculty task force has been formed at the direction of Provost Hadley to begin exploring questions relating to undergraduate students' writing abilities and experiences. At our first meeting, the Task Force agreed to gather ideas, impressions, and recommendations from the faculty about the current state of undergraduate writing across campus, the sorts of strategies that we might productively pursue to address identified problems, and the quality of students' current experiences with writing.

We want to emphasize that we are in the early stages of planning—our next few meetings will be largely exploratory. To help us with our work, we are inviting you to give us your thoughts. How would a university-wide program to increase attention to writing across our campus affect you, your department, and your work? What are some ways in which we might pay greater attention to writing in our courses and majors?

Please rest assured that we will hold your response in confidence if you mark it so, and the Task Force will send you a personal response to your ideas and feedback based on our discussion of your comments.

We thank you in advance for your help with this important issue and look forward to your responses.

Chikilah Johnson, Chair

By the next morning, the emails and notes were starting to come in—a good sign, Chikilah initially thought, that faculty at least were interested enough to respond. The first had been from Terence Jones, professor of astronomy. Chikilah had met him during a term on the University Senate but hadn't gotten to know him very well. She noticed that Jones had sent his message in the wee hours of the morning after her request went out.

Subject: Writing at TRU
Date: Fri, 09 April 2:18:42
From: Tjones@TRU.edu
To: WAC-COMM@TRU.edu

This is a brief note in response to your call for ideas and reactions regarding the initial planning stage of a possible writing-across-the-curriculum program on campus.

I'll be brief. I value good writing from students. But I was trained as an astronomer, not a writing teacher. I think I know good, correct writing when I see it (I think we all do), but I don't feel confident teaching students about grammar, punctuation, thesis points, and similar areas.

This is not unlike asking someone who appreciates good music and can probably plunk out a few tunes on a piano to give violin lessons. It's just not something I feel either confident or professionally prepared to do. Consequently, I must weigh in against the proposal to increase attention to writing across the campus if that means putting it into the hands of astronomers, physicists, and other people like me.

Next was an email from P. Stanover of the psychology department—Chikilah didn't know him (or was it a her?).

Subject: Task Force Reply
Date: Fri, 09 April 8:33:41
From: pstan@TRU.edu
To: WAC-COMM@TRU.edu

Thank you for the opportunity to respond to the idea that all departments and faculty should increase attention to writing in their curricula and courses.

Whatever model is chosen to do this, I must say that it represents a real difficulty for those of us in the Department of Psychology. Every year there is more information in my field to impart to students—more research, more theory, more background.

I assume from the Committee's campus-wide email that we are being called upon to engage in some needed remediation for students with poor writing skills. But why is it that the English department cannot fix the problem of poor student writing? We have enough to do. After all, we don't ask English to teach psychology.—P. Stanover, psychology

The history department, one floor down from Chikilah's own Department of Humanities, was near enough for Florence Argyle to drop a folded printout of her typed response into Chikilah's mailbox. On her way to make a few photocopies, Chikilah retrieved Florence's note and read it standing at the machine.

To: Chikilah Johnson, Chair
From: Prof. Florence Argyle, History Dept.
Re.:   Student Writing Skills
Date: April 9

I speak for many of my colleagues when I say that the Department of History applauds the effort to increase the attention to writing across the University. Students are woefully unprepared for the demands of communication in higher education. Unfortunately, the general lack of skills development in the public schools has created an increased burden on the colleges and universities in this country to do what should have been done years before students even apply to college.

We in the Department of History do not anticipate the need for much new activity here. Some of us already require a research paper in our smaller classes, and these, which are one component of the student's performance, we grade rigorously. In my Western Civilization class, for example, students are docked two points (of 100) for every spelling, grammatical, or punctuation error they make in their papers. About 15–20% do very poorly on the paper for this reason.

Under these circumstances, I believe that many of our faculty would rather spend their time on some of the other teaching-related activities going on, including especially the use of computers in the teaching of history.

Good luck with your efforts.

By the time she had copied the note for her task force members and returned to her office, the inbox on Chikilah's email program had already received several more responses to the task force call. One was from someone in the Department of Biology.

Subject: Task Force on Writing
Date: Fri, 09 April 10:14:23
From: rsantiago@TRU.edu
To: WAC-COMM@TRU.edu

Thank you for the chance to respond to the Committee's recommendation that we begin building writing systematically into courses across the curriculum.

While calling attention to students' poor writing skills is a good idea (as you know, I'm all in favor of increased standards and the weeding out of those who are not suited for college-level work), I am wary of putting too many resources into yet another "initiative." Writing across the curriculum strikes me as another short-lived educational fad, destined to go the way of all the previous fads, leaving behind a costly infrastructure and outdated requirements.

Instead, we need to use our scarce resources to increase faculty salaries, attract first-rate scholars, and invest in maintaining our laboratories and buildings. I hope we may take up these other pressing needs at our next Faculty Senate meeting.

Another response came from Lucinda Abrams, an assistant professor in the Department of Studio Arts.

Subject: Task Force
Date: Fri, 09 April 10:23:49
From: labrams@TRU.edu
To: WAC-COMM@TRU.edu

This serves as a brief response to your invitation to the faculty to express our ideas and concerns about writing across the campus.

Our department would be among the last to resist a project that could tie into the creative potential of students across the campus. Writing can be a wonderful mode of self-expression and self-exploration.

In our department, however, we work with our own media: the visual arts. We do not envision the need for development in the area of writing. Otherwise, who is to say that students shouldn't be sculpting their versions of a personal essay in the freshman composition course, or painting their way to a rendition of the Battle of the Bulge in history?

Each discipline has its own primary modes of expression and communication. Philosophy, history, anthropology—these are founded on the written word, on language, on story. But painting, sculpting, dancing, have their own ways of speaking. One might expect the accountants, mathematicians, and logicians to make the same claims, but I will let them make those claims for themselves.

The phone rang as Chikilah was skimming Lucinda's note. It was Terry Aken, one of the other women on the task force and a strong advocate of writing across the curriculum who had almost singlehandedly helped to build a requirement for a senior thesis in her own Department of Business and Accounting. Terry had called to share her thoughts about the email responses with Chikilah.

"I can't believe some of these responses," Terry said. "Do these faculty think that they can just lecture and test, or what?"

"Well, it's pretty early to get much consensus," Chikilah replied. "Maybe these first notes are from the people who are the most worried and scared."

Terry made a snorting sound. "Remember that we can't just read and ignore these. We promised we'd respond to everyone who wrote to us. Are *you* up to figuring out a way to reply to Stanover? You know what he's like, don't you?"

Chikilah was already glancing at another email that had just come in, this one from someone in the English department. She was just about to ask Terry to look at it too when she realized it had been sent to her own personal email address. After reading the first few lines, she interrupted Terry.

"A message just came to my personal account from someone named Victor Ramstadt in English. Want to hear it?"

"Fire away," Terry said.

Subject:	Not Wise!
Date:	Fri, 09 April 11:04:55
From:	vramstadt@TRU.edu
To:	chikjohn@TRU.edu

I am one of the few dissenting voices in a department champing at the bit to begin taking writing across the campus in this latest crusade.

The writing-across-the-curriculum movement in this country has grown steadily for at least two decades. In some cases, it has done good. But I am also convinced that in most such programs, a complex ability that requires years of experience and training to teach well is being handed over to unqualified faculty who may do more harm than good in preparing students to write well. A few, I might add, are themselves deplorable writers whose own prose makes a poor model for aspiring students. Worse still, there are even some disciplines, especially in the social sciences, that daily produce and publish prose unfit for the discerning eye.

While I suppose, however, there is no great harm in writing being taught in various majors—preferably in the senior year—by faculty who have extensive experience in the writing of their own fields, I believe that the University's resources for general education ought to be channeled into our existing English department, where reducing class size and teaching loads would go a long way toward improving students' abilities.

PS: Please honor your promise to hold letters in confidence when requested. My colleagues have already pilloried me for making some of my views known about writing and related issues.

Dr. Victor Ramstadt, PhD, MA, BA, Associate Professor of English

As Chikilah reached the PS in her colleague's email, she immediately stopped reading aloud and thought about what to do.

"You still there?" Terry asked.

"Yes, yes," Chikilah said hesitantly. "This person asked to remain anonymous. I guess I blew it."

"Why?" Terry said. "I'm on the task force, remember?"

"Well, I know. But he sent it just to me. Are we supposed to share these with each other?"

There was a slight pause, and then Terry blurted out, "Oh, no! Here's another one from my own department!"

The email had come from M. Kim (who everyone on campus called just "M").

Subject: Task Force
Date: Fri, 09 April 11:12:07
From: mkim@TRU.edu
To: WAC-COMM@TRU.edu

I want to thank the Committee for its hard work on a subject of great importance.

My response focuses on the problem of large classes. In my department, most of the faculty teach at least regularly, and some constantly, in large lecture classes because of the size of the Business College and the number of students we teach, both majors and in general education courses. In these classes, it is impractical or even impossible to teach writing. Collecting one paper from 50 or more students can destroy a teacher's entire weekend, and the gains may be negligible.

The Committee should exempt from any writing plan all those departments that routinely teach students in large lecture/test sections, where it is already difficult enough just to manage our machine-scorable tests and post the results in a timely fashion without extensive help from graduate students.

We usually do ask students in our graduate seminars to write something, because those classes are so small and the work load is manageable.—M. Kim, Business and Accounting

As the two women read M's note and thought about its implications, yet another email arrived in their mailboxes simultaneously. This time it was from a colleague in Chikilah's own Department of Allied Health Sciences, James Saroyan, a faculty member in the division of medical technology. Chikilah had met him a number of times at faculty meetings and social occasions but wouldn't consider him among her close colleagues.

Subject: Writing
Date: Fri, 09 April 11:17:34
From: jsaroyan@TRU.edu
To: WAC-COMM@TRU.edu

If we are to expect students to write proficiently at this institution, irregardless of our teaching, we must be ourselves models of clear, concise, and grammatically correct prose. To that end, I note with considerable discomfort an egregious error in the very document asking us for our responses. (There is a comma missing after "identified problems" at the end of the first paragraph.) As a faculty member concerned about writing, this kind of problem makes me wonder whether we should first offer courses for the faculty before we raise the bar for our students.

"You still there?" Chikilah asked this time.

QUESTIONS FOR REFLECTION AND DISCUSSION

Note: If you are "assigned" to a specific response to the Task Force's call, apply the following questions to that response. The questions are equally applicable to all the responses received by the task force.

1. Imagine that you are a member of the Task Force on Writing at TRU State. Formulate a reply to your chosen or assigned faculty response. How do you react to the author's claims or perspective? Are there any false or problematic assumptions in his or her response? Are there any accurate assumptions? How would you respond to either?

2. Pinpoint specific sources of resistance to writing across the curriculum in your chosen or assigned response. What are some strategies (campus-wide or person/department-specific) that could overcome this resistance?

3. The task force members, as Chikilah characterizes them, are well-established senior faculty with strong feelings about the importance of formal writing in their courses. On the basis of their own collective dispositions, how you would advise them, if you were Chikilah, to respond in writing to the author of your chosen or assigned response?

4. Clearly, the responses from faculty at TRU State aren't predicted by their departments or disciplines. Would they be on your campus? Are there some disciplines where the integration of writing is perceived to be easy or difficult, and if so, how might we go about helping members of those disciplines to use writing in their courses?

5. Imagine that a member of the task force is, like Terry Aken, from the same department as the author of your chosen or assigned response. What are the possible advantages and disadvantages of having that task force member respond to his or her colleague's reaction? Do members of a discipline make the most effective proponents of writing across the curriculum among their colleagues?

6. Consider again the task force's call for reactions, especially the way they have described their charge versus the specific request they make of faculty at Two Rivers State. Would you suggest any change in their approach and/or their call for responses? Why or why not?

READINGS FOR FURTHER CONSIDERATION

Fulwiler, Toby, and Art Young, eds. *Programs That Work: Models and Methods of Writing Across the Curriculum.* Portsmouth: Boynton/Cook, 1990.

Glick, Milton D. "Writing Across the Curriculum: A Dean's Perspective." *WPA: Writing Program Administration* 11 (Spring 1988): 53–57.

McLeod, Susan H., and Margaret Soven. *Writing Across the Curriculum: A Guide to Developing Programs*. Newbury Park: Sage, 1992.

Swanson-Owens, Deborah. "Identifying Natural Sources of Resistance: A Study of Implementing Writing Across the Curriculum." *Research in the Teaching of English* 20 (1986): 69–97.

43

"We Hate You!"
WAC as a Professional Threat

Carol Peterson Haviland and Edward M. White

As she began to implement the impressive projects she had designed in the spring WAC seminar, Escriba Weil was exhilarated. She could see how these new ways of using writing to learn would help her engineering students, both as they wrestled with design concepts and as they wrote proposals for prospective customers. Unfortunately, all of the energy she felt with the WAC group quickly dissipated in the "We hate you!" looks she received from her students and her engineering colleagues. Some of the disdain was open: students strutted in brazenly to drop her sections as soon as they learned about the required writing and thumped her roundly on their student evaluations.

Some of the hostility was more subtle. When she was asked to talk about her WAC experience at a department meeting, no one attended. When she came up for tenure and promotion to associate professor, her low student evaluations were offered as evidence of poor rather than challenging teaching. When she asked for her dean's support, he noted that although he thought writing was important in engineering, he had more pressing issues to contend with as he struggled to get faculty to accept the increasingly heavy teaching and research assignments on their "14,000 and growing rapidly" state university campus.

"Our WAC seminar leaders were wrong," she wrote to the campus WAC listserv the following February. "My quarter in the WAC seminar was personally enriching but professionally disastrous. No one speaks to me in our halls, I get 8 a.m. and 8 p.m. classes in the temporary classrooms, and my once-sure tenure path is very shaky. Why didn't they issue me some sheep's clothing and warn me to wear it even in the summer rather than encourage me to take 'good news' back to an eager department?"

Because they knew that they weren't always celebrated in the English department, the WAC seminar leaders expected that WAC participants would hit some reluctance when they returned to their own departments and shared the ways they had been thinking about incorporating writing into their teaching. In fact, the leaders had focused parts of several seminars on the mixed responses to their own enthusiasms participants could expect. They shared their own stories, encouraging participants to enact the seminar model of asking questions and listening rather than evangelizing. They also invited participants to turn to the seminar group for support when they became discouraged.

However, Escriba's experience was sobering to these leaders and all of the spring seminar participants when they read her listserv post because it was clear that she was in greater trouble than any of them had experienced. When they had applauded the projects she had devised in the spring, none of them had predicted the level of opposition or the professional repercussions she was going to encounter. Some of them even began to wonder about their own new uses of writing as they followed her struggles and watched her rethink her commitments to using writing. "What's the point?" she wrote one afternoon, midway through another set of papers written by her resentful students. "I spend time devising assignments and reading papers, only to carry them back to students who glare at me in class and thrash me on my evaluations. My colleagues think that at best I'm a fool and at worst I'm a threat they need to run out of the department before I get tenure. The more I think about the messy business of writing, the more I think I should just return to my less writing-infused pedagogies."

Escriba had begun, she thought, very intelligently and modestly. For example, instead of quizzing students about their reading, she asked them to pose questions, to critique and offer alternative ways of approaching the design problems the chapters posed. Then, she asked them to write proposal letters, describing the design solutions they thought best met the customers' needs and, in effect, promoting their companies' products. After polling engineering professionals and hearing her colleagues disparage students who "couldn't get jobs because they didn't sound like engineers," she insisted that their proposal letters and memos follow American business conventions, and reduced their grades substantially if they ignored these forms.

Students complained that no one else made them write, that if they'd wanted to write they would have been English majors, and that engineers had to get only the numbers right. Escriba countered that they wouldn't learn everything they needed to know before they graduated so they would need to think about alternatives as well as memorize existing facts, that they would need to write up their proposals so that buyers could understand them, and that if their proposals were sloppy, buyers might think that their calculations as well as their spelling might be faulty.

Her students didn't care, and they told her so. In fact, one day they embarrassed her openly by gathering to complain outside her door when the dean was meeting faculty in an adjacent conference room. "Weil is just trying to show how tough she is by nitpicking at our writing. We want to learn engineering, and she's grading us on how our letterheads look. Why can't she be like other regular engineering faculty?" And, of course, they whacked her soundly in their course evaluations.

Escriba did bubble a bit about her encounter with writing, but she didn't overtly try to reform her colleagues. Nevertheless, several, particularly those who rationed their time on campus because they also had lucrative consulting careers, chose to criticize her work rather than reevaluate their own teaching. Others had received negative responses to their own writing and felt threatened by her concern with abilities they did not possess. Instead of giving her credit for her professional growth and course development, senior faculty members emphasized her lower course evaluations and held up her first request for promotion. Even though she finally was promoted and tenured, the squabble was demoralizing and later costly in terms of departmentally assigned merit pay. Very simply, her colleagues, too, hated her in very tangible ways.

QUESTIONS FOR REFLECTION AND DISCUSSION

1. How can WAC participants work constructively with colleagues who, rightly or wrongly, are so defensive about their own writing that they see WAC as a professional threat?
2. How can WAC leaders prepare seminar participants to change their pedagogies without alienating their colleagues?
3. How can student evaluations of teaching effectiveness be revised so that responses do not penalize teachers who implement WAC practices?
4. How can WAC programs gather support for faculty who take risks such as devising writing-rich pedagogies?

READINGS FOR FURTHER CONSIDERATION

Barnett, Robert W., and Jacob S. Blumner. *Writing Centers and Writing Across the Curriculum Programs*. Westport: Greenwood, 1999.

Mullin, Joan A. "Writing Across the Curriculum." *Administrative Problem-Solving for Writing Programs and Writing Centers*. Ed. Linda Myers-Breslin. Urbana: National Council of Teachers of English, 1999.

Haviland, Carol Peterson, and Edward M. White. "How Can Physical Space and Administrative Structure Shape Writing Programs, Writing Centers, and WAC Projects?" *Administrative Problem-Solving for Writing Programs and Writing Centers*. Ed. Linda Myers-Breslin. Urbana: National Council of Teachers of English, 1999.

44

Forget Everything You Learned About Writing

Dennis Baron

"Well, what do you say when the student complains, 'But that's not how my high school English teacher wanted us to write'?"

"I just tell them, 'Forget everything you ever learned about writing in high school.'" With that piece of wit, which was met with appropriate chuckles and murmurs of agreement, Roy Kumar ended the opening session of the Summer Writing-Across-the-Curriculum Faculty Orientation Workshop.

Roy directed first-year writing at Central Illinois State College, and the provost had put him in charge of the college's new WAC orientation, which began meeting just as the hot, humid, windy, and all-around unforgiving Illinois summer went into high gear. As Roy told the participants at the start of the morning, "To coin a phrase, I'd rather be sailing. Unfortunately, Central Illinois is pretty well landlocked."

Silence. Well, they're not going to laugh at everything, he thought.

Faculty in the WAC workshop had ranged from enthusiastic anthropologists, well up on the latest literary theories and convinced that their students would benefit from this new approach to writing, to downright skeptical physicists, who seemed convinced, like Alan Sokal, that all humanists were frauds, and who signed up for WAC training only to collect the generous stipend the provost had allocated to encourage attendance. Regardless of their motives, the workshop participants were all certain that Central Illinois State's first-year writing program had not prepared its undergraduates for the writing tasks that lay before them. The science professors, the engineers, the business school faculty all agreed when one of Roy's English department colleagues, Mike-the-radical-Marxist-theorist, complained at the start of the workshop, "My students can't write. They obviously need more instruction. Aren't you teaching them anything down there in English 101?"

Ignoring the location of writing "down there" and the class structure that the statement implied, Roy asked Mike-the-Marxist, "What do you mean when you say they can't write?"

Mike's answer was simple and direct: "They can't punctuate. They can't spell. And they don't know MLA formatting." Roy saw heads nodding all around the room. Mike was ready to trash late capitalism and storm the barricades at the drop of a hat, but the conventions of standard English and proper footnoting were sacred to him. Here was something the anthropologists and physicists could agree on. Roy knew this was going to be a tough crowd.

Since the first-year writing program had failed to inculcate in students the habits of good writing, the university had dealt with this crisis in student literacy by adding a writing-across-the-curriculum component to its general education requirements. Courses fulfilling the new Comp II requirement had to have writing as an ongoing, regular activity in the class, not just something reserved for exams and a term paper. Students in these courses were to receive writing instruction throughout the semester, as well as instruction in the course content. And students were promised significant and frequent feedback on their writing. Though students could test out of English 101, now renamed Comp I, there was no getting out of Comp II.

That was all well and good. Roy Kumar believed students should write more in college because they would have to write a lot once they got out of college, whatever field they went into. But adding a writing requirement wouldn't necessarily produce students who could punctuate, spell, or master MLA citation forms. Nor would it necessarily produce students who could use prose to create knowledge or solve problems, or who could write like social scientists or managers or poets. It seemed to Roy that adding an extra writing course wouldn't solve whatever literacy crisis was supposed to exist at Central Illinois State.

Of course, the university would train the faculty who would be teaching the new writing-intensive course, and because of his experience training the staff for the much-maligned Comp I course, Roy found himself facing a crowd as tough to please as the typical set of 101 students.

At least they laughed at some of my jokes, Roy thought to himself as he walked down the hall to his office. He'd check his mail, grab a cold soda, and go back for session two, where the participants were going to do an actual writing assignment and then talk about it.

As he stood by his desk swigging his diet cola, Roy read through his mail—a few book ads, a call for papers, some administrivia from the dean's office. There was one piece of real mail, an anxious letter, passed on to Roy with the comment "Please handle" by his department head. It was from someone with the unlikely name of Jeanne Picard, who identified herself as the chair of the English department at Soybean Country Community High School, and obviously a lot of her students were coming to Central Illinois State. This is what she wrote:

Dear English Department Chairperson:

I am writing as a result of reports made by several recent Soybean Country High School graduates. These students claim their freshmen writing teachers remarked that the writing instruction in high school would best be forgotten. Additionally, "Power Writing" and the "five paragraph essay" are not useful tools.

As a high school English teacher, I am frustrated. I teach at the sophomore and senior levels. At the tenth grade, I am required by the State of Illinois, therefore the local curriculum as well, to prepare students for the Illinois Goals Assessment Program (IGAP) tests. The informative and persuasive essays, demanded by the state, require a five-paragraph essay. The scoring rubric used ensures this approach. Ideally, the conventions of "Power Writing" make the whole process a logical one. Therefore, I implement both techniques.

Of course, the seniors are required to write extensively. They use power writing for any informative or persuasive essay. At the same time, creative writing assignments are also an integral part of the curriculum. These include satires, sonnets, ballads, epics, and the like.

Quite frankly, I want to know what you want from me. I want my students to go into their college classes as prepared as possible. With the constraints of state requirements and local district demands, my teaching format does not have the same liberties as yours. Considering my dilemma, would you please provide suggestion as to the direction I might pursue in my instruction of writing?

Obviously, my attempt is to achieve as much of an instructional continuum as possible. Our professional objectives are the same; a complementary relationship will be a benefit to all.

Sincerely,

Jeanne Picard
English Chairperson
Soybean Country Community High School

Roy sat down hard when he got to the part about forgetting everything you learned about writing in high school. Guilty as charged, he admitted under his breath. Sometimes it's tough enough just getting students through the level they are in, let alone preparing them for the next level. Yet he often felt his undergraduates had come out of high school with little or nothing to show for it. And how many times had he looked at the writing of a new graduate student and said, "You may have been able to get away with this in college, but you're in grad school now, and this sort of thing just won't do"? He himself bitterly remembered the first time an editor had told him, "You're not in graduate school any more. Now you've got a real audience. Forget this phony, academic writing and do it right."

Wasn't this what Mike-the-Marxist was saying, too? "Forget everything you learned in 101—that is, ha ha, if you learned anything at all . . . ."

Roy began mentally to compose a reply to Jeanne Picard. She was clearly convinced that her students would need later on all the writing tips she was giving them. He had heard these high school rules of writing from his students—don't use the first person; avoid the passive voice; don't start a sentence with "and" or "but"; never end a sentence with a preposition. Or the endless formulas, "Tell your readers what you're going to tell them. Tell it to 'em again. Then tell 'em what you just told them." And, "Give three supports for every claim you make." Some of his students felt liberated when he told them to throw out those rules. Others felt threatened.

Roy didn't think Jeanne Picard would feel liberated if he told her that she was wrong. "Dear Ms. Picard," he typed at his computer, "forget everything you ever taught in high school." No, scratch that. Must be the humidity making me punchy, he thought. Better try again.

"Dear Ms. Picard, there are so many demands on writing teachers, from so many constituencies, who would not be frustrated by the experience?" He looked at the screen. He knew it wouldn't do, either.

What could Roy reply to this Jeanne Picard? He had never heard of the five-paragraph theme till he began teaching college writing and half his students told him about the universal formula for writing success they had mastered in high school. Roy was suspicious of writing formulas. He believed that the five-paragraph theme couldn't exist outside the writing classroom. And he had no idea what Jeanne Picard meant by "power writing." Sounds like edubabble to me, he thought.

But were his own methods any better? He tried to get students to write the way real writers did, but did he have any idea what "real writers" did? Weren't students real writers? Their school-based writing had significant repercussions, just as work-place writing did. How many times had he told students who questioned his writing assignments, which he thought of as not being formula driven, "You'll need this later on"? Guilty, once again. In fact, he had come to realize that his own assignments, designed to elicit a critical take on a subject, were as ideologically loaded as any five-paragraph formula, and often as unsuccessful.

Moreover, Roy often had no idea what his students would need later on, in terms of writing or anything else, for that matter. He had never written a business report or an engineering proposal or a legal brief. A confirmed English major, even in college his forays into writing papers for history, philosophy, or music appreciation had been less than successful. Outside his own area of expertise, he was a rank amateur. He even had trouble writing effective absence notes when his children missed school. Yet he considered himself both a good writer and a good writing teacher. Was this a paradox? Was he a hypocrite and a fraud, as he sometimes suspected?

So Roy couldn't say to Jeanne Picard, "Here at Central Illinois State we have found the answer. This is what you should do. . . ." Instead, he sat there, staring at his blank computer screen, thinking how writers adapt to new demands as they move from level to level, from assignment to assignment, and wondering how to begin work on the writing assignment he had just been given, a reply to Jeanne Picard's call for help.

And then it came to him. He grabbed Picard's letter and ran to the copy room and fired up the copier. Clutching twenty copies of the letter, he rushed into the workshop five minutes late and said, "OK, here's your first assignment. It's a case study. Write a reply to this urgent call for help. . . ."

QUESTIONS FOR REFLECTION AND DISCUSSION

1. What are the strengths and shortcomings of the writing programs at your institution?

2. In what ways can WAC, writing-intensive courses, and increased general education requirements effectively address the needs of student writers in your classes? Are there other ways of getting students to write better?

3. How do you respond to Roy Kumar's suggestion that we all blame our students' writing deficiencies in part on their previous instruction?

4. Roy says that outside his own area of expertise, he is a rank amateur when it comes to writing. What constitutes expertise in writing, and how can we fairly measure student writing progress or success?

5. Jeanne Picard assumes that colleges are looking for one particular kind of writing, and Roy Kumar assumes that high schools teach writing in a uniform way. Neither assumption matches the reality of what goes on in high schools or in colleges. What assumptions do you make about what goes on in other people's writing classes? What really does go on there?

6. Jeanne Picard is torn between teaching to a test and teaching what she thinks her students need to learn. How do you respond to those conflicting pressures in your own classroom?

7. How would you reply to Jeanne Picard's plea for advice?

READINGS FOR FURTHER CONSIDERATION

Baron, Dennis. "The Myths of Teaching English." *Declining Grammar and Other Essays on the English Vocabulary*. Urbana: National Council of Teachers of English, 1989. 49–62.

DeVota, Bernard. "English A." *The American Mercury* 13 (1928): 204–12.

Faigley, Lester. "What Is Good Writing? Views from the Public." *The English Language Today*. Ed. Sidney Greenbaum. Oxford: Pergamon, 1985. 99–105.

Knoblauch, C. H., and Lil Brannon. "The Development of Writing Ability: Some Myths About Evaluation and Improvement." *Rhetorical Traditions and the Teaching of Writing*. Ed. C. H. Knoblauch and L. Brannon, Upper Montclair: Boynton/Cook, 1984. 151–71.

"Students Right to Their Own Language." Urbana: Conference on College Composition and Communication/ National Council of Teachers of English, 1974.

"Why Johnny Can't Write." *Newsweek*, 8 Dec. 1975: 58–62, 65.

45

Learning About Learning Communities

Nancy S. Shapiro

Sara was an experienced, nontenure-track writing instructor (ABD) who had been a member of the English department's composition program for five years. During that time, she taught freshman composition courses, as well as the required upper-division professional writing courses, including business writing, technical writing, and writing in the health sciences. At the end of her fifth year, Sara was ready for something different, and when the university decided to pilot a new interdisciplinary, residential learning community program, she volunteered to join one of the faculty teams.

The university-wide learning community, known around campus as LINC (Learning in Communities) was a serious attempt at creating a new approach to undergraduate education on a large research campus. The goals for the program included recruiting and retaining a diverse group of academically talented undergraduates into a large, state research university, and redesigning undergraduate education by incorporating research-based reforms, including undergraduate research, service learning, and writing across the curriculum.

When Sara went for an interview with Susanna Everly, director of the LINC program, she had lots of questions. "What is a 'learning community?'" she wanted to know. "How will my class in the learning community be different from my usual classes?"

"Let me start with the first part of your question," Susanna said, "then you'll better understand the answer to your second question." Susanna had obviously had lots of practice talking about learning communities, since she was part of the yearlong task force that made the recommendations to the campus to implement this curricular innovation.

"Campuses that support learning communities," she began, "use them to restructure the undergraduate experience in ways that promote greater student involvement in learning. I've been trying to recruit faculty for our LINC program who would agree that the essential goal of 'liberal education' is not merely the acquisition of specific content knowledge, but some broader understanding on the part of students about the complexity of ideas, the relationship between and among disciplines, and the development of more mature intellectual capacities."

Sara interrupted, "You talk about recruiting faculty. Do you mean that there is a special faculty for these communities?"

"Well," said Susanna, "we try to bring faculty from different disciplines together who are willing to collaborate, to work together to shape interdisciplinary courses and syllabi, and to work with some of the student affairs folks as well to create learning experiences both in and out of the classroom. In some ways, our LINC program is like a 'college-within-a-college.' Our program links courses together so students travel to two or sometimes three classes together, and every course cluster contains a first-year writing section—that's why it's so important to bring people like you in on the ground floor, so you can begin to collaborate with the other faculty members in your cluster and work together to plan learning activities around some big, integrated themes."

Susanna's excitement about the program was clear from her description and her body language—she was sitting on the edge of her seat throughout this whole explanation, willing Sara to share her enthusiasm.

Sara was drawn to this program and its potential as a truly innovative undergraduate curriculum model. "How many students are in a learning community?" she asked.

"Different programs on different campuses are organized differently," explained Susanna. "Our program has about seventy students in each of five themes: Body and Mind; Life Sciences; International Global Change; Science, Technology and Society; and Arts and Imagination. Each faculty director leads a one-credit weekly integrating seminar on their themes. The students in each of the learning communities are registered for the same sections of larger lecture classes, so they are sure to meet each other throughout the week. They also share the same writing sections—that's where you come in. You'll be working with the Life Sciences cluster, and have three sections of writing in that cluster. You can expect that your three sections of students will also be in the same sections of their biology class, and will come together once a week with their faculty director for the seminar."

Sara was slowly forming another question in her mind. "Am I supposed to attend these linked classes?" she asked.

"Not necessarily," answered Susanna, "although you may want to go to some of the seminars. I understand Jerry Stillman has begun lining up some really interesting speakers, including the world's most famous bat scientist and a member of the science team working on decoding the human genome! But you and Jerry will be expected to work together to plan some collaborative assignments, and you and he might plan some joint assignments—with reading and writing around the Life Sciences themes."

They talked some more, and Sara learned more about her learning community colleague Jerome Stillman, entomologist and faculty director of the Life Sciences cluster. Jerome specialized in tropical rain forest insects, and was well known for collecting fuzzy tarantulas, which he kept in his office in glass aquariums.

The summer planning meetings between Sara and Jerry were very different from her collaborations with her English department colleagues. For the most part, the regular faculty in the English department took the writing instructors for granted as a necessary service component of the department. In fact, they considered themselves to have engaged in an enlightened act when they recently revised the by-laws of the department to allow a handful of instructor-representatives to cast votes in regular faculty meetings.

Jerry, on the other hand, was extremely respectful and almost in awe of Sara's experience and expertise as a writing instructor—never mind that she was an untenured instructor. Although he was a nationally known microbiologist, he shared a private insecurity with her right off the bat. "I was never a good writer," he self-consciously admitted to her on their first meeting. And later, when they began discussing their collaborative planning, he said, "I have no idea how to assign these journals—or whatever they are called—in my LINC seminar. What should we ask students to write about? How are we supposed to grade these things?" And he added with a self-deprecating chuckle, "I know I'll need help grading the grammar and punctuation!"

Early on Sara found herself mentoring a full professor on the finer points of writing across the curriculum, on the basis of her extensive study of composition theory and her professional development at numerous local and national composition conferences. Together they explored the ideas of writing-to-learn, reflective journaling, and freewriting. Jerry was a willing and excited student, and Sara felt for the first time in her professional career that her academic expertise was being valued and appreciated. Although her office was now in the residence hall, she returned to visit with her fellow composition instructors to describe her new "campus-level" perspective on the role of writing at the university.

Together, Sara and Jerry set about designing a syllabus for both the LINC Life Sciences seminar and the first-year composition course that revolved around current controversies and themes in the life sciences. During the course of the first year, students would be given opportunities to attend lectures on ozone depletion, human genome theory, killer bees and army ants, and AIDS research, among others. Sara developed assignments around the weekly seminar topics that Jerry identified, and incorporated the seminar readings into her own syllabus. She even attended the seminar meetings to hear the guest lecturers and participated in the planned field trips to local peat bogs and conservation habitats.

She drew her assignments from the engaging content of the learning community seminar. She had students define major terms or concepts in life sciences, such as cloning, bioethics, and ecosystem; identify the range of audiences for life sciences essays and articles; argue sides of controversial life science topics; and research current issues. Jerry, for his part, gave students close-up tours of the research labs on the campus, invited world famous researchers to attend the weekly seminars, and staged debates on current topics that included campus faculty and invited guests.

The collaboration had everything going for it: intellectual excitement, interdisciplinary collaborations, and a focused curricular structure that integrated coursework for the students. For Sara, working with faculty from a different college who valued her expertise as a rhetorician and a writing instructor increased her sense of self-confidence and was a catalyst to get her thinking about finishing her dissertation.

Yet toward the middle of the first semester, the rosy glow began to fade. One day, Sara met Molly, one of her writing instructor friends at the coffee bar. "How's it going?" asked Molly. "You know we're all so jealous that you have your own office now, and we hear that LINC is the darling of the administration! What kind of students do you have? Is it still as good as you described in September?"

Sara cupped her hands around her coffee mug and smiled. "It's still great to be in LINC, with so many faculty who really care about the quality of undergraduate education around all the time, but, since you asked, I could use some advice. I still love working with Jerry—he is one of the most dedicated professors I've ever met. But recently, he's been using our planning time together to get my input on his writing assignments for his seminar, and I'm not sure how much I should do for him."

"What do you mean?" asked Molly.

Sara sighed. "Jerry seems to be relying on me more and more to help him define, develop, and even prepare his weekly seminar topics for reading and writing. He always does it in the most complimentary way, alluding to my great writing assignments, to my 'way with words,' to the apparent ease with which I summarize ideas and get to the controversial core of a reading or lecture. But I have to admit, I'm feeling overburdened right now. He also just started asking me to take a look at some of the journals his students have been turning in—he wants to talk to me about how we can help them improve their writing."

"That doesn't sound so bad," said Molly. "In fact, it sounds like you've made a WAC convert already!"

"It's a bit more complicated. You see, he wants me to read his students' journals and correct them for grammar and punctuation, to 'improve' their writing—always acknowledging, whenever he asks for that favor, that I'm such an 'expert!' " But I have my own work to do, and I'm even hoping to carve out some time to work on the dissertation again. I don't want to let down my LINC partner, and I hesitate to remind him that I'm still just an instructor. He treats me like an equal faculty collaborator, and I don't want to jeopardize that relationship."

Molly promised to think about the problem, and they agreed to meet next week. But when they got together, Sara was consumed with another issue—and described it to her friend this way:

"You know how we all experience that class-bonding that happens about midway through the semester, when the individual students begin to feel comfortable with each other and with us as teachers? In my classes, I've always looked forward to that time when we begin to joke around, loosen up, and really take some intellectual risks out loud. Well, I think I just discovered a down-side of these small learning communities—maybe you could call it 'hyperbonding.'"

"Hyperbonding?" laughed Molly, "What are you talking about?"

"Well, you see, in a learning community, students are together a lot. In LINC our students don't just go to three classes a week together, they also live together on the same floor of the residence hall, they eat together, they take the same seminar together, and most of them are in the same sections of chemistry and calculus, too. So they're together all the time!"

Sara continued, "This week they all had an important biology lab, and they all decided to postpone doing my assignment in favor of their biology assignment. When I called them on it, they tried to jolly me out of the consequences. I held my ground, and they began to get nasty. Threatened to go to the director en masse and complain about my class. They gave me a really hard time. I know they're probably flexing their 'postadolescent' muscles, but I got a glimpse of a little monster hatching there in the classroom."

"Have any of the other learning communities had this happen? Or is it just your class?" asked Molly.

"I don't know about the others yet, but I do know that our group has more classes together because of the lab schedule." Sara cast her eyes down to the table. "I'm afraid there is one more issue that is raising it's ugly head," she said.

"Let me guess," said her friend. "Plagiarism."

"How did you know?" asked Sara.

"Well, as you drew the picture of a group of students spending all this time together in and out of class, I can just imagine how they'd be up in their rooms sharing notes, drafts, and generally mixing it up. Add to that the normal competition among students to get better grades (or at least equally good grades) as their friends and roommates, and it is kind of an obvious outcome."

"Well, you're right on the money. I gave the normal plagiarism lecture the first or second week of class, but for these kids who share so much, so much of the time, I'm beginning to think that they, themselves, are not sure which ideas are their own, and which they imported from someone else. All I know is that I'm seeing a lot of very similar work being turned in."

Sara and Molly continued talking for a while longer about the difference between teaching a regular section of first year composition, and the advantages and disadvantages of teaching in a learning community with linked courses and faculty collaboration. In the end, while they enthusiastically agreed that the learning community model had some great advantages for both students and teachers, there were still some problems to solve. As they parted ways outside the coffee shop and Sara headed back to her office, she thought ahead to the next LINC faculty meeting and created a mental list of questions for next year's planning.

QUESTIONS FOR REFLECTION AND DISCUSSION

1. What is a fair description and definition of the roles of the faculty in learning communities? How can learning communities avoid exploiting writing faculty?

2. How real are the dangers of "hyperbonding" in a learning community, and what are some solutions? How can learning communities develop a community response to this pitfall?

3. When faculty share the same students, it is possible for prejudices to get passed around from one faculty member to another. How can learning communities ensure that each student is treated as an individual without prejudice all the time?

4. Faculty in learning communities sometimes try to impress each other with the rigor of their standards—raising the bar for their own purposes, not necessarily in the best interests of their students. Can faculty arrive at some set of common understandings (performance outcomes) about freshman level work?

READINGS FOR FURTHER CONSIDERATION

Gablenick, Faith, et al., eds. *Learning Communities: Creating Connections Among Students, Faculty and Disciplines*. New Directions for Teaching and Learning, no. 41. San Francisco: Jossey Bass, 1990.

Schneider, Carol G., and Robert Shoenberg. *The Academy in Transition: Contemporary Understandings of Liberal Education.* Washington: Association of American Colleges and Universities, 1998.

Shapiro, Nancy S., and Jodi H. Levine. *Creating Learning Communities: A Practical Guide to Winning Support, Organizing for Change, and Implementing Programs.* San Francisco: Jossey Bass, 1999.

Best Online Resources for Writing Across the Curriculum

Shaun P. Slattery, Jr.

One of the most convenient ways of learning about WAC theory and practice is to look online. Many campus programs support their efforts with Web sites that provide constantly accessible information. But not all Web sites are created equal. Most are designed to serve only faculty at a particular university. Others provide only contact information or descriptions of a particular program.

Fortunately, a few Web sites are structured to provide information for faculty and students more broadly. The sites detailed in this appendix represent the most thorough and informative WAC-related resources on the Internet. The selections are based on a 5-point ranking system I devised to analyze and document the current national status of cross-curricular writing and/or communication programs. After testing several online search engines, I collected 131 relevant Web sites that I subsequently organized by URL, sponsoring institution of higher learning, and visit date. The contents of each site were summarized and each was ranked on a scale of one to four stars. The criteria for four-star sites required that the sites provide information on WAC theory (including rationale, history, and recommended readings) and practice (including sample syllabi and assignments). Many of these practical resources are discipline specific.

Here are the annotations for four-star sites identified in the study.

> **Sponsor:** Colorado School of Mines, Golden, CO—Doctoral II
> **URL:** ⟨http://www.mines.edu/Academic/lais/wc/⟩
> **Rating:** ★★★★
> **Visit:** 3/21/00
> **Program Name:** Campus Writing Program
> **Focus:** WAC
> **Highlights:**
> Faculty Resources include:
> Effective Writing Assignments
> • Designing Effective Assignment Sheets

- Creating Collaborative Writing Assignments
- Assignments That Work
- Writing to Learn (Many Example Assignments)
- Scaffolding Formal Assignments

Grading Strategies

- The Grading Process
- How to Reduce Grading Time and Stress
- Responding and Evaluating
- Making Grades More Than Just Letters
- Holistic Grading
- Portfolio Grading
- Using Essay Exams
- Why Writers Make Mistakes

WAC Program description ("Undergraduate Council Approval of WAC")

- Goals and Objectives
- Assessment Plan
- Writing-Intensive Course Guidelines

Notes: Includes mission statement, committee and liaison list, links to Colorado State University resources including WAC Clearing House, Guides for Teachers and FAQ about WAC (see entry for Colorado State University)

Sponsor: Colorado State University, Fort Collins, CO—Research I

Rating: ★★★★

Visit: 3/15/00

URL: ⟨http://aw.colostate.edu/⟩, also ⟨http://aw.colostate.edu/resource_list.htm⟩ (WAC Clearinghouse) or (older link with re-direct ⟨http://www.colostate.edu/Depts/WAC⟩)

Program Name: *academic.writing* (journal) and *academic.writing*'s WAC Clearinghouse

Focus: WSAC and WAC

Highlights:

- Extensive Introduction to WAC including pedagogy, practical advice and answers to common questions/concerns, example write-to-learn assignments, WID discussion, principles of effective writing assignments, peer review guidelines, evaluation strategies, and collaborative writing.
- Dissertations, theses and research related to CAC
- Extensive CAC link list (Websites and other resources including: Good Places to Start, WAC and CAC Programs, CAC Bibliographies, Online Articles and Papers about CAC, Electronic Support for CAC, Listservs, Learning Communities, Teaching/Learning Centers and Instructional, Computer-Mediated Communication Resources, Electronic Journals)
- Link list of upcoming and past CAC and WAC conferences
- Information on "WAC-L", a writing across the curriculum listserv

Notes: Includes submission procedures and guidelines for contributing to *academic.writing* (and forthcoming subscription form). Also Submission Guidelines, Subscription Information, and Back Issues (in Adobe Acrobat Format) of *Language and Learning Across the Disciplines— on the Web*.

Sponsor: Colorado State University, Fort Collins, CO—Research I

Rating: ★★★★

Visit: 3/15/00

URL: ⟨http://www.colostate.edu/Depts/WritingCenter/⟩

Program Name: The Writers' Center

Focus: WAC/WID

Highlights:

- Extensive Resources for Writers and Teachers (Including: Interactive Tutorials, Writing & Teaching Guides, Interactive Demonstrations, Library Links & Guides, and Writing & Teaching Links)
- Link to Guides for Teachers (extensive) at CSU Writing Center ⟨http://www.colostate.edu/Depts/WritingCenter/references/teaching.htm⟩
  - Using Peer Review, Designing and Evaluating Writing Assignments
  - FAQ about WAC includes: (Writing to Learn, WID, and answers to common questions from faculty new to WAC) ⟨http://www.colostate.edu/Depts/WritingCenter/references/teaching/wac-faq/wac-faq.htm⟩
- Writing & Teaching Guides include: Writing & Reading Processes, Types of Documents, Speeches & Presentations, Library, Internet, and Field Research, Working with Sources, Social Science and Qualitative Research, Working with Graphics and Tables, and Reference Materials for Teachers
- Course Pages and Assignments Page includes course materials from 21 different disciplines (Agricultural Science, Applied Human Sciences, Chemical and Bioresource Engineering, Civil Engineering, Composition, Design and Merchandising, Education, Electrical Engineering, English, Environmental Health, Foreign Language and Literature, Honors Program, Human Development, Journalism & Technical Communication, Key Academic Community, Mechanical Engineering, Microbiology, Physics, Political Science, Speech, Women's Studies)

Notes: Includes online Q&A for students' writing (questions of grammar/style) and sponsor-specific writing center information.

Sponsor: Mary Washington College, Fredericksburg, VA—Master's II

Rating: ★★★★

Visit: 3/19/00

URL: ⟨http://www5.mwc.edu/~spkc/speakint.htm⟩

Program Name: Speaking-Intensive Program

Focus: Speaking Across the Curriculum (SAC), Speaking Intensive (SI) courses, CXC

Highlights:

- Speaking Center description—sections: Speech Consultation Services, Videotapes of Speeches (title list), Instructional Videos (title list), Reading Materials (an exhaustive list of the Center's resource titles, though none are available online or listed with bibliographic information).

- Student Resource page with speaking tips—sections: Nervous?, Preparing Your Presentation, Group Presentations, Researching Your Presentation.
- Faculty Resource page—sections: Leading Discussion Groups, Suggested Criteria for Evaluating Group Presentations, Suggested Criteria for Evaluating Oral Presentations, Preparing the Main Points of a Presentation, Preparing Speaking Notes, Dealing With Speaking Anxiety, Using Supporting Materials in an Oral Presentation.
- Course requirements section with excellent tips "Make Your Class Speaking-Intensive"—sections: Speaking-Intensive Course Requirements, Suggested Speaking-Intensive Class Assignments, Resources To Help Make Your Class Speaking-Intensive (bibliography), MWC Speaking-Intensive Course Proposal Form (with examples of approved proposals), Proposal Deadline Update.

Notes: Includes, program overview with speaking-intensive requirement at MWC, program goals. A list of speaking-intensive courses at MWC.

Sponsor: Northern Illinois University, DeKalb, IL—Doctoral I

Rating: ★★★★

Visit: 3/20/00

URL: ⟨http://www.engl.niu.edu/wac/⟩ Also, ⟨http://www.niu.edu/acad/english/wac/wac.html⟩

Program Name: WAC@NIU, NIU English Department

Focus: WAC/WID

Highlights:

- Proposal forms and examples of WAC grants at NIU
- ESL Clinic page—sections: A Grammar Guide for ESL Students, A Place to Ask Questions, Dave's ESL Café, Frizzy University Network (link), How to Join a Listserv for ESL
- Student Resource page: links to online writing centers, documentation/style guides, reference/research resources
- Faculty Resource page. Link heading: English Related Professional Organizations, Handouts, Online Journals and Discussion Groups, Writing and Rhetoric Resources for English Faculty, Internet Resources.
- Faculty Resource page includes NIU's English Sourcebook
  - Designing Assignments (includes sequencing, thesis statements, freewriting, critical thinking, collaboration)
  - Editing/Revising (includes Cooperative Editing)
  - Paragraph Concerns
  - Peer Reviews
  - Style/Clarity/Coherence
  - Grammar & Punctuation
  - Modes of Writing (includes Writing to Learn, Narrative, Interview, Comparison & Contrast, Persuasive & Argumentative)
  - Writing the Research Paper (Source Analysis, Thesis Statements, Citation, Samples)

- Networked Classrooms (includes Internet & E-mail, Sample Syllabi)
- Links to Other On-Line Writing Centers
- Extensive WAC link list
- Extensive Writing Consultant Handbook
- Extensive WAC bibliography [not directly linked] ⟨http://www.niu.edu/acad/english/wac/wacbib.html⟩

Notes: Includes "A Short History of WAC," Writing Center link, faculty writing consultant list, and brief WAC/WID philosophy.

Sponsor: Panitz, Ted, MA
Rating: ★★★★
Visit: 3/15/00
URL: ⟨http://www.capecod.net/~tpanitz/tedspage/⟩
Program Name:
Focus: cooperative learning and WAC
Highlights:
- Ted's Cooperative learning e-book
- Ted's WAC e-book
  - Preface
  - Reasons for using WAC
  - Table of contents for writing assignments
  - Writing assignments in expanded form
  - WAC Web Sites (non-linked)
- WAC Web pages (link list)
- Writing ideas list of assignments (loosely organized, a bit overwhelming) ⟨http://www.capecod.net/~tpanitz/tedspage/ewacbook/wacapproaches.htm⟩ (includes: writing to learn, informal writing, microthemes, note-taking, journals, portfolios, in class writing, exploratory writing, critical thinking, formal writing, personal writing)
- Ted's articles (on cooperative learning: definition, benefits, assessment, cooperative learning in mathematics classes)
- Cooperative learning Web Sites (link list)

Notes: Includes Internet discussions on cooperative learning.

Sponsor: Southern Illinois University—Carbondale, IL—Research II
Rating: ★★★★
Visit: 3/20/00
URL: ⟨http://www.siu.edu/departments/cac/⟩
Program Name: Communication Across the Curriculum at SIU
Focus: WSAC/WID
Highlights:
- Introduction to CAC (includes history and rationale, philosophy)

- Extensive link list includes: CAC Resources and Programs at SIUC, Model CAC and WAC Programs, and Resources for Teachers and Students (General to Discipline-Specific)
- "Integrating Written, Oral, Visual and Electronic Communication Across the Curriculum: A Guide for Faculty and Graduate Teaching Assistants"
- Extensive Faculty resources, Student resources, and Writers' resources
- Writing Centers link, extensive handouts
- CAC Research link includes: CAC Research on the Web and Bibliographies. Includes "Selected Bibliography of Journal Articles and Dissertations on Communication Across the Curriculum" (General, Disciplinary: Biology, Business and Management, History, Mass Communication, Math, Nursing, Science, Sociology, and Technology and CAC)

Notes: Includes news/announcements page and CAC Task Force and minutes.

Sponsor: University of Hawai'i at Manoa, Honolulu, HI—Research I
Rating: ★★★★
Visit: 3/20/00
URL: ⟨http://www2.hawaii.edu/~uhmwrite/⟩
Program Name: The Manoa Writing Program
Focus: WAC/WID, Writing Intensive (WI) Courses
Highlights:
- WI Faculty teaching resources include:
  - Assignment Design & Sequencing
  - Freewriting & Journals
  - Responding, Evaluating & Grading
  - Publishing Student Writing
  - Discipline-Specific Resources (Architecture, Art, Chemistry, Civil Engineering, Dance, Education, Food Science, Geography, History, Indo-Pacific Languages, Linguistics, Mathematics, Nursing, Philosophy, Poetry, Psychology, Science, Sociology, Spanish)
- Writing Activities
- *Writing Matters* online writing newsletter (under "Faculty Information")
- Extensive WI Course philosophy, policy, materials, FAQ, and proposal forms
  - Manoa Writing Program: History, Research, & Staff Contains:
  - Assessment Research & Publications (Guide and Bibliography) Sections:
  - Designing Effective Writing Assignments
  - Responding to Student Writing
  - Writing and Research
  - Overcoming writing errors
  - Helping students make connections
  - Working with ESL Students' Writing: Opportunities for Language Learning
  - Peer Review & Feedback Forms

- Teaching Your Field's Forms of Writing
- Brief program background
- Extensive Writers' Links for Students and Teachers

Notes: Includes link list, description of Writing Placement Exam, description of Undergraduate Writing Requirement. WI Student Information includes list of current WI courses (no sample materials) and writers' links.

Sponsor: University of Minnesota, Twin Cities (Minneapolis and St. Paul), MN—Research I

Rating: ★★★★

Visit: 3/20/00

URL: ⟨http://cisw.cla.umn.edu/⟩

Program Name: The Center for Interdisciplinary Studies of Writing

Focus: WAC/WID, Writing Intensive (WI) courses

Highlights:

- WI Course philosophy, guidelines, proposal form (and sample proposals from several disciplines, syllabus checklist and resources
- Several WI Course Sample Syllabi and Assignments (Arts and Humanities, Social Sciences, Sciences, Engineering, Technology, Business, Health Sciences, Education, and Other Professional Schools)
- Responding and Grading (including peer response and group work)
- Instructional Strategies (designing and sequencing assignments, informal writing, large classes)
- Technology and Writing tips and teaching resources links
- Abstracts of CISW-Sponsored Research (Language, Arts, and Humanities; Sciences; Social Sciences; Business and Professional Communication; Cross-Disciplinary)
- The Minnesota Writing Project: Brief history, goals, programs and information

Notes: Brief description of new Writing-Intensive requirements (includes FAQ), writers' resource link list, sponsor-specific grants and development, and news page.

Sponsor: University of Richmond, Richmond, VA—Master's I

Rating: ★★★★

Visit: 3/20/00

URL: ⟨http://www.richmond.edu/~wac/⟩

Program Name: WAC Program and University Writing Center

Focus: WAC

Highlights:

- Extensive Program Information includes: program description, history, rationale & goals, overview, and evaluation
- Description of Writing Fellows program (and Technology Fellows)

- Resource page includes:
  - WAC newsletters, WAC brochure, and Writing Fellows handbook
  - For Instructors—Extensive Write-to-Learn activities list (including: freewriting, collaborative writing, double entry notebooks, microthemes) and related web site links
  - For Writing Tutors—online writing handbooks, tips for conducting conferences and responding to student papers, sample online WAC projects, and related web site links (WAC and writing programs, writing centers, tools for writing instructors, ESL, and online journals)
  - For Students—extensive link list for writers

Notes: Welcome page with brief program statement, contact information, description of faculty and student development, and submit form for suggestions.

Sponsor: University of South Florida, Tampa, FL—Research II

Rating: ★★★★

Visit: 3/20/00

URL: ⟨http://www.usf.edu/~lc/wac/⟩

Program Name: USF Learning Communities—WAC & Information Literacy (ILIAD)

Focus: WAC/WID

Highlights:

- Brief History (Russell article summary) and WAC Bibliography (some annotations and websites)
- Learning Communities philosophy, models, assessment, and link list
- Future of WAC section (includes: "Major Assumptions Underlying WAC" and role of WAC in Learning Communities)
- Information Literacy and WAC (includes: Information Literacy Goals, bibliography of online resources)
- Strategies for Implementing Writing Across the Curriculum
  - Designing Research Paper Assignments That Support WAC Initiatives
  - Writing To Learn with Response papers
  - Developing Writing Prompts That Support Writing Goals
  - Developing Writing Assignments That Enhance Thinking Skills
  - Handling the Paper Load
  - Responding to WAC Student Writing
- WAC Websites sorted by Discipline (Accounting, Anthropology, Agriculture, Bilingual Education, Biology, Economics, Geology, Government, Health and Recreation, History, Hospitality Management, Literature, Management, Modern Languages, Political Science, Physics, Plant Biology, Social Sciences, Social Work, Women's Studies, Writing)

Notes: Includes section on WAC program assessment, Service Learning, WAC and Instructional Technology (links to MOOs, online writing labs, and FSU Learning Communities).

Sponsor: Virginia Polytechnic Institute and State University, Blacksburg, VA—Research I

Rating: ★★★★

Visit: 3/26/00

URL: ⟨http://www.edtech.vt.edu/uwp/⟩

Program Name: University Writing Program

Focus: WAC/WID, Writing Intensive (WI) courses

Highlights:

- WI courses, Guidelines and Proposals (includes extensive description of sponsor-specific WI information)
- WAM (Writing Across the Major), Guidelines and Proposals
- Informational Flyer Series (online newsletters on WAC issues), subjects include: effective assignment design, grading, syllabus design, active learning, minimal marking, writing to learn, writing assessment and critical thinking
- Teaching With Writing (Includes: Grading and Responding to Student Writing, Handling Error in Student Writing, Ten Ways to Emphasize the Writing Process, Assignment Design: Some Considerations, Assignment Sequencing, Writing-to-Learn/Informal Writing, Using Peer Review Groups, Using Writing on the Web)

Notes: Includes "About UWP," listing of WI courses (no sample materials), extensive link list.

About the Scenemakers

Chris M. Anson is professor of English and director of the Campus Writing and Speaking Program at North Carolina State University, where he helps faculty in nine colleges to use writing and speaking in the service of students' learning and improved communication. He has written or edited twelve books and has published fifty articles. Before coming to NC State in 1999, Chris spent fifteen years at the University of Minnesota, where he directed the Program in Composition from 1988 to 1996 and was Morse-Alumni Distinguished Teaching Professor. He is the recipient of numerous awards, including the State of Minnesota Higher Education Teaching Excellence Award, which was given by the state legislature to one of three thousand faculty in the U of M system. He has led over seventy-five faculty workshops in thirty-eight states and six foreign countries. ⟨http://www2.chass.ncsu.edu/cwsp⟩

Ian G. Anson is an eighth-grade student at Cary Academy in Cary, North Carolina, where he has experienced firsthand the benefits of a truly outstanding communication-across-the-curriculum program. A consistent honor roll student, he has a passion for writing and music, and has sung or performed in many local, state, and regional musical events. When he isn't working on an academic project, he's playing soccer, listening to music, or cooking "world cuisine" with his mom, dad, and younger brother.

Dennis Baron is professor of English and linguistics and head of the department of English at the University of Illinois at Urbana-Champaign. He has taught writing in high school and college for 33 years, and for 11 years he directed the first-year writing program at Illinois. He has written seven books about various aspects of the English language and is currently writing about literacy and technology.

Wendy Bishop teaches writing at Florida State University and has conducted spring faculty writing workshops at Emory University. She is the author or editor of fourteen books, including *In Praise of Pedagogy: Poems, Flash Fiction and Essay on Composing* (editor, with David Starkey; Calendar Islands, 2000); *The Subject Is Reading: Essays by Teachers and Students* (editor; Boynton/Cook, 2000); *Thirteen Ways of Looking for a Poem: A Guide to Writing Poetry* (Longman, 2000); *Ethnographic Writing Research: Writing It Down, Writing It Up, and Reading It* (Boynton/Cook, 1999); and *The Subject Is Writing: Essays by Teachers and Students,* 2nd ed. (editor; Boynton/Cook, 1999). She lives in Tallahassee, Florida, with her daughter Morgan, son Tait, and husband Dean.

Rebecca E. Burnett is professor of rhetoric and professional communication in the Department of English at Iowa State University where she is the director of Advanced Communication and teaches undergraduate and graduate students. She has been named as a master teacher by ISU's College of Liberal Arts & Sciences. Her research focuses primarily on investigating the nature of the interaction and decision-making among team members and collaborators. She works as an expert witness and is a regular consultant in academia and industry. Her publications include the fifth edition of *Technical Communication* (Harcourt, 2001). She is currently editor of the *Journal of Business & Technical Communication*. Since 1991, she has been working with ISU faculty—especially those in engineering and in AgComm, the communication-across-the curriculum program in the College of Agriculture—who are interested in integrating oral, visual, and written communication into their technical courses. When she's not in her office, she's likely to be digging in her perennial garden. ⟨rburnett@iastate.edu⟩

William Condon has taught writing for just over half his life—beginning as a seventh- and eighth-grade teacher in 1974. Along the way, he has been a writing program administrator at a wide variety of institutions—the University of Oklahoma, Arkansas Tech University, the University of Michigan, and Washington State University, where he is director of campus writing programs and professor of English. Coauthor (with Wayne Butler) of *Writing the Information Superhighway* (Allyn and Bacon, 1997) and *Assessing the Portfolio: Principles for Theory, Practice, and Research* (with Liz Hamp-Lyons; Hampton, 2000), Bill has also published several articles in the areas of writing assessment, program evaluation, and computers and writing.

Patricia Connor-Greene is Alumni Distinguished Professor of Psychology at Clemson University, and has taught in the University of Pittsburgh's Semester at Sea program. She teaches abnormal psychology, psychology and culture, women and psychology, and theories of psychotherapy. Her current research interests include the cultural construction of psychiatric disorders and treatment, and the role of narrative in art and psychology.

Deanna P. Dannels is an assistant professor of communication at North Carolina State University, where she serves as assistant director of the Campus Writing and Speaking Program. Her cross-curricular work at NC State includes faculty development, TA training, curricular revision, undergraduate consulting, and instructional design. She is the recipient of several awards for her cross-curricular work and her teaching. Her most recent publication, "Learning to Be Professional: Technical Classroom Discourse, Practice, and Professional Identity Construction," (*Journal of Business and Technical Communication,* 2000) explores ways in which classroom instruction contributes to the learning of professional, communicative identities in the technical disciplines.

Christine Farris is associate professor and director of composition at Indiana University, where she teaches undergraduate and graduate courses in composition and cultural studies, literacy, and literature. She is the author of *Subject to Change: New Composition Instructors' Theory and Practice* (Hampton, 1996) and coeditor with Chris M. Anson of *Under Construction: Working at the Intersections of Composition Theory, Research, and Practice* (Utah State UP, 2000), as well as of several book chapters on research and consultation in writing across the curriculum.

Michael C. Flanigan is the Earl A. and Betty Galt Brown Professor of Rhetoric and director of composition at the University of Oklahoma. He runs workshops for faculty on using writing as a way of enhancing learning in the disciplines, and he conducts research on learning and writing across the disciplines. He especially enjoys team teaching in various disciplines and has team taught classes in history ("Wine, Women and Work: 19th and 20th Century Laboring Women"), in art/literature ("Art, Literature and Writing: The Work of Diego Rivera in Pan-American and European Contexts"), art history ("Reading Medieval Art: The Interactions of Visual and Verbal Texts"), and other disciplines.

Tom Fox chaired the University Writing Committee for ten years at Calfiornia State University, Chico. He now administers the first-year composition program and directs the Northern California Writing Project. Whenever possible, he teaches first-year writing and advanced courses in rhetoric and composition. His most recent book is *Defending Access* (Heinemann/Boynton-Cook, 1999).

Toby Fulwiler has directed the writing program at the University of Vermont since 1983. Before that he taught at Michigan Tech and the University of Wisconsin where, in 1973, he also received his PhD in American literature. He conducts writing workshops for teachers in all grade levels and across the disciplines, including the over 40 two-day workshops for the faculty at UVM. His most recent books are *The Letter Book*, coedited with Susan Dinitz (Boynton-Cook, 2000) and *The Journal Book for Teachers in Technical and Professional Programs*, coedited with Susan Gardner (Boynton-Cook, 1998). His other books on writing across the curriculum include: *When Writing Teachers Teach Literature* (Boynton-Cook, 1995) and *Programs That Work* (Boynton-Cook, 1990), both coedited with Art Young; *College Writing* (Boynton-Cook, 1992); *Teaching with Writing* (Boynton-Cook, 1986); and *The Journal Book* (Boynton-Cook, 1987).

Joan Graham directs the University of Washington's Interdisciplinary Writing Program, which offers writing courses linked with lecture courses in disciplines across the curriculum. Because of her interest in the effects of writers' contexts and the roles of writing in learning, she has become increasingly involved in curriculum and faculty development and in the mentoring of teaching assistants. She has codirected a large, longitudinal study of students' writing experience at the University of Washington, and she serves frequently as a consultant on writing assessment and program development at other institutions.

Sharon Hamilton, Chancellor's Professor of English and director of Campus Writing, has been at the Indianapolis campus of Indiana University (IUPUI) for 14 years. She is currently the director of the IUPUI Portfolio, an electronic institutional portfolio that provides quality assurance in the areas of student learning, research, and scholarship, and civic engagement to multiple stakeholders, including accrediting agencies and state legislators. She is concurrently developing student electronic portfolios to provide evidence of improvement throughout each student's academic career. She has published widely on collaborative learning and is the author of a literacy autobiography, *My Name's Not Susie: A Life Transformed by Literacy*

(Heinemann/Boynton-Cook, 1995) and a play, *My Brother Was My Mother's Only Child.*

Patricia C. Harms is a doctoral student in the rhetoric and professional communication program at Iowa State University. She is currently conducting an ethnographic study of a learning community link between first-year composition and first-year engineering at ISU. She has taught in collaborative, interdisciplinary course links and has consulted on writing across the curriculum. She recently conducted a series of faculty focus groups as part of an interdisciplinary research project on undergraduate communication across the curriculum at ISU (ISUComm).

Richard Haswell is Haas Professor of English at Texas A&M University, Corpus Christi. For a number of years he conducted faculty workshops and reading sessions in connection with the cross-curricular junior portfolio at Washington State University. He is author of *Gaining Ground in College Writing: Tales of Development and Interpretation* (Southern Methodist UP, 1991) and, with Min-Zhan Lu of Drake University, of *Comp Tales* (Longman, 2000). He is general editor of *Beyond Outcomes: Assessment and Instruction within a University Writing Program* (Ablex, 2001).

Carol Peterson Haviland is associate professor of English and Writing Center director at California State University, San Bernardino. She teaches in both the undergraduate and graduate composition programs and coordinates the faculty WAC seminars. Haviland is coeditor of *Weaving Knowledge Together: Writing Centers and Collaboration* (NWCA Press, 1998), and is currently working on *Teaching Writing in the Late Age of Print.*

Dona J. Hickey is the associate dean for research support and director of A&S graduate school at the University of Richmond, where she initiated the WAC program in 1992. She is author of *Developing a Written Voice* (Mayfield, 1993), *Figures of Thought for College Writers* (Mayfield, 1999), and with Donna Reiss, co-editor of *Learning Literature in an Era of Change* (Stylus, 1999). Hickey and Reiss frequently collaborate in leading faculty development workshops on technology and writing.

Thomas Hilgers has directed the WAC program at the University of Hawai'i for the past 10 years. The program's published research reports show how a major requirement (five writing-intensive courses for a bachelor's degree) can be successfully implemented at a large research university. The program's Web site (http://www.hawaii.edu/uhmwrite) is a portrait of the current program. During 2000, Hilgers was a Fulbright scholar in Thailand. He conducted faculty workshops at six Thai universities on using writing (in Thai and in English) to improve student learning.

Rebecca Moore Howard chairs and directs the Writing Program at Syracuse University. She has conducted WAC workshops for faculty and students and has published a variety of articles on the subject. Among her published books are *The Bedford Guide to Teaching Writing in the Disciplines* (Bedford, 1995) and *Coming of Age: The Advanced Writing Curriculum* (Heinemann Boyton/Cook, 2000).

Keith Hjortshoj directs Writing in the Majors, a program for advanced instruction in the disciplines in the Knight Institute for Writing in the Disciplines at Cornell University. He has led numerous seminars and workshops for graduate students and faculty, at Cornell and at other institutions. His most recent publications include *The Transition to College Writing* (a freshman text; St. Martins, 2001) and *Understanding Writing Blocks* (Oxford UP, 2001), based on his studies of blocked writers in undergraduate and graduate education.

Jeffrey Jablonski is an assistant professor of professional writing at the University of Nevada-Las Vegas. His scholarly interests include WAC, professional writing, and writing program administration. His dissertation, *Reconceiving Interdisciplinary Collaboration: Locating the Intellectual Work of Writing Across the Curriculum Consultants* (Purdue Univ.), grows out of his interest in collecting, describing, and developing methods for writing consulting in academic contexts. He has published recent work and reviews in *Academic Writing, Business Communication Quarterly*, and *Technical Communication Quarterly*.

Sandra Jamieson is associate professor of English and director of composition at Drew University, in Madison, NJ. She teaches in the college and in the PhD program, and supervises and trains writing teachers. She has organized writing-in-the-disciplines workshops, and runs the writing component of Drew's two annual faculty development workshops for first- and second-year seminar instructors. The author of *The Bedford Guide to Teaching Writing in the Disciplines: An Instructor's Desk Reference*, with Rebecca Moore Howard (Bedford, 1995), her research explores the relationship between theory and pedagogy in writing instruction. She has collaborated with faculty from several disciplines to design text and assignments for an academic writing textbook she is developing.

David Jolliffe is professor of English and director of the First-Year Program at DePaul University. He is the author of *Writing, Teaching, Learning: Incorporating Writing throughout the Curriculum* (HarperCollins, 1993) and contributing editor of *Writing in Academic Disciplines* (Ablex, 1988).

Joan Mullin, director of WAC and the Writing Center at the University of Toledo, started both programs in 1987. She publishes in various journals across the disciplines. Her coedited collection, *Intersections: Theory-Practice in the Writing Center* (NCTE, 1994), won the 1994 National Writing Center Association Award for Outstanding Scholarship, and the coauthored book, *ARTiculating: Teaching Writing in a Visual Culture* (Heinemann—Boynton/Cook, 1998) indicates her current research interest in visual literacy across the curriculum. Past president of the National Writing Centers Association, she coedits *The Writing Center Journal*.

Joan Perkins works as editor for Pacific Resources in Education and Learning, one of ten regional educational laboratory programs supported by the U.S. Department of Education. She taught composition and literature for five years at the University of Hawai'i at Manoa, where she also served as academic coordinator of the Manoa Writing Program. She is employed as an artist/instructor in Hawai'i's Poets in the

Schools Program, and has presented many workshops on composition pedagogy and development of children's rhetorical skills through poetry writing.

Thomas Polito is director of Student Services for the College of Agriculture at Iowa State University and assistant professor of agronomy and of agricultural education and studies. He worked for two years in the fertilizer and chemical industry before returning to the university. His research focuses on fertilizer management in no-tillage corn and soybean production systems. He has been active in ISU's learning community movement as well as in efforts to include WAC in the College of Agriculture's curriculum. In his teaching, he has included communication-intensive assignments in his courses for many years. He is a co-instructor in ISU's only upper-level learning community that integrates a soil science course with a junior-level writing course. To get away from the university, he spends time outdoors with his family and shares his administrative skills with the local youth hockey association. October through March finds him following his son's hockey team through as many as six states. ⟨tpolito@iastate.edu⟩

Sharon Quiroz is editor of the WAC journal, *Language and Learning Across the Disciplines.*

Donna Reiss is associate professor of English at Tidewater Community College (Virginia), where she teaches computer-enhanced and Web-based writing, literature, and humanities. Her recent writing and faculty workshops focus on electronic communication for teaching writing, literature, and other courses throughout the college curriculum. She serves on the editorial boards of *Computers and Composition* and *Academic.Writing: Interdisciplinary Perspectives on Communication Across the Curriculum.* She coedited *Electronic Communication Across the Curriculum* (with Dickie Selfe and Art Young; NCTE, 1998) and *Learning Literature in an Era of Change: Innovations in Teaching* (with Dona Hickey; Stylus, 2000), which includes her chapter, "Epistolary Pedagogy and Electronic Mail: Online Letters for Learning Literature." She also has written feature articles for regional periodicals and has edited books for a regional press. She sometimes teaches introductory swing dancing. ⟨dreiss@wordsworth2.net; http://www.wordsworth2.net/⟩

David Roberts is associate professor of rhetoric and professional communication and assistant chair for curriculum in the Department of English at Iowa State University. He teaches courses at every level, from freshman composition to graduate seminars, and in March 2000, he received the university's Louis Thompson Award for Distinguished Undergraduate Teaching. His major research interests are visual rhetoric and information design, and with Charles Kostelnick he is coauthor of *Designing Visual Language* (Allyn & Bacon, 1998). He is a work-place consultant, focusing on the development of service proposals and other sales documents. A devoted baseball fan, he has been known to miss committee meetings and cancel office hours during October. ⟨droberts@iastate.edu⟩

Hephzibah Roskelly teaches courses in rhetoric, women's studies, and American literature at the University of North Carolina Greensboro. She is associate director of the Women's Studies Program and often conducts workshops in and out of the university on using reading and writing effectively across the curriculum.

David R. Russell is professor of English at Iowa State University, where he teaches in the PhD program in rhetoric and professional communication. His book *Writing in the Academic Disciplines, 1870–1990: A Curricular History* (Southern Illinois UP, 1991) examines the history of American writing instruction outside of composition courses. He has published many articles on writing across the curriculum and coedited *Landmark Essays on Writing Across the Curriculum* (Hermagoras, 1994), and a special issue of *Mind, Culture, and Activity* (Erlbaum, 1997) on writing research. He has given many workshops on WAC, nationally and internationally.

Carol Rutz has directed a modified WAC program at Carleton College in Northfield, Minnesota, since 1997. She has organized faculty development workshops on a number of campuses, and with Chris Anson and two others, she coedited a volume of cases for faculty development: *Dilemmas in Teaching*, published by Mendota Press in 1998. In addition to faculty development, her research interests include writing pedagogy and response to student writing. ⟨crutz@carleton.edu⟩

John Schafer is professor of agronomy at Iowa State University. He teaches three Web-based introductory soils courses for three different student audiences, a distance-learning introductory course, and an upper-level soil management course that is part of an integrated learning community. He has offered short courses on soils in China and Hungary. His research has been in the area of manure management. He has received department, college, and university teaching awards and a faculty citation from the ISU Alumni Association. He is a fellow of both the Soil Science Society of America and the American Society of Agronomy. Over the years, as he has traveled and hiked throughout the United States, Europe, Asia, and Africa, he has become acquainted with many farmers and agriculturalists. He especially enjoys visiting them to learn about the changes that are taking place at the local level around the world, and then he incorporates what he's learned into his courses. ⟨jschafer@iastate.edu⟩

Dickie Selfe directs the Center for Computer-Assisted Language Instruction at Michigan Technological University, a communication-oriented computer facility, and teaches computer-intensive first-year English, technical communication, and graduate computer studies courses. His interest is in communication pedagogy as well as in the social/institutional influences of electronic media on our culture and that pedagogy. Selfe's recent publications include the coedited volume *Electronic Communication Across the Curriculum* (NCTE, 1998), and a chapter in the forthcoming volume *New Words, New Worlds* (Hampton Press) titled "What Are We Doing to and for Ourselves? The Material Process of Adapting to Electronic Spaces."

Nancy S. Shapiro is director of the K-16 Partnership for Teaching and Learning in the Office of Academic Affairs, University System of Maryland. She was the founding director of the College Park Scholars Living-Learning Program at the University of Maryland. In her current position as associate vice chancellor for academic affairs, she develops university-school programs to enhance teaching and learning, K-16. She also serves as a National Learning Communities Project fellow. Her publications include *Creating Learning Communities* (with Jodi H. Levine; Jossey-Bass, 1999) and *Scenarios for Teaching Writing* (with Chris Anson, et al; NCTE, 1993), as well as articles, essays and edited collections.

Hayley Shilling graduated from Clemson University with a major in psychology and minor in journalism. She was secretary of the Psychology Club at Clemson, as well as a member of Psi Chi, Golden Key National Honor Society, and Phi Kappa Phi, and completed general honors in Clemson's Calhoun College Honors Program. She is interested in clinical psychology and hopes to continue her interest in writing by attempting to freelance entertaining feature stories, especially about personal hobbies like travel, tumbleweed collection, and vegetarian cuisine.

Shaun P. Slattery, Jr. holds his masters in English from North Carolina State University. While pursuing his MA with a concentration in composition and rhetoric, he was a consultant for the Campus Writing and Speaking Program, working with faculty in civil engineering, electrical and computer engineering, and marine, earth, and atmospheric sciences. Shaun currently teaches first-year composition and business and technical writing.

Monica Stitt-Bergh is the assessment coordinator for the Manoa Writing Program at the University of Hawai'i. She carries out research projects related to teaching with writing, creates support materials for instructors teaching writing-intensive courses, and offers workshops on using writing to improve student learning. She has coauthored several articles about the WI program at UH and has also taught first-year writing courses.

Chris Thaiss is professor of English at George Mason University, where he chairs the department and regularly teaches courses in advanced composition, the writing of nonfiction, the teaching of writing and literature, and theories of composition. For many years the director of WAC and English composition at Mason, he coordinates the National Network of Writing-Across-the-Curriculum programs and serves on the editorial boards of *The Journal of Language and Learning Across the Disciplines* and the electronic journals *academic.writing* and *Inventio*. Thaiss has authored or edited nine books, most recently *The Harcourt Brace Guide to Writing Across the Curriculum* (1998) and a series of discipline-specific writing guides in psychology, theatre, and law enforcement (1999–2000) that he cowrote with faculty in those fields.

Martha A. Townsend directs the University of Missouri's Campus Writing Program, a sixteen-year-old WAC initiative. A member of the English department, she also teaches first-year composition, the department's capstone course required for majors, and graduate seminars in WAC/WID, writing assessment, and the practicum for new composition instructors. Her work with WAC has taken her to Romania, Korea, Thailand, South Africa, and China. She regularly conducts faculty workshops in and out of the university on using writing in the disciplines and integrating writing into general education programs.

Irwin Weiser is professor of English and director of composition at Purdue University. He regularly teaches a graduate practicum in the teaching of writing, as well as seminars in writing across the curriculum and writing assessment. In his most recent book, *The Writing Program Administrator as Researcher*, coedited with Shirley K. Rose (Heinemann Boynton-Cook, 1999), he explains the value of surveys of faculty from across the curriculum in designing composition curriculum.

Edward M. White is professor emeritus of English at California State University, San Bernardino, and adjunct professor of English at the University of Arizona. He has written, edited, or coedited nine books on writing and assessment, most recently *Assessment of Writing: Politics, Policies, Practices* (MLA, 1996). For over a decade he led a faculty seminar in "the uses of writing in all disciplines" at Cal State, a seminar now continuing under the leadership of Carol Haviland.

Stephen B. Wiley began experimenting with online communication environments as a teaching assistant at the University of Illinois, Urbana-Champaign, where he codeveloped the Writers' Workshop Online Writing Guide and worked through the Sloan Center for Asynchronous Learning Environments to help faculty incorporate computer-mediated communication into their teaching. Steve is currently an assistant professor in the Department of Communication at North Carolina State University, where he teaches about the social shaping of communication technologies and the globalization of communication infrastructure and policy. His research examines communication infrastructure as social space and focuses on the role of media and information technologies in shaping national and transnational spaces in Latin America and the United States.

Kathleen Blake Yancey is Roy O. Pearce Professor of English at Clemson University, where she also directs the Roy and Marnie Pearce Center for Professional Communication, an endowed center that fosters communication-across-the-curriculum activities for faculty and students. She has given WAC workshops at many institutions across the country, and in 2001 will be one of three keynoters for the fifth national Conference on Writing Across the Curriculum. With Brian Huot, she edited *Assessing Writing Across the Curriculum* (Ablex, 1997), and she has edited or written some five other volumes, most recently *Self-Assessment and Development in Writing: A Collaborative Inquiry* (Hampton Press, 2000).

Art Young is Campbell Chair in Technical Communication and professor of English and professor of engineering at Clemson University, where he founded and coordinates the communication-across-the-curriculum program. His most recent book, coedited with Donna Reiss and Dickie Selfe, is *Electronic Communication Across the Curriculum* (NCTE, 1998). He teaches writing and literature, and he is taking swing dance lessons.

Steven Youra directs the Engineering Communications Program at Cornell University, where he works with writing across the curriculum and teaches technical communication. His articles on writing, literature, and film have appeared in such journals as *Computers and Composition, Journal of Technical Writing and Communication,*

American Transcendental Quarterly, Film Criticism, and *PMLA.* He also edited "Communications Across the Engineering Curriculum," a special issue of *Language & Learning Across the Disciplines* (2001).

Julie M. Zeleznik is a PhD student in rhetoric and professional communication in the Department of English at Iowa State University. For the last three years she has conducted her dissertation research on the ways in which students' writing, problem-solving, and collaborating abilities have been affected by their participation in integrated pairs of first-year and upper-level agronomy and English courses. She has co-presented the preliminary results of this research with participating faculty at several university and national conferences. In another line of research, she investigates the ways in which radiologic technicians communicate with their patients while they administer mammograms, exploring how communication affects the quality of the mammograms and the emotional well-being of the patient. She teaches courses in technical communication, business communication, report and proposal writing, and visual communication. When she's not working on her research, she enjoys traveling home to visit her family in Michigan's Upper Peninsula. ⟨juliez@iastate.edu⟩